ESSENTIAL
SPIRITUALITY

ESSENTIAL SPIRITUALITY

THE 7 CENTRAL PRACTICES TO AWAKEN HEART AND MIND

ROGER WALSH, M.D., PH.D.

John Wiley & Sons, Inc.

New York • Chichester • Weinheim • Brisbane • Singapore • Toronto

Published by John Wiley & Sons, Inc.
Published simultaneously in Canada

This publication is designed to provide accurate and authoritative information in regard to the subject matter covered. It is sold with the understanding that the publisher is not engaged in rendering professional services. If professional advice or other expert assistance is required, the services of a competent professional person should be sought.

Library of Congress Cataloging-in-Publication Data:
Walsh, Roger N.
    Essential spirituality : the 7 central practices to awaken
heart and mind / Roger Walsh.
        p. cm.
    Includes bibliographical references and index.
    ISBN 0-471-33026-4 (alk. paper)
    1. Spiritual life. 2. Self-realization—Religious aspects.
3. Psychology and religion.   I. Title.
BL624.W335   1999
291.4′4—dc21   99-14640

Printed in the United States of America

10 9 8 7 6 5 4 3 2 1

This book is dedicated

✳

to
Judith Skutch Whitson, Rob Lehman, and Wink Franklin
who have given so much inspiration and support
to so many people,

to
my teachers,
who learned the seven practices
and then shared them with the world,

and to
the well-being and awakening of all

CONTENTS

THE SEVEN PRACTICES

FOREWORD

In our increasingly materialistic world, we are driven by a seemingly insatiable desire for power and possessions. Yet in this vain striving, we wander ever further from inner peace and mental happiness. Despite our pleasant material surroundings, many people today experience dissatisfaction, fear, anxiety, and a sense of insecurity. There seems to be something lacking within our hearts. What we seem to be missing is a proper sense of human spirituality.

As human beings, our requirements cannot be fulfilled by material means alone. We need material facilities for physical comfort, but these alone cannot provide mental comfort. Under such circumstances, religious traditions are very relevant. If religion were not of much value in our day-to-day life, I believe we would be quite right to abandon it. But I continue to believe that religion actually provides us with tremendous benefit.

Each religion has its own philosophy, and there are similarities as well as vast differences among the various traditions. What is important is that which is suitable for each particular person. All our different religions have a special role to play in the awakening of compassion. They all realize the importance of compassion and have the potential to increase and enhance compassion and harmony. It is on the basis of this common potential that they can all understand each other and work together.

At the same time, I believe that qualities such as compassion and forgiveness are fundamental human qualities and are thus of great importance even without a religious belief. I believe religion strengthens and increases our natural positive qualities. The population of this planet is more than five billion, of which perhaps only one billion follow a formal religion. The remaining four billion do not have such strong beliefs, but as human brothers and sisters, I believe, they can be inspired by the need for compassion.

In this book, Roger Walsh examines seven practices that he has identified as common to world religions. He discusses ways to purify our motivation, to cultivate love and compassion, to train our attention, to clarify our awareness, to develop ethics, to cultivate wisdom, and to engage in the service of others. I believe that all these practices are essentially linked to the development of compassion, which involves not only thinking about others and wanting to do something for them, but actually putting these good wishes into effect.

Human nature is such that we can change ourselves for the better. However, the benefits that religion and spiritual values can bring and the contribution they can make to mankind depend on ourselves as individuals and whether we really put them into practice. Therefore, if we all spend a few minutes every day thinking about the practices described here and trying to develop compassion, eventually compassion will become part of our lives.

The Dalai Lama
December 29, 1998

ACKNOWLEDGMENTS

I would like to express my deep gratitude to the many people who helped make this book possible. Foremost among them are the following:

The many spiritual friends who have inspired and instructed me. These include especially Ram Dass, Joseph Goldstein, Sharon Salzberg, Jack Kornfield, Surya Das, Tsokni Rinpoche, Sonja Marguiles, Reb Anderson, Les Hixon, and Michael Harner.

Those religious scholars who both studied and practiced the great religions and were therefore able to explain them on the basis of both their direct experience and intellectual understanding. These include especially Huston Smith and Ken Wilber.

Gary Lapid, who was the first to show me that there is a path.

My therapist, Jim Bugental, who, with extraordinary humanity and skill, started me on this wondrous journey.

Frances Vaughan, who provided invaluable support for the journey, the book, and life.

My mother and sister, Patricia and Penelope Walsh, who always offered unswerving support.

My editors, who offered invaluable feedback: Stephanie Gunning, Ben Yalom, Alan Rinzler, and Shoshana Alexander. The religious scholar Philip Novak edited the book for factual accuracy.

Reviewers who were kind enough to read the manuscript and offer suggestions: Penelope Walsh, Tony Schwartz, MaryAnn Ready, Jim Fadiman, and especially Ken Wilber.

Those psychiatrists in our meditation group who read the manuscript and gave feedback: James McQuade, Kristine Panik, Gary Dylewski, and Tony Kassir.

My teaching assistants, Sharon Weldon and Rhonda Higdon.

Those people who were kind enough to provide endorsements.

The members of my meditation teacher's group who supported me during this project: Sylvia Boorstein, Caroline Palden

Alioto, Surya Das, Claude d'Estree, Jack Kornfield, Yvonne Rand, Lewis Richmond, and John Tarrant.

Those people who offered assistance at crucial times, especially Wink Franklin, William Andrew, Irvin Yalom, and Judith Skutch-Whitson. Linda Gaudiani proved a wonderfully compassionate physician during a medical crisis.

Bonnie L'Allier, who provided impeccable and never-failing assistance.

My agent, Ling Lucas, for excellent suggestions and bubbling enthusiasm.

Tom Miller, my editor at John Wiley, who proved the type of editor every author dreams of.

The Fetzer Institute, whose support of this and other projects has been invaluable, and who, more than any other organization I have known, really walk their talk.

PERMISSIONS

The following were kind enough to grant permission to reprint:

The Vietnam veteran's story is by Dr. Lloyd Burton. Lloyd Burton has been a student of Joseph Goldstein, Jack Kornfield, and Sharon Salzberg since 1975 and is cofounder of both the Spirit Rock Meditation Center in Northern California and the Insight Meditation Community of Colorado.

The story of the aikido student on the Tokyo train is by Terry Dobson. Permission to reprint it was kindly given by his widow, Riki Moss.

CHAPTER 1

UNVEILING
THE SACRED

When you seek God,
Seek Him in your heart.
—*Yûnus Emre,*
Islamic sage

Life is not always easy, but it can be ecstatic. How to manage the difficulties and taste the ecstasy is a central challenge of life and a goal of any spiritual practice.

The difficulties are many. Even the most fortunate of us suffers times of sorrow and sickness, disappointment and despair. All of us know fear and frustration, sadness and depression. Sooner or later, we all watch loved ones die, and we eventually die ourselves. This is hardly a new discovery. More than two thousand years ago the Buddha centered his teaching on the recognition that difficulty is part of life, while from Israel, the Jewish Psalms wailed forth their lament:

Our years come to an end like a sigh....
Their span is only toil and trouble; they are soon gone.

Life is difficult to understand. We are born dazed and helpless, finding ourselves in a world overflowing with mystery. Yet our world is only a speck of cosmic dust in a remote uncharted corner of a vast, unfathomable universe. No wonder life feels so mysterious and we sometimes reel in bewilderment.

Yet life can be exciting and joyful. There are countless wonders to explore and people to meet, and the world holds places of breathless beauty. We all have opportunities to love and play, to learn and heal. Our lives are rich with opportunities and our challenge is to live them to the full. All of us can be the creative artists of our lives.

Life can be ecstatic. There are experiences so profound and meaningful that life and the world seem nothing less than sacred. There are moments of such bliss that they outshine ordinary pleasures as the sun does a firefly, moments of such love and compassion that we fall helplessly in love with all creation. A single such experience can transform your life forever.

❋

Richard Bucke was such a person. Born in 1837, he was raised on a remote Canadian farm. At age seventeen he set off wandering throughout the United States, working as a gardener, miner, and Mississippi steamboat deckhand. Seeking more adventure, he signed up to help drive a wagon train 1,200 miles across open country to Utah, and he barely survived starvation and multiple Indian attacks. Undaunted, he decided to try his hand at mining in Nevada, but then his luck ran out. In midwinter his friends died and he and one other survivor were left alone in the wilderness. They made a desperate gamble and set out for the West Coast. It was a horrendous journey: His companion died and at the last moment Bucke was rescued by a mining party. But his feet were frozen; one had to be partly amputated, the other completely. At age twenty-one he was maimed for life.

But that year he also received his inheritance and used it to put himself through medical school. He began an entirely new life and rapidly distinguished himself as a prominent psychiatrist.

At age thirty his life took yet another turn. A visitor to his house quoted some verses by the poet Walt Whitman, and their effect on him was dramatic. He became increasingly reflective and in 1872, at age thirty-five, he had an experience that utterly transformed his life, and that has affected hundreds of thousands of his readers. The introduction to his famous book *Cosmic Consciousness* tells us that he had spent the evening with two friends reading the poetry of Wordsworth, Keats, Shelley, Browning and Whitman. At midnight they parted and he began the long drive home in his carriage. He was still under the influence of the poets' ideas, and his mind was calm and happy. Suddenly without warning:

> All at once I found myself wrapped in a flame-colored cloud. For an instant I thought of fire, an immense conflagration somewhere close by in that great city; the next, I knew that the fire was within myself. Directly afterward there came upon me a sense of exultation, of immense joyousness accompanied or immediately followed by an intellectual illumination impossible to describe. Among other things, I did not merely come to believe, but I saw that the universe is not composed of dead matter, but is, on the contrary, a living Presence; I became conscious in myself of eternal life. It was not a conviction that I would have eternal life, but a consciousness that I possessed eternal life then; I saw that all men are immortal; that the cosmic order is such that...all things work together for the good of each and all; that the foundation principle of the world, of all the worlds, is what we call love, and that the happiness of each and all is in the long run absolutely certain.

So profound was the impact that Bucke devoted the rest of his life to researching such experiences.

Obviously, it would be wonderful to have a way to deal with all kinds of experiences: sorrow, mystery, happiness, and ecstasy. Our lives would be transformed if we could learn to heal and to withstand sorrow better, to uncover meaning in the midst of mystery, to cultivate happiness, and to invite ecstasy. Fortunately, these are the goals of spiritual practices, and these practices offer a life-changing feast of benefits.

BENEFITS OF SPIRITUAL PRACTICES

We need to distinguish between two crucial terms: *religion* and *spirituality*. The word *religion* has many meanings; in particular it implies a concern with the sacred and supreme values of life. The term *spirituality*, on the other hand, refers to *direct experience* of the sacred. Spiritual practices are those that help us experience the sacred—that which is most central and essential to our lives—for ourselves.

Psychological and Spiritual Benefits

The ultimate aim of spiritual practices is awakening; that is, to know our true Self and our relationship to the sacred. However, spiritual practices also offer numerous other gifts along the way. For thousands of years wise men and women from all traditions have sung the praises of the many benefits that flow into the lives of practitioners as they progress along the spiritual path. Gradually, the heart begins to open, fear and anger melt, greed and jealousy dwindle, happiness and joy grow, love flowers, peace replaces agitation, concern for others blossoms, wisdom matures, and both psychological and physical health improve. Virtually all aspects of our lives are touched and transformed in some way.

In the past, such claims had to be taken on faith, if they were believed at all. Now the climate has changed dramatically. Out of modern laboratories has poured a flood of data that support many ancient claims and demonstrate psychological and physical benefits, some of them undreamed of by the practitioners of old.

Among psychological benefits, the relaxation response, which reduces anxiety and develops peace, is the best known. Other effects are even more exciting, including intellectual gifts of enhanced creativity, intelligence, and academic achievement. Spiritual practitioners experience greater self-control and self-actualization. They develop greater sensitivity, deeper empathy, and greater marital satisfaction. They use less alcohol and drugs and suffer fewer conflicts around sex and aggression.

Physical Benefits

Physical benefits are also dramatic. Spiritual practices can reduce stress, blood pressure, and cholesterol levels. They may help alleviate insomnia, muscle spasms, and diseases ranging from migraine to chronic pain. They may even reduce the effects of aging and lengthen the life span. One Harvard study showed that nursing home patients who were in their eighties when they first began meditation felt happier, functioned better, and lived longer than nonmeditators.

The Greatest of All Discoveries

Over time, spiritual practices work their transformative wonders on our hearts, minds, and lives. As the heart opens and the mind clears, we see further and further into the boundless depths of the mind.

There, within ourselves, we finally find the most profound, the most meaningful, and the most important discovery any human being can make. Within ourselves we find our deepest self, our true Self, and recognize that we are not only more than we imagined but more than we can imagine. We see that we are a creation of the sacred, intimately and eternally linked to the sacred, and forever graced and embraced by the sacred.

This is the greatest of all discoveries, the secret of all secrets, the priceless gift that is both the source and goal of the great religions. This is the aim of all our seeking, the answer to a lifetime of longing, the cause of the mystic's bliss, the source of overwhelming and enduring joy. This is the central message at the heart of the great religions and the basis for their ecstatic cries, such as those in the Western traditions.

> The kingdom of heaven is within you. (Jesus, Christianity)

> Those who know themselves know their Lord. (Mohammad, Islam)

> He is in all, and all is in Him. (Judaism)

Centuries earlier, similar words were already pouring from ecstatic Chinese practitioners.

> Those who know completely their own nature, know heaven. (Mencius, Confucianism)

> In the depths of the soul, one sees the Divine, the One. (The Chinese *Book of Changes*)

Indian traditions also offer the same gift, the recognition that, in their words,

> Atman [individual consciousness] and Brahman [universal consciousness] are one. (Hinduism)

Look within, you are the Buddha. (Buddhism)

Ecstatic recognitions such as these represent the deepest goal and fullest flowering of spiritual development. Though the words may differ, the experiences that underlie them point to commonalities among the world's religions, chief among which are the perennial philosophy and perennial practices.

THE PERENNIAL PHILOSOPHY AND PRACTICES

Thanks to global communication, for the first time in history, we have all the world's religions, their wisdom and their practices, available to us. Unprecedented numbers of people are now sampling practices from multiple traditions. Yet the sheer richness of possibilities has left many people confused, even dazed, by the variety of apparently competing claims and practices. What do the different traditions have in common?

Beneath the hundreds of different cultures, claims, and customs, there lies a common core of both wisdom and practice at the heart of each authentic tradition. By "authentic tradition," I mean one capable of offering a direct experience of the sacred, and of fostering true spiritual growth and maturity in its practitioners.

What an amazing discovery: For thousands of years countless people have fought, tortured, and killed over the differences between the world's religions. Differences certainly exist, as a glance at any newspaper makes painfully clear, yet now we are increasingly recognizing similarities and a common core.

The Perennial Philosophy

Scholars call the essential, common core of religious wisdom the perennial wisdom or perennial philosophy. Why perennial? Because these profound insights into life have endured across centuries and cultures and have been taught by the great sages of all times.

Developed over thousands of years, the perennial philosophy is a treasure house of humankind's accumulated wisdom. Vast in scope, profound in depth, it offers numberless insights into the nature of life and love, health and happiness, suffering and salvation.

At its heart lie four crucial claims—actually observations, since they are based on direct insights by advanced spiritual practitioners—about reality and human nature.

1) *There are two realms of reality.* The first is the everyday realm with which we are all familiar, the world of physical objects and living creatures. This is the realm accessible to us via sight and sound and studied by sciences such as physics and biology.

But beneath these familiar phenomena lies another realm far more subtle and profound: a realm of consciousness, spirit, Mind, or Tao. This world cannot be known through the physical senses and only indirectly through the physical instruments of science. Moreover, this realm creates and embraces the physical realm and is its source. This domain is not limited by space or time or physical laws, since it creates space, time, and physical laws, and hence it is unbounded and infinite, timeless and eternal.

2) *Human beings partake of both realms.* We are not only physical but also spiritual beings. We have bodies, but we also have, at the core of our being, in the depths of our minds, a center of transcendent awareness. This center is described as pure consciousness, mind, spirit, or Self and is known by such names as the *neshamah* of Judaism, the soul or divine spark of Christianity, the atman of Hinduism, or the buddha nature of Buddhism. This divine spark is intimately related to—some traditions even say inseparable from and identical with—the sacred ground or foundation of all reality. We are not divorced from the sacred but eternally and intimately linked to it.

3) *Human beings can recognize their divine spark and the sacred ground that is its source.* What this implies, and this is absolutely crucial, is that the claims of the perennial philosophy do not have to be accepted blindly. Rather, each of us can test them for ourselves and decide their validity based on our direct experience. Although the soul or innermost Self, being nonphysical, cannot be known by the senses or the instruments of science, it can be known by careful introspection.

This is not necessarily easy. Although anyone can be graced with spontaneous glimpses, clear sustained vision of our sacred depths usually requires significant practice to clarify awareness sufficiently. This is the purpose of spiritual practice.

When the mind is still and clear, we can have a direct experience of our Self. This is not a concept of, nor an intellectual theory about, the Self. Rather, it is an immediate knowing, a direct intuition in which one not only sees the divine spark but also identifies with and recognizes that one *is* the spark. Sages from Judaism and Sufism, from Plato to Buddha, from Eckhart to Lao Tsu have agreed on this. "Not by reasoning is this apprehension attainable," say the Hindu Upanishads, while the famous Christian mystic St. John of the Cross wrote that

> the arguments of the wise
> Are unable to grasp it....
> And this exalted wisdom
> Is of such excellence,
> That no faculty of science
> Can hope to reach it

Compared to this direct realization of the sacred, mere book learning and theoretical knowledge are very poor substitutes, as far removed from direct experience as a text on human reproduction is from the embrace of a lover. The Buddha drove the point home by comparing a person satisfied with mere theoretical understanding to a herdsman of other people's cattle, while Mohammad was even more blunt, comparing such a person to an ass carrying a load of books.

4) *The perennial philosophy's fourth claim is that realizing our spiritual nature is the* summum bonum: *the highest goal and greatest good of human existence.* Beside this, all other goals pale; all other delights only partly satisfy. No other experience is so ecstatic, no other attainment so rewarding, no other goal so beneficial to oneself or others. So say the wise of diverse traditions and ages.

Again, this is not wild dogma to be accepted merely on the word of others or on blind faith. Rather, it is an expression of the direct experience of those who have tasted these fruits for themselves. Most importantly, it is an invitation to all of us to test and taste for ourselves.

If we distill these four claims down to their essential essence, what do we find? The central ringing cry of the perennial philosophy is this: We have underestimated ourselves tragically. We are sadly mistaken when we see ourselves as merely temporary bodies instead of timeless spirit; as separate, suffering selves instead of blissful Buddhas; as meaningless blobs of matter instead of blessed children of God.

The words differ from one tradition to another, but their central message is the same: You are more than you think! Look deep within, and you will find that your ego is only a tiny wave atop the vast ocean that is your real Self. Look within, and at the center of your mind, in the depths of your soul, you will find your true Self, that this Self is intimately linked to the sacred, and that you share in the unbounded bliss of the sacred.

This recognition is the goal of the great religions and it is known by names such as *salvation* and *satori, enlightenment* and *liberation, fana* and *nirvana, awakening* and *Ruah Ha-qodesh.* But whatever the name, the great religions all exist to help us discover our true Self and our true relationship to the sacred. This discovery, they agree, is the supreme joy and greatest goal of human life.

The Perennial Practices

How to achieve this discovery of our true self is the central question of life, and it is here that the great religions offer their greatest gift. Each of them contains a set of practices designed to help us reach this goal. Whether they be the commandments and contemplations of Judaism, Islam, and Christianity, the yogas of Hinduism, or the disciplines of Taoism, each tradition offers spiritual practices that awaken.

Among the many spiritual practices, there are seven that are common to authentic religions and that we can therefore call *perennial practices.* These perennial practices were discovered by the religious founders and have been used by millions of men and women around the world. Now their universal nature can be recognized. *Essential Spirituality* explains the seven perennial practices and offers exercises for applying them in all aspects of life so that you, too, can enjoy the many benefits they offer.

CHAPTER 2

DISCOVERING THE
SEVEN PRACTICES

By exhaustively examining one's own mind,
one may understand his nature.
One who understands his nature understands Heaven.
—*Mencius, Confucian sage*

This book is the result of twenty-three years of research in and
practice of the world's spiritual disciplines. Before then, I was an
agnostic with no belief in the value or validity of religion of any
kind. Raised in outback Australia, far removed from movies and
television, I read voraciously and rapidly fell in love with science.
By my late teens, science was my god. I bowed to its researchers
and worshipped in its laboratories, and as far as I was concerned,
what could not be measured with its instruments did not exist.

I spent more than a decade at universities, stuffing myself with
data and honing my intellect into a precise scientific machine. I collected degrees in psychology, physiology, neuroscience, and medicine, obtained clinical licenses in medicine, psychology, and
psychiatry, and published articles and books on the brain and behavior, occasionally taking time off to tease my religiously oriented
friends for what I believed to be their primitive, outmoded thinking.

INNER EXPLORATIONS

Fascinated by the mysteries of the mind, I left Australia for the
United States to continue my brain research and study psychiatry.

There I found myself desperately trying to help patients whose bizarre mental states and behavior bewildered me. Curious to learn more about the mind, I entered psychotherapy as a client, expecting no more than a few interesting weeks of introspection.

I could not have been more wrong. Therapy taught me how to turn attention inward, and as I explored my own mind, I discovered an unsuspected universe within me as vast and mysterious as the external universe around me. It was literally the greatest shock of my life. Here was an inner world of thoughts and fantasies, images and intuitions, and subterranean motives and emotions of which I had been utterly unaware. Yet this inner world was clearly the key to understanding the mind and myself, and offered invaluable wisdom and guidance about life. I had been internally blind and out of touch with myself, and as I looked around with my newly opened eyes, it seemed that most people suffered a similar blindness.

To continue this exploration, I began to sample a variety of meditation practices. They proved powerful techniques for training the mind and developing qualities such as calm and concentration, sensitivity and self-awareness. Meditation unveiled ever-greater depths of mind. It became increasingly apparent that the part I had previously known was merely a tiny fragment, and that the mind was actually far more vast and mysterious than I had ever suspected.

I was incredibly excited but also painfully puzzled. Why was I, a scientist and religious skeptic, doing meditation, which is a religious technique? And why did it seem to be so helpful if religious practices were merely leftovers from prescientific times? How could I possibly be benefiting from a relic of primitive thinking?

I spent months puzzling over this paradox. Then, one evening as I was getting ready for dinner, I walked lost in thought from my bedroom into the bathroom. As I opened the bathroom door there was a flash of understanding that changed my life forever. I gasped as I recognized that at their spiritual center, the great religions contain a common core of practices for training the mind. These practices cultivate the same profound states of mind, and qualities such as wisdom and love, that the religious founders had originally discovered. Yes, religions contain an enormous amount of popular nonsense, but they also contain a core of wisdom and practices of remarkable transformative power.

With this new appreciation my life changed direction completely. I plunged into intensive study of religions and spiritual practices. At first I gravitated towards Asian traditions. I learned Buddhist meditation and spent many months in retreats, where I devoted myself to full-time practice. I traveled around the world in search of wise men and women, studied with theologians and philosophers, and devoured the words of the Buddha, Confucius, Lao Tsu, and other sages.

After several years, I turned back to explore my native tradition, Christianity. To my amazement and delight, I found that I could now recognize depths of wisdom within it that I had once completely missed.

My previous exposure to Christianity had been limited to Sunday school and conventional churches. Now I found that behind these conventional institutions existed a rich two-thousand-year-long tradition of spiritual practices and contemplative wisdom, though most Christians knew very little about them. My meditation practice had given me the gift of sufficient spiritual experience and understanding to appreciate teachings that I had once overlooked. I eagerly took up Christian contemplative practices and continue them to this day.

This new appreciation of Christianity led to an interest in its Jewish roots. I began to explore Jewish spiritual practices, many of which had been reserved for advanced students and carefully hidden from public view until recently. When an opportunity became available, I also began the study of Islam, the other world religion which, along with Christianity, sprang from Jewish roots. Along the way I made brief forays into other traditions, including the earliest of all traditions, shamanism, which resulted in my book *The Spirit of Shamanism*.

DISCOVERING THE SEVEN PRACTICES

Gradually I began to recognize certain practices common to these religions. The first hint came from Ram Dass, probably the only Harvard professor ever to drop out and become a spiritual teacher. He suggested that all spiritual traditions emphasize three qualities of mind and contain practices for developing them: practices of developing ethics, concentration, and wisdom.

Ethics, he explained, are essential. If we live unethically and deliberately hurt others, we also hurt ourselves, because our minds become ridden with guilt and fear. Concentration is necessary in order to calm our restless minds and to disentangle them from the countless worries and obsessions that typically preoccupy us. Wisdom must be developed if we are to understand life and ourselves and to live well. These certainly made sense, but over time I began to recognize that there are also other essential common practices.

Transforming emotions was the first to become obvious. Each tradition recognizes the painful destructive power of such feelings as fear and hatred and offers methods for reducing them, while cultivating beneficent emotions such as love and compassion. The result of these techniques is a slow but remarkable transformation of emotional life and the development of emotional wisdom.

Next, I recognized the practice of shifting motivation. Most of us focus on and even become addicted to things like money, possessions, praise, and power. Spiritual traditions, however, all cry out a warning that to obsessively crave such things is to suffer, because they offer only temporary solace, are ultimately unsatisfying, and all too easily distort our values. "Even wise men cannot deal with wealth and fame. So how can you?" asks Taoism. The traditions therefore offer techniques to reduce such cravings and to replace them with healthier, more satisfying desires.

As my own awareness gradually became clearer, I recognized that clearing awareness is also a common practice. Usually perception is clouded by our fears, craving, and wandering attention, so that, as the Christian St. Paul said, we see through "a darkened glass." Clearing our awareness and awakening spiritual vision is therefore crucial if we are to see ourselves and the world sensitively and accurately. Spiritual disciplines provide methods for doing so.

Finally, I began to appreciate the vital importance of service: the practice of consciously contributing to others. Service reduces destructive motives such as greed and cultivates healthy alternatives such as kindness and generosity. Deep spiritual practice is not done for oneself alone, but also to benefit others. In fact, a central goal of spiritual work is to transform yourself so as to be effective at what Mohammad, the founder of Islam, considered the "most excellent of all virtues": helping others.

Though the seven practices can be done in any order, the following sequence is particularly helpful for learning them, as the progression of chapters in the book will make clear. The seven perennial practices are:

- Transform your motivation: reduce craving and find your soul's desire.
- Cultivate emotional wisdom: heal your heart and learn to love.
- Live ethically: feel good by doing good.
- Concentrate and calm your mind.
- Awaken your spiritual vision: see clearly and recognize the sacred in all things.
- Cultivate spiritual intelligence: develop wisdom and understand life.
- Express spirit in action: embrace generosity and the joy of service.

In calling these the seven perennial practices, I am distinguishing practices from techniques and exercises. I am using the term *practice* to refer to the discipline of cultivating a crucial capacity of mind, such as wisdom or concentration. Practices are rehearsals of desired qualities, which eventually become spontaneous, natural ways of being. By contrast, I use the words *technique* and *exercise* to indicate the specific methods used in a practice. For example, the specific techniques of meditation and reflection are part of the practice of cultivating wisdom.

This distinction makes clear why some well-known techniques, such as music and prayer, are not listed among the perennial practices. Things get a little tricky because the word practice can do double duty in spiritual language and people sometimes speak of practicing a technique, such as practicing a meditation. However, for our purposes, it will be valuable to maintain a distinction between the more general practices and the more specific techniques and exercises they employ.

CHAPTER 3

USING THIS BOOK

The fragrance of blossoms soon passes;
the ripeness of fruit is gone in a twinkling.
Our time in this world is so short,
better to avoid regret:
Miss no opportunity to savor the ineffable.

—Loy Ching Yuen,
20th-century Taoist Master

Each practice, exercise, and idea in this book is applicable to life and helpful in transforming it. Test them for yourself. This book allows you to do just that.

These practices require no specific religious belief, nor do they require giving up any specific religious belief. This book is much more concerned with learning and living than with believing. All that is necessary is an open mind and a willingness to experiment. The crucial question is whether the practices are helpful to you.

This is not to imply that spiritual practice is easy. It takes courage to examine yourself and your life carefully. It takes effort to do the exercises regularly and commitment to keep doing them during difficult times. Fortunately, the more you practice, the more these essential qualities grow. Above all, be patient. Transforming yourself and your life is a gradual process.

ABOUT THIS BOOK

Each of the following sections presents one of the seven perennial practices. It begins by describing the importance and benefits of the practice. Then suggestions for doing the practice are offered, accompanied by a variety of exercises for applying it in daily life. Finally, I describe some of the practice's more advanced stages and ecstatic experiences.

Spiritual Exercises

Each religious tradition provides both the seven perennial practices and an array of exercises to implement them. *Essential Spirituality* offers some of the most powerful, yet simple and easy, exercises that are directly applicable to daily life.

These exercises are either ancient exercises taken directly from one or more religions, or modern modifications adapted to contemporary needs. In most cases I have modified and updated exercises myself, and occasionally I have borrowed from contemporary teachers. This updating makes the practices more relevant to our modern lives. For example, the religious founders emphasized the importance of being peaceful. However, they did not say much about how to do this while driving a car or talking on the phone. As we all know, driving and talking on the telephone can leave us angry and anxious or calm and relaxed. Therefore, some exercises focus on these and other modern activities to foster spiritual qualities.

Each exercise is a potent tool for self-transformation and awakening. I say this on the basis of three things: the recommendations of wise people throughout the ages, my own experience, and that of my students. At some time over the last twenty-three years I have done each of the exercises myself and found them helpful. In addition, I have taught many to students, who also found them valuable. The exercises have been selected for their simplicity and immediate effects, and with only three exceptions, which I will point out, they usually offer benefits the first time they are done.

These exercises are especially valuable because they can all be done in the midst of daily life. There is no need to abandon your job or flee to a monastery. Monasteries can be wonderful for intensive spiritual practice, but so too can ordinary life. These exercises are designed to transform daily activities into opportunities for spiritual awakening.

The Focus of the Book

For the sake of simplicity and effectiveness, this book is highly focused: on the practical, the major world religions, and the most eminent teachers.

1) *The focus is highly practical.* Over the centuries each religion has accumulated large amounts of theory and also a great amount of nonsense. While theories are interesting to scholars, they usually offer little practical benefit and can be terrible time-wasting distractions. Consequently, I have minimized the theoretical, discarded the nonsensical, and presented only those ideas and exercises that are clearly practical and effective.

2) *I have focused on seven major religions: The monotheisms of Judaism, Christianity, and Islam, and the Asian religions of Hinduism, Buddhism, Taoism, and Confucianism.* These traditions are called the "world religions" or "great religions" because they have been so enormously influential.

Of course, each tradition has numerous branches, and not every branch contains all seven practices. Yet if we look at the totality of each authentic tradition, we certainly find these practices. For example, Confucius lived in a time of great social unrest and desperately wanted to heal the injustices he saw around him. Consequently he focused primarily on practices such as ethics, wisdom, service, and compassion. There was, however, very little emphasis on developing concentration or spiritual vision, and some scholars argue that classical Confucianism cannot be considered a religion. But over the centuries Confucianism developed a strong contemplative spiritual dimension, especially after it absorbed ideas from Buddhism and Taoism and flowered into neo-Confucianism, in which all seven practices hold an honored place.

3) *I have drawn mainly from the most eminent figures in each tradition.* Where possible I have used the words of the founders, such as Jesus, Mohammad, Lao Tsu, Confucius, and the Buddha.

Using Evidence from Science and Psychology

Mature spirituality cannot be limited to ancient ideas and long-dead teachers. Rather, if spirituality is to live in us and through us, it must embrace our modern world and incorporate relevant findings from contemporary science.

Science and religion have long been at each other's throats in a battle extending over centuries. Some criticisms have certainly been valid. For example, scientists have rightly scoffed at religious myths that Lao Tsu was born at 900 years of age, that Buddha walked within minutes of birth, and at Archbishop James Ussher's seventeenth-century claim that "the world was created on the twenty-second of October, 4004 B.C. at six o'clock in the evening." Fortunately, Ussher was corrected by Dr. John Lightfoot, Vice Chancellor of the University of Cambridge, who from his reading of the Bible proclaimed that "man was created by the Trinity on the twenty-third of October, 4004 B.C., at nine o'clock in the morning."

Likewise, religious scholars and philosophers have shredded the claims that science is the only way to obtain valid information and that science can encompass all reality. Science cannot, for example, directly assess subjective experience and can say next to nothing about such vital dimensions of life as meaning and purpose.

However, this war is really waged between pseudoreligion, with its untestable, dogmatic claims, and pseudoscience, especially *scientism:* the belief that science is the only means to acquire valid knowledge. The fatal reply to the scientismist is, "Please show me your scientific proof that science is the only means for acquiring valid knowledge," to which there can be no answer, only stunned silence. There is no such proof.

There is no war between mature spirituality, with its emphasis on directly testing claims and practices for ourselves, and mature science, with its similar emphasis on direct observation and testing. Consequently we can, and should, take note of relevant findings from modern science whenever they throw light on spirituality. Psychology in particular is now exploring relevant areas such as meditation, states of consciousness, and transpersonal development. These studies have thrown light on how spiritual practices work, confirmed some of their benefits, and led to the birth of "transpersonal psychology," a field of psychology dedicated to integrating perennial wisdom and modern science. *Essential Spirituality* includes contemporary ideas and research findings wherever they illuminate spiritual practices. This makes possible a new way to assess spiritual claims.

Until recently there were only two ways to validate spirituality: faith and personal experience. With faith we simply take the word of spiritual authorities—a person or a book—and accept that if they say something is true, then it must be so. But of course, teachers and books can be very, very wrong. This kind of "untested faith," as Buddhists call it, or "proof by authority," as modern philosophers describe it, can lead to disasters. Better to test these claims for ourselves by doing the relevant practices, thereby producing "tested faith."

A third approach is now possible. For the first time in history we can test claims ourselves, and we can also see how some of them hold up against relevant research. This dual approach is the method emphasized throughout this book.

THE CHALLENGE OF CHANGE

Changing ourselves is a challenge. Fortunately, there are some general principles that make it easier and that can be used with each of the seven practices. These principles are introduced briefly here, and will be applied specifically in the following chapters.

- *Start easy.* It is a good idea to start with habits and situations that are relatively easy to master. Save the really tough challenges for later, after you have had a few successes and built up your confidence. Jewish wisdom says that "The key to everything is the way you start," and recommends, "Start in a modest way, maintain an earnest effort to aspire to higher and higher realms, and [eventually]...you will have attained undreamed-of heights."
- *Decide how long.* Commit to a trial period for doing the exercises. Deciding never to eat unhealthy food again for the rest of your life sounds wonderful but will probably be overwhelming. It is much better to experiment with a

healthy diet for one day, give it all your attention, and succeed, than to try halfheartedly for months and fail.

- *Make no exceptions.* Until a new habit is firmly established, it is best not to make exceptions. If you commit to being at meetings on time for a week, try to get to *all* of them on time.
- *Look and learn.* With each experiment in change, explore your experience as you proceed. How do you feel? What resistances do you experience? How do other people react? The idea is to learn as much as possible during the process of change.
- *Be gentle.* Be kind and forgiving with yourself. If you make mistakes or fall short of your goals, accept the fact that you are human and humans are imperfect creatures. Remember, these are practices. If you could do them perfectly you would not need to practice.
- *Start again.* If you slip up (and who doesn't?), start again as soon as possible. It doesn't matter if you fall short or make a mistake as long as you start the exercise again. In order to triumph, you only have to succeed one time more than you fail.
- *Write it down.* It helps to keep a diary or notebook in which you record your goals as well as your insights and observations, mistakes and successes. Writing down goals clarifies and strengthens commitment. Research shows that people who write down their goals are far more likely to succeed than those who don't.

   Keeping a diary need not be a major chore—just a few minutes of notes each day can be valuable. Writing crystallizes insights, fools the defense of forgetfulness, and builds a collection of ideas and reflections that can spur further insights even years later. For centuries Jewish and Islamic teachers have praised the benefits of diary-keeping, and modern psychologists now echo their recommendations.
- *Enjoy yourself.* This is a little-known secret of spiritual practice. It's okay—even great—to have a good time! We've been conditioned to think of religious life as a

teeth-gritting sacrifice, and of saints as solemn martyrs. We forget that one of the goals of spiritual practice is joy (and ultimately bliss). The saints and sages I have met are among the happiest people I have ever known. (In this book I am using "saint" to mean a spiritually mature person and "sage" to indicate an individual who is both spiritually mature and especially wise).

There is nothing selfish about enjoying yourself. In fact, as wise people have long said and psychologists have since discovered, happiness makes people less self-focused and more altruistic.

Above All, Do *the Practices*

What is most crucial is that you actually *do* the practices and their exercises, and not just read about them. Fast readers could probably rocket through this entire book in a few hours and come away with lots of fascinating ideas but little personal change. We get out of practice what we put into it. The exercises transform you to the extent that they are done and applied in your daily life. You may not want to do all the exercises the first time you go through the book, but I recommend doing at least some from each chapter and then returning to the others later. In the words of the Buddha, spoken 2,500 years ago and still true today:

> However many holy words you read,
> However many you speak,
> What good will they do you
> If you do not act upon them?

CHAPTER 4

SPIRITUAL PRACTICES

WHAT DO THEY DO
AND HOW DO THEY DO IT?

Little by little, wean yourself.
This is the gist of what I have to say.
From an embryo, whose nourishment comes in the blood,
move to an infant drinking milk,
to a child on solid food,
to a searcher after wisdom,
to a hunter of more invisible game.

—*Rumi*

What do spiritual practices do and how exactly do they do it?
The most venerable answers are that the gods intervene in our
lives—and that practices modify life energy, for example, by rais-
ing kundalini energy or by balancing yin and yang. However, the
most common and vivid descriptions involve metaphors.

METAPHORS OF SPIRITUAL GROWTH

Metaphors are figures of speech in which we describe one
thing—usually something subtle or difficult to grasp—in terms
of something else more concrete and comprehensible. Spiritual
experiences and transformations, by their very nature, are often
subtle and indefinable, and metaphorical descriptions therefore
abound. Each of the metaphors illustrates an aspect of spiritual

development, and together they paint a rich, multifaceted picture of the ways spiritual practices work their many effects. The following are some of the most potent "metaphors of transformation" that guide and describe spiritual growth.

Awakening: Our usual condition is semiconscious, say the sages, and spiritual practices awaken us from our slumber.

Dehypnosis: Our slumber is said to be a kind of trance or hypnosis. Hypnotized people suffer a constricted state of mind in which their awareness and behavior are largely limited by the suggestions of other people. Yet hypnotized people usually recognize neither their limitations nor the fact they have been hypnotized. Only when dehypnotized do they become free and know that they were entranced. Spiritual practices free us from the collective trance in which we all slumber.

Enlightenment: According to this metaphor, we stumble about in inner darkness, but spiritual disciplines bring understanding, light, and vision.

Uncovering: Our true nature or Self is said to be covered or veiled from awareness, but spiritual disciplines dissolve these veils and restore awareness of our true identities.

Freedom: We are said to be enslaved by our wayward motives and emotions, but taming them brings freedom.

Metamorphosis: As nature transforms the caterpillar into an exquisite butterfly, so too do spiritual practices transform us.

Unfolding: The beauty of the rose may be hidden but is already present within the bud. Likewise, our transcendent beauty and potential are hidden within, and spiritual practices help us unfold and blossom.

Wholeness: Both spiritual traditions and modern psychology suggest that our minds are sadly splintered and dissociated into warring fragments. Spiritual practices heal and whole the mind and restore us to unity of mind and purpose.

Journey: The metaphor of the journey implies that we are traveling to a goal. This goal can seem a far-off distant place, but spiritual wisdom reveals that the goal is our Self and is forever here and now, awaiting only our recognition and remembrance, in this and every moment.

Death and Rebirth: The old, false self must yield to make way for
the new and true. Spiritual practices make us strong enough
to be willing to die—the surrender of our former self-image
can feel like dying. Out of the ashes of the ego arises,
phoenix-like, a new self-image. This new self-image will itself die and be reborn repeatedly, until we finally recognize
that who and what we really are is far beyond all images and
concepts. Then there is no self-image left to die, and only
the deathless remains.

ACCELERATING YOUR DEVELOPMENT

Authentic spiritual practices also foster development. Spiritual
disciplines restart or accelerate psychological and spiritual
growth, taking us at whatever level we are stuck on and helping
us to grow beyond it. This idea fits beautifully with contemporary research.

Stages of Development

Psychologists now agree that human development proceeds
through three major stages: preconventional, conventional, and
postconventional, also known as prepersonal, personal, and
transpersonal. We are born bewildered and unsocialized at the
prepersonal and preconventional stage, with no coherent sense
of ourselves as people and with no sense of the conventions of
society. We are then gradually enculturated, informally by family and media, formally by the educational system.

In this way we are introduced to—and hypnotized into—
the conventional view of things. For the most part, we come to
see and act as society suggests. We tend to assume that our culture's beliefs are valid, its morals appropriate, and its values fulfilling. We also accept its worldview—its picture of the universe
and ourselves. We mature to the conventional/personal stage
and become firmly entrenched in its view of reality. Fortunately, there is much that is valuable in the conventional worldview.

Limits of Conventional Living

Across centuries and societies, though, wise people have also lamented the limitations of conventional development. Conventionality is associated with clouded awareness and inauthentic, unfulfilling ways of life. In Asia this distorted awareness is described as *maya*, an illusion or a dream.

Western traditions make a similar diagnosis. Both Islam and Christianity describe our vision as veiled, while existential philosophers complain that conventional living is unreflective and superficial. Some psychologists lament that we live in a "consensus trance," or a "shared hypnosis," and that at its worst, as in barbarous wars or mass genocide, this becomes a "collective psychosis." William James, often regarded as America's greatest psychologist and philosopher, summarized our condition in his usual pungent way:

> Compared to what we ought to be, we are only half-awake.
> Our fires are dampened, our drafts are checked; we are making use of only a small part of our mental and physical resources.

These views from East and West, from religion, philosophy, and psychology, all converge on a startling conclusion of enormous importance: *We are only half-grown and half-awake.* Development has proceeded from preconventional to conventional, but then grinds to a halt in a semiconscious trance. We do not usually recognize this trance for several reasons: we have been hypnotized since infancy, we all share in it, and we live in the biggest cult of all, namely *culture.* Much of the misery in our lives, the turmoil in our relationships, and the tragedies in the world begin to make sense once these facts are appreciated.

The Benefits of Further Growth

The good news is that the conventional stage of life can be a stepping-stone rather than a stopping place. Psychology has recently rediscovered what philosophers such as Plato and Hegel have long claimed, and what the great religions have long proclaimed: further development is possible. Our usual conventional condition may be a form of collective developmental arrest, but development can proceed far beyond what we thought were the limits of health and normality. All of us harbor enormous but usually unrecognized potential for growth, and the higher reaches of transpersonal, transconventional maturity merge into the higher stages of spiritual growth. Spiritual practices are the tools that make this growth possible.

Those who reach the higher stages live, love, relate, and play in far more satisfying and helpful ways than less mature people do. Exactly what these higher stages feel like will be the subject of later chapters, but the following story gives a taste of their importance in one arena: ethics.

A psychological study offered terrifying evidence of the extent to which ordinary, well-meaning, but conventional people will follow orders and inflict torture on innocent victims. It also demonstrated that people who have matured to postconventional levels are far more independent and unwilling to inflict pain on others.

In this experiment, actors were strapped into chairs and wired to electrodes connected to a fake shock generator. A gauge on the generator ranged from "Slight Shock" at one end to "Danger: Severe Shock" and finally "XXX" at the other end.

Experimental subjects were told they were part of a study on learning. They were instructed to give the actor (who they did not know was only acting) a shock of increasing intensity every time he gave a wrong answer (which he did deliberately). With each increase of apparent shock, the actor pretended to suffer more severely, until he screamed at the top of his lungs and begged to be released. If the experimental subjects hesitated to apply the shock, the experimenter told them they must continue. Almost two-thirds of the subjects administered the highest-level "XXX" shock even though they believed it was potentially lethal.

People at different levels of moral development responded in very different ways. In general, those people at the conventional level obeyed, while those at transconventional levels stood their ground and refused to obey orders blindly.

The same principle holds in the real world and under far more tragic circumstances. One of the grimmest episodes of the Vietnam War occurred in 1968 when an American infantry patrol entered the village of My Lai and slaughtered over 300 civilians. Subsequent studies of the soldiers showed that those at postconventional moral levels were less likely to follow unethical orders and inflict suffering.

BLOCKS TO TRANSPERSONAL DEVELOPMENT

While society supports development from the preconventional to the conventional, it usually neglects or even violently resists development beyond. Why? Because postconventional wisdom can seriously undermine conventional assumptions and ways of life, the innumerable shared myths (such as that money can guarantee happiness or that our nation is superior) that lull individuals and societies asleep and maintain the social status quo. Though these myths may comfort, they do so at considerable cost. A person attempting to grow beyond the usual conventional level cannot expect much support from society.

Growth means overcoming our own personal resistances as well. Surprisingly, we fear our potential greatness almost as much as our present weakness. One reason is that we are wary of seeming vain, inflated, or grandiose. We also fear that if we grew into our greatness we would be very different people. Who would we be, what would we do, what new responsibilities would we face? All would be new and unfamiliar because real growth involves movement from the known into the unknown. We would have to give up our old familiar myths and stories about who we are because, as psychologist Jean Houston recognized, we are required:

> to die to one story, one myth, in order to be reborn to a larger one.... Development involves giving up a smaller story in order to wake up to a larger story.

This fear of our own potential is a very real and powerful force, well known to both spiritual teachers and psychotherapists. It has been called by many names: "the evasion of growth," "voluntary self-crippling," "fear of one's own greatness," and "the Jonah complex," after Jonah, an Israelite prophet who tried to resist a divine call to preach.

Fortunately, most of the discomfort associated with growth is only temporary, but it is hard to recognize this fact beforehand. Before making the leap, growth looks like a sacrifice. Only afterward is it apparent that the only sacrifice was the loss of the cold comfort of one's formerly constricted way of life. According to the twentieth-century Indian sage Aurobindo:

> This is why it is so difficult to explain the path to one who has not tried; he will see only his point of view of today, or rather the loss of his point of view. And yet, if we only knew how each loss of one's viewpoint is a progress and how life changes when one passes from the stage of the closed truth to the stage of the open truth—a truth like life itself, too great to be trapped by points of view because it embraces every point of view and sees the utility of each thing at every stage of an infinite development; a truth great enough to deny itself and pass endlessly into a higher truth.

Requirements for Transpersonal Growth

Given these difficulties, it is not surprising that we require help in order to grow to the transpersonal stage. Fortunately the great religions offer support at all developmental stages. In childhood they can provide a sense of comfort and security. In conventional adulthood, traditional religious institutions offer comfort and community, a code of conduct and a creed: a belief system to explain life and the world.

But though institutional religions offer meaning and guidance for a conventional lifestyle, this is usually not sufficient to propel people into growth beyond the conventional. For that, something more is needed, a spiritual discipline, a set of practices designed to foster further growth.

Ideally that discipline will be accompanied by a spiritual community, a group of like-minded people similarly dedicated to transpersonal growth. This community will provide the support that the larger community cannot, and ideally will include one or more advanced practitioners who can act as guides or teachers. It is possible to make progress alone, but the support of a group and the guidance of a teacher are invaluable.

TRANSFORM YOUR MOTIVATION

REDUCE CRAVING AND FIND YOUR SOUL'S DESIRE

All you want is to be happy. All your desires, whatever they may be, are of longing for happiness. Basically, you wish yourself well.... Desire by itself is not wrong. It is life itself, the urge to grow in knowledge and experience. It is the choices you make that are wrong. To imagine that some little thing—food, sex, power, fame—will make you happy is to deceive oneself. Only something as vast and deep as your real self can make you truly and lastingly happy.

—*Sri Nisargadatta Maharaj,*
20th-century Hindu sage

CHAPTER 5

THE SECRET OF HAPPINESS

To a land where people cease from coveting peace comes of course.

—Lao Tsu

Everyone wants to be happy. This is the all-consuming drive that powers everything from our daily routines to the growth of civilization. Spiritual practices are so rewarding because they not only make us happier, but ultimately open the door to bliss, a type of happiness that is infinitely more profound and satisfying than any of our usual fleeting pleasures.

Although everyone wants happiness, most people suffer from tragically mistaken ideas about what brings it. Worse still, once we decide on what we think will make us happy—whether it be fame or fortune, people or possessions—we tend to become attached to them. To know happiness and bliss, we need to change our motivation. This means reducing craving for those things that do not bring true happiness and redirecting desires to those that do. The first practice helps us change our motives by:

- recognizing our mistaken ideas about what brings happiness
- relinquishing attachments
- recognizing and seeking what truly fosters happiness

MISTAKEN IDEAS ABOUT
WHAT BRINGS HAPPINESS

What leads to true happiness? A glance at our possessions and priorities, our society and media, makes it very apparent what most people *believe* will bring true happiness: *things*—and lots of them. Each billboard and neon sign, every radio and television wails forth a siren song suggesting that if we just buy this, own that, taste this, then real contentment will finally be ours. Our culture is fixated on the physical foursome of money, sensuality, power, and prestige—we are lost in the seductive illusion that if we can somehow just get enough of them, we will finally be fully and forever happy.

By contrast, the great religions are downright heretical. They practically scream in horror at such ideas, which they regard as absolute nonsense. Certainly we need enough money to live on, and the physical foursome can indeed be pleasant. But to believe that one of them or all of them can produce profound, enduring happiness, let alone bliss, is a delusion.

Century after century and sage after sage, all the great religious traditions have begged us to recognize a crucial fact: No outside sensation or possession can ever give us full or lasting satisfaction. In fact, obsession with wealth and possessions tranquilizes us with trivia and distracts us from what is truly important in life. As Chuang Tzu, one of the greatest Taoist sages, warned, "You use all your vital energy on external things and wear out your spirit." Mohammad summarized the problem by pointing out that "It is difficult for a person laden with riches to climb the steep path that leads to bliss." Jesus asked, "For what is a man profited, if he shall gain the whole world, and lose his own soul?"

True happiness and bliss are available *if* we know where and how to look for them. Before we explore this possibility, we need to ask two crucial questions:

1) What evidence is there to back up the great religions' claim that external pleasures are less than fully satisfying?
2) If this claim is true, why do we become so hypnotized by these pleasures and how can we free ourselves from their spell?

The Science of Satisfaction

Never in human history have so many had so much. Though more than half the world suffers horrendous poverty, the other part enjoys riches undreamed of by history's greatest kings. Cars and computers, telephones and televisions, faxes and refrigerators, fresh food and frozen delicacies: the list of possessions and possibilities is virtually endless. We are awash in technological wizardry, labor-saving devices, and pleasant pastimes. The richest person in past history had only a tiny fraction of the pleasures available to many of us.

Are we happier for having them? According to psychologist David Myers, who wrote *The Pursuit of Happiness*, the answer is "a little bit." Considerable research shows that once we have escaped poverty and our basic needs are met, further income and possessions add remarkably little to our well-being. Myers summarized the situation:

> Strangely, however, there is only a slight tendency for people who make lots of money to be more satisfied with what they make. It's true: Satisfaction isn't so much getting what you want as wanting what you have.

Take the case of the United States. During the thirty years from 1960 to 1990, the average person's buying power and possessions doubled. Did this double happiness? Myers's painful conclusion:

> Our becoming much better-off over the last thirty years has not been accompanied by one iota of increased happiness and life satisfaction.

These facts come as an enormous shock to most people. They demolish the central assumptions about happiness around which so many lives and cultures revolve. Millions of people sacrifice their health to become rich; capitalists and economists believe that money is the central human motive; countless consumers are forever buying the latest gadget; and politicians keep dangling the lure of expanding wealth before hypnotized voters. Of course we need to help people escape from crushing poverty. But recent

research agrees with the world religions: more and more money
and possessions do not bring more and more happiness.

A Balanced Life

> The richest among you is the one who is not entrapped by greed....
> The miser is the poorest of all.
>
> —*Mohammad*

There is a very common misunderstanding that has caused enormous amounts of unnecessary suffering. Physical pleasures such
as money, sex, and possessions are not inherently bad, nor is having them evil. They are some of the pleasures of life and certainly
we can enjoy them. In fact, the monotheistic traditions—Judaism,
Christianity, and Islam—sometimes refer to them as gifts of God
and describe our world as a garden of earthly delights. However,
if we make the fatal mistake of believing that these pleasures are
the best, or the *only* source of joy, we become addicted to them as
surely as heroin users become slaves of their drug.

What we need is a comprehensive, balanced view—a philosophy of life—that recognizes and honors the appropriate pleasures
and accords each an appropriate place in life. The world religions
do this, and Hinduism offers a particularly clear account.

The Four Aims of Life

Hinduism acknowledges four major aims of life: *artha, kama,
dharma*, and *moksha. Artha* is the acquisition of material possessions and of all the things necessary for a comfortable and con-
tributory life. *Kama* is sensual pleasure and love, and its classic
text, *The Kamasutra*, is a book on lovemaking that is known worldwide. The third aim is *dharma*, a word rich with meaning but in its
essence referring to the broad range of moral and religious duties.

Each of these three aims of life is regarded as appropriate and
pleasurable. Each can be honorably pursued and enjoyed as part of
a full life, provided that the fourth aim is also honored and pursued.

The fourth aim, *moksha*, provides the context and balance for
the first three and gives profundity to Hindu philosophy and life.
Moksha is spiritual release, enlightenment, or liberation, and is re-

garded as the ultimate goal and good of human life. The first three aims are to be pursued not only for the pleasures they bring, but also for spiritual growth. Integrating the four aims ensures that the first three are not pursued unethically or excessively, and orients all of life and its many delights to the inconceivable delight of enlightenment.

THE CURSE OF CRAVING

Attachment, or craving, and its full-blown cousin, addiction, are very different from simple desire. Attachment is a compulsion that screams, "I *must* have what I desire if I am to be happy." For example, if I simply desire an ice cream and get it, that's wonderful; if I don't get it, it is no big deal. But if I am attached to ice cream, I *must* have it or I suffer. Desire is simple wanting, attachment a compulsive necessity. Unfulfilled desires produce little impact; unfulfilled attachments yield frustration and pain.

The Costs of Craving

All the great religions regard craving as a major cause of human suffering. Interestingly, Western psychology and society are beginning to agree. Recently we have begun to recognize just how pervasive and destructive attachments are and how powerfully they warp lives and cultures. Our attachment to consumption is poisoning our planet while nicotine, the most addictive and dangerous of all drugs, murders millions of people each year.

In the West we focus on drugs. But the great religions have long pointed out that we can become attached, even addicted, to practically anything: money, power, fame, sex, status, beliefs, food, clothes, self-image—the list is virtually endless. Once we are hooked, our attachments distort our priorities and blind us to the true source of happiness, as Tibetan Buddhism graphically portrays:

> You are deceived by your addiction to and desire for sensuous objects,
> As is the moth by the flame of a lamp.

No one has ever made this point as clearly as the Buddha. Born 2,500 years ago, the man who was to become the Buddha lived for twenty-nine years as a prince in pampered luxury. At first he reveled in his royal lifestyle and indulged in every possible pleasure. But shortly before his 30th birthday, while out riding in his chariot, he saw three things that were to change his life and eventually the world: a very old man, someone who was desperately ill, and a corpse. In a moment of shattering insight, he recognized:

1) he and everyone else would inevitably age, sicken, and die;
2) none of his many pleasures and pastimes would last; and
3) none would bring enduring happiness or meaning to his life.

The result was dramatic. He abandoned his palace, his wealth, and even his family and spent the next six years wandering through India in a fierce and unrelenting search for the supreme happiness and goal of life. He tried every known method one after another. He studied philosophy, took up yoga, and practiced such severe asceticism and fasting that he almost died of starvation. In his own words:

> As I took such small quantities of solid and liquid food, my body became extremely emaciated.... Just as is the camel's hoof, even so were my hips for want of food. Just as is a string of beads, even so did my backbone stand out and bend in, for lack of food.... And I, intending to touch my belly's skin, would instead seize my backbone.

Having pursued the path of asceticism to its mortal limits, he realized that neither it nor its opposite, a life of luxury and sensuality, could offer the goal he sought. Instead he settled on what he called the "middle way" between the extremes of asceticism and indulgence.

After taking enough food to ensure his health, he decided on one last supreme effort. Seating himself under a tree, he vowed that he would not get up again until he reached enlightenment, even if he died in the attempt. Throughout that day and night he confronted every craving and fear and probed the utmost depths of his mind until, just before sunrise, understanding dawned and he awoke. Thus he became "*the Buddha*," which means "the Awakened One."

During his first thirty-five years he had tried every spiritual practice, tasted every pleasure, forsaken every pleasure, and finally attained the supreme pleasure of enlightenment. When the

Buddha spoke about happiness and the means for finding it, he knew what he was talking about.

The Four Noble Truths

He summarized his discoveries in the Four Noble Truths, which constitute the very heart of Buddhism:

1) Life is imbued with difficulties and suffering.
2) The cause of suffering is attachment.
3) Freedom from attachment brings freedom from suffering.
4) Freedom from attachment and suffering can come from practicing the Eight-Fold Path, which centers on ethics, wisdom, and meditation.

At the center of his teachings lies the recognition of the absolutely pivotal role played by attachment. The Buddha observed that while everyone seeks happiness, nearly everyone proceeds in the wrong way. They waste their lives in a never-ending and ultimately futile struggle to fulfill attachments instead of releasing them.

Addictive craving is unquenchable and can never be fully satisfied. Feeding our cravings brings temporary satisfaction but ultimately fuels them further. The Buddha claimed that "The rain could turn to gold and still your thirst would not be quenched."

Along with craving come its inevitable painful companions: destructive emotions such as fear, anger, jealousy, and depression. These emotions are intimately tied to attachment and reflect the ways it operates in us. We fear that we will not get what we crave, boil with anger toward whoever stands in our way, writhe with jealousy toward people who get what we lust after, and fall into depression when we lose hope. Jewish wisdom claims, "To be too fond of this world and of that which is therein provoketh the wrath of Heaven." Maybe so, maybe not. But it certainly provokes our own wrath and other painful emotions.

The amount of suffering in our lives reflects the gap between what we crave and what we have. Craving creates suffering by producing emotional anguish and by being insatiable.

There are subtle spiritual costs as well. Attachment keeps us chained to little pleasures and deprives us of the greatest pleasure of all. Jesus summarized the dilemma by pointing out, "No one can serve two masters.... You cannot serve God and wealth." St. John of the Cross, a sixteenth-century Spanish monk and one of the most influential Catholic mystics, expanded on this theme in the following exquisite lines:

> The Soul that is attached to anything, however much good there may be in it, will not arrive at the liberty of divine union. For whether it be a strong wire rope or a slender and delicate thread that holds the bird, it matters not, if it really holds it fast; for, until the cord be broken, the bird cannot fly. So the soul, held by the bonds of human affections, however slight they may be, cannot, while they last, make its way to God.

No wonder that one of the ten commandments of Judaism and Christianity is "You shall not covet [crave]." The neo-Confucian sage Wang Yang-ming claimed:

> The learning of the great person consists entirely in getting rid of the obscuration of selfish desires [attachments]...so as to restore the condition of forming one body with Heaven, Earth, and the myriad things.

The Cause of Craving

The message from the great religions is clear: we are all addicts. Why do we cling so deeply and desperately to our toys and trinkets if they ultimately cause so much pain?

The great religions suggest that the answer lies in our false sense of identity. They claim that we are separated from the sacred and are thereby unaware of our true nature. This separation is described in various ways. In Judaism and Christianity it is called "the fall." In Hinduism and Buddhism it is specifically the fall into the semiconscious state of *maya*, while in Taoism it is the apparent deviation from the Tao.

But whatever it is called, its underlying message is the same: in falling into illusion we have forgotten our boundless, spiritual nature. Consequently, we underestimate ourselves terribly, believing we are merely little egos isolated in our fragile bodies, and that we are fundamentally fearful and deficient. How could we feel otherwise when we have constricted ourselves so terribly and torn ourselves away from our Source? Believing we are fundamentally deficient and defective, we crave whatever seems to hide, compensate for, or distract us from our deficiencies.

STRATEGIES FOR HANDLING ATTACHMENTS

There are two very different ways we try to quench our attachments. The first of these is common and catastrophic; the second is rare, liberating, and ecstatic.

Strategy 1: Try to Satisfy Attachments

With this approach we try to satisfy our attachments: to eat, own, copulate, or consume as much as possible. Whatever we crave, we try to get. With this strategy we attempt to fill our sense of internal deficiency with external stimulation: with pleasant sensations, more possessions, and greater power. We struggle to reduce the painful gap between what we crave and what we have by having more. Using this approach, we try to arrange the world to fit our attachments, and our lives are spent in searching, *and paying*, for variations of sight, sound, touch, and taste.

This strategy has severe problems. It is hard, never-ending work to get the world shaped up the way we want it. Even if we succeed, the inevitable happens: the world changes.

Even worse, once we get what we thought we wanted, we find it isn't enough. We want more. In order to get the same high, the drug addict needs a larger dose, the miser more wealth, the consumer another shopping binge. In religious language, greed grows; in psychological terms, we habituate. But whatever the language, the results are the same. Attachments swell while satisfactions shrink, a fact David Myers describes as "ever-rising desires mean never-ending dissatisfaction." We keep hearing from advertisers, "You can have it all." What they don't tell us is that having it all is never enough.

Substitute Gratifications Never Satisfy

Why should this be? The answer is very simple but rarely recognized: All these fleeting pleasures are neither what we really need

nor what we really want. They are merely substitute gratifications, futile attempts to compensate for our inner sense of deficiency, whereas our deepest desire is to awaken to our true Self,
in which there is no deficiency.

"What destroys craving?" asked Shankara, who lived in ninth-
century India and is often regarded as the greatest of all Hindu
sages. "Realization of one's true self," he replied.

The hopeless quest for substitute gratifications inevitably fails
because we can never get enough of what we don't really want. Yet
countless people and cultures frantically pursue this quest, while
the polluted, plundered earth around us attests to our insatiable
appetites. Gandhi summarized our situation by pointing out that
the world has enough for everyone's need, but not enough for
everyone's greed.

Once we understand attachments and the diminishing satisfactions they offer, a startling but ultimately liberating conclusion leaps
into awareness: *No thing is ever going to make us fully or lastingly happy!*

We are never, ever going to get enough money, sex, power, possessions, or prestige to be completely satisfied. Paradoxically, this is
not a message of gloom, but rather of freedom and hope, for it liberates us from the painful belief that one more thing will finally and
forever satisfy us, even though every previous thing ultimately failed.
It frees us from the frantic, hopeless quest for some person or possession outside ourselves capable of filling the aching void within.

Strategy 2: Change Your Mind

The good news is that there is a way to reach lasting satisfaction.
This way involves changing our minds about what we think we
need, and it is beautifully portrayed in a story popular among the
Islamic mystics known as Sufis.

One of the Sufis' favorite characters is the trickster Nasrudin.
Often Nasrudin appears to be a complete idiot, but he is actually
a wise and cunning man whose tricks contain brilliant lessons
about life.

One day Nasrudin was out walking and found a man sitting on the
side of the road crying.

"What is the matter, my friend?" asked Nasrudin. "Why are
you crying?"

"I'm crying because I am so poor," wailed the man. "I have no money and everything I own is in this little bag."

"Ah-ha!," said Nasrudin, who immediately grabbed the bag and ran as fast as he could until he was out of sight.

"Now I have nothing at all," cried the poor man, weeping still harder as he trudged along the road in the direction Nasrudin had gone. A mile away he found his bag sitting in the middle of the road, and he immediately became ecstatic. "Thank God," he cried out. "I have all my possessions back. Thank you, thank you."

"How curious!" exclaimed Nasrudin, appearing out of the bushes by the side of the road. "How curious that the same bag that made you weep now makes you ecstatic."

Happiness lies not in feeding and fueling our attachments, but in reducing and relinquishing them. Nowhere is this summarized more succinctly than in the Buddha's Third Noble Truth: "Freedom from attachment brings freedom from suffering."

Likewise, Shankara asked: "How is heaven attained?" and responded, "The attainment of heaven is freedom from cravings."

Countless other sages have agreed. Some have even argued that freedom from attachment—sometimes called *detachment*, *nonattachment*, or *acceptance*—is the greatest of all virtues. Meister Eckhart, who lived in fourteenth-century Germany and is regarded as one of Christianity's greatest mystics, wrote:

> I have read many writings both by the pagan teachers and by the prophets...to find which is the greatest and best virtue with which man can most completely and closely conform himself to God....And as I scrutinize all these writings, so far as my reason can lead and instruct me, I find no other virtue better than a pure detachment from all things.

How does the end of attachment lead to the end of sorrow? Remember that unhappiness reflects the difference between what we crave and what we have. If we relinquish our attachments by accepting what we have, the gap dissolves and so too does our unhappiness. This is why Gandhi, when asked to describe his philosophy of life, needed only three words: "Renounce and rejoice!" and why Meister Eckhart promised that "No one is happier than those who have the greatest nonattachment."

CHAPTER 6

EXERCISES TO
REDUCE CRAVING

Free yourself from greed, for greed is itself an
impoverishment.

—*Mohammad*

Let's be honest. Reducing craving is rewarding but also demanding. We need to be gentle and patient with ourselves and not add to our problems by becoming attached to getting rid of attachments. This is especially true for full-blown addictions such as alcohol and nicotine that have a strong physical basis and that therefore respond best to a combination of physical, psychological, and spiritual treatments.

Reducing attachments is usually a long-term process that takes more than a single exercise, or even several exercises. However, when specific exercises are combined with consistent spiritual practice, attachments gradually weaken over time. The following are some gentle exercises to begin this process by fostering awareness and understanding of the experience of craving.

EXERCISE 1:
RECOGNIZE PAIN AS FEEDBACK

Suffering is a call for inquiry, all pain needs investigation.
—*Sri Nisargadatta Maharaj*

An enormous opportunity opens up once we recognize that our psychological and spiritual sorrows are rooted in attachments.

Sorrows then become valuable feedback because mental pain is like physical pain. It is a warning signal that something is amiss, that we crave something and are bewitched by an attachment. The great religions therefore urge us to recognize our attachments so we can begin releasing them.

To do this, either think of some situation in your life that feels painful or, the next time you feel mental pain—whether it be fear, anger, jealousy, or anything else—stop what you are doing and look for the attachment that underlies it. For example, if you feel angry, it is probably because you believe someone is preventing you from satisfying an attachment. If you reach for a chocolate and become enraged because someone beat you to the last one, it's a good bet that your fondness for chocolate has become an attachment. Likewise, if you feel embarrassed, you are doubtless attached to having people think well of you; if you are jealous, you crave what others have.

It is not that there is necessarily anything bad about some of the things we are attached to. It isn't bad to want to get a degree, a good job, or a good reputation. But when wanting becomes craving, we are setting ourselves up for problems.

※

Once we recognize an attachment, a whole new array of possibilities opens up. Now when we suffer, we have a choice. We can continue to cling and suffer, or we can relinquish the attachment and end the suffering. At this stage the crucial question becomes, "How much pain am I willing to put up with before relinquishing this attachment?" Surprisingly, the answer is often "a lot," for after a lifetime of clinging and believing that fulfilling craving is the only route to happiness, attachments are not always easy to relinquish. The following exercises can help.

EXERCISE 2: EXAMINE THE EXPERIENCE OF CRAVING

Bringing greater awareness to our experience and behavior is crucial if we are to understand and change them. This is one reason why developing clear awareness is one of the seven practices. Yet usually when we are caught in an attachment, we focus attention on what we are trying to get rather than on the actual experience of craving.

Spiritual traditions recommend deliberately examining the sensation of craving itself. To do this, when you next notice yourself captured by a craving, take the opportunity to analyze it carefully and to identify the components of the experience. Stop whatever you are doing. Then carefully explore the experience. See if you can identify the underlying emotions, body sensations, thoughts, feelings, and tensions.

Usually what you find is not terribly pleasant. Craving can feel like a burning in the body accompanied by a contraction and tension of the mind. There may be clusters of painful emotions, such as anxiety and fear. Fantasies of who or what you crave may fill your awareness. Your mind becomes agitated, and bursts of self-destructive thoughts such as "If I don't get this I'll never be happy" race through. Exploring the experience of craving helps you understand it, recognize its painful effects, and naturally helps you want to relinquish it.

Awareness heals, which is another reason why developing clear awareness is one of the seven practices. Simply bringing greater awareness to craving can begin to weaken it and sometimes, as Nisargadatta Maharaj pointed out, "Weak [attachments] can be removed by introspection and meditation." Examining craving is an essential first step in understanding and healing it.

EXERCISE 3: REFLECT ON THE COSTS OF CRAVING

Reflection is a fundamental technique in each of the great religions. It essentially consists of pondering or thinking about an issue or experience in order to understand it and yourself better. As you will see, it is a vital tool for developing wisdom. Here you can use it to recognize the costs of craving.

To do this, find a time and place where you can reflect quietly for several minutes without interruption. Begin by thinking of one of the more powerful attachments running your life. It might, for example, be for nicotine or a fancy car. Then consider all the time and energy that go into acquiring it. Reflect on the effort and money that you sacrifice. Recall the painful emotions that accompany it, such as anger at people who stand in your way, depression when you feel hopeless about getting what you crave, and worry about losing it once you have it.

Simply allow these costs and any accompanying insights to come into awareness. There is no need to force any particular insights to emerge, and there is certainly no need to judge or condemn yourself for having the attachment. Self-condemnation and self-attack only leave us feeling more deficient and therefore more prone to cling to the illusory consolations of our attachments. The aim of this reflection, and of all reflection, is to understand, not to condemn.

EXERCISE 4: RECOGNIZE UNDERLYING THOUGHTS AND BELIEFS

Beneath the emotions and sensations that accompany addictions lurk destructive thoughts and beliefs, and it is extremely helpful to identify them. Perhaps the most common belief is, "I must have *something* in order to be happy." This something can be almost anything: more money, sex, power, a new spouse, or whatever else it is we crave. A closely related belief is the basis of the "if only" game. Here we moan that "If only I had (fill in the blank), then I could be happy."

These beliefs emerge into our awareness as thoughts. Unrecognized thoughts are extraordinarily powerful and hypnotize us into believing them. Their power was suggested by the Buddha, who began his teaching with the words:

> We are what we think.
> All that we are arises with our thoughts.
> With our thoughts we make the world.

Fortunately, these thoughts begin to lose some of their grip on us when we recognize them. Then we see them as what they are: simply thoughts that we do not necessarily have to believe.

For example, suppose you are attached to having people think you are smart, but you do something foolish (as we all do, regularly) and are writhing with embarrassment. If you explore the thoughts racing through your mind, you may find ones such as, "I'll die if anyone finds out about this" or "I'm the stupidest person in the world." A moment's reflection makes it clear that these thoughts are certainly nothing you have to believe. You won't die of embarrassment, and there is an awful lot of competition for the position of world's stupidest person. You probably aren't even in the running. Recognizing the unreality of such thoughts begins to free us from their grip.

A good time to do this exercise and to recognize such thoughts is when you are in the grip of an attachment, with all the emotional turmoil it brings. Then the mind is agitated and related thoughts race through it. The problem is that unless we take time to stop and examine the thoughts, we succumb to believing them.

The first crucial step, once you recognize you are being run by an attachment, is to stop whatever you are doing. Take a moment to relax and breathe deeply. Then take several minutes to see what you are telling yourself about your attachment. If you find yourself thinking, for example, "I must have that" or "I'll die if anyone finds out about this," then recognize that these are just thoughts and are certainly nothing you have to believe.

Once thoughts are recognized as what they really are—just thoughts—another step is possible. Then you can begin to substitute saner, more realistic and accepting thoughts such as, "Okay, I made a mistake, but everyone does that," or "Well, maybe it doesn't matter if people don't think I'm smart." In this way we can begin to recognize that the thoughts and beliefs that perpetuate our attachments are ridiculous, need not be believed, certainly don't have to be obeyed, and can be replaced with healthier ones.

Because they are so subtle and quick, thoughts are masters of seduction, seducing us into believing that what they say is invariably true. Consequently, identifying thoughts is an important but demanding process. We will therefore return to it during the practice of developing clear awareness, at which stage it will be somewhat easier. However, there is benefit in recognizing even a few attachment-related thoughts and beliefs now, because recognizing them reduces their grip, and the grip of attachment, on us.

EXERCISE 5:
INDULGE AN ATTACHMENT

One of my meditation teachers was an Indian man who had devoted years to spiritual practice. He had studied many spiritual texts, lived in monasteries under austere conditions, and done long meditation retreats. He had had some very deep experiences. Yet in spite of all this he still had one problem he had not been able to overcome: he was utterly attached to sweets. In fact, he spent a significant amount of the very little money he had buying them.

Finally, one day he went to the market with a large box. Going from one sweet stall to another, he filled the box with delicacies until his money ran out. Then he went home, laid the sweets out on his table, and meditated. When his mind was clear, he took his first mouthful.

Summoning all his awareness, he noted every aspect of the experience. He observed his eager anticipation as he reached for the first morsel, the sensations as the sweets filled his mouth, and the first taste of sweetness and the rush of pleasure that immediately raced through his mind. Then he watched himself swallow and immediately reach for more.

Mouthful after mouthful, sweet after sweet, he continued to eat and observe. After a while, he began to notice a change. The sharp, sweet taste began to cloy rather than stimulate, and the rush of pleasure disappeared.

Still, he continued eating and watching. Now the eager anticipation became distaste. The intense sweetness, which had initially seemed so exciting, now felt vaguely sickening, and the sight of the remaining sweets only increased the feeling. He continued to eat until he had to force himself to pick up another sweet. By the time he finally got up from the table, he had cured his attachment to sweets forever.

Of course, indulging a craving is no guarantee of a cure. If it were, alcoholics would drink themselves sober instead of dead. However, when indulgence is used occasionally and skillfully, with careful awareness and in the context of a spiritual practice, it can sometimes be very valuable.

Mindfully indulging or frustrating an attachment offers an opportunity to learn a great deal about it. Often we feel so guilty about our attachments that we don't allow ourselves to really enjoy them. On the other hand, because they overwhelm us, we may never find out what it is like to do without them completely. This exercise and the next offer an opportunity to do both.

Select an attachment and for one day indulge and enjoy it to the full. If you crave chocolates, follow the example of my meditation teacher. Buy several boxes and eat as many as you can as mindfully as you can. If you want to watch television, find a period when you have a long stretch of unbroken time, sit yourself in front of it, and don't get up unless you have to. The only restriction is that you must not indulge an attachment in a way that would significantly harm yourself or, of course, anyone else.

The key to success in this, and many other spiritual exercises, is to be as aware as you can of your experience. How does the twentieth chocolate taste compared to the first? Is the fifth hour of television as enjoyable as the first, or are you simply too brain-dead to get out of the chair? Mindfully indulging an attachment can make its limitations painfully clear.

This realization hit me during my first meditation retreat. I had been meditating daily for over a year, experimenting with a variety of techniques, and found it fascinating and helpful. The obvious next step was to go on a retreat where I would be able to practice without distraction for several days and have teachers available for guidance.

The day after a long night celebrating my thirtieth birthday, I climbed bleary-eyed onto a plane bound for Oregon. A few hours later I stumbled into an isolated country school that was closed for the summer and was to serve as the retreat center. There, with fifty others, I braced myself for ten days of meditation. In order to make the experience as deep as possible, we were asked to practice full time and to minimize any distractions.

It was quite a contrast from the previous night of loud music, singing, good food, and champagne. Now all we did was sitting and walking meditation. There was no talking, no music, and of course no alcohol or sex. I was less than happy.

The food was nutritious but far from gourmet. With nothing to distract me, I found myself increasingly lost in fantasies of food. Memories of birthday cake and champagne floated tantalizingly through my mind; visions of gourmet meals paraded by.

Finally I broke down, snuck out of the retreat center, and walked the three miles into town. I stuffed a pillowcase with every delicacy I could lay my hands on. With the bulging pillowcase thrown over my shoulder, I looked like Santa Claus, yet the only person I planned to give these gifts to was myself. Then I went to a restaurant and ordered a fancy meal.

What a letdown! It took only a few mouthfuls to learn several lessons. While the food was nice, eating it was nowhere near as satisfying as I had fondly imagined in my fantasies. Nor did it remove the underlying feelings of fear and loneliness which, I now recognized, had flared up in response to the unfamiliar retreat environment and seduced me into trying to console myself with food. Greatly disillusioned, I trudged the three miles back to the retreat center, staggering under the weight of the heavy pillowcase stuffed with food that I no longer wanted.

This experience was not much fun, but it certainly offered some valuable lessons. It taught me how cravings can fill the mind with fantasies, overwhelm good judgment, and consume enormous amounts of time and energy. Yet indulging them may prove nowhere near as satisfying as we imagine. In addition, they can hide deeper fears and longings that must be recognized if we are to free ourselves from their grip and be happy.

The retreat itself, though difficult at first, proved invaluable. My meditation deepened dramatically and remained deeper afterward, and I learned an enormous amount about the mind and myself.

I even came to appreciate the silence and simple, uncluttered lifestyle. At first it felt austere and difficult, but over time I came to love the freedom from ceaseless activity and distractions as well as the peace and healing that silence offers. Consequently, retreats continue to be a regular and valued part of my life.

EXERCISE 6:
FRUSTRATE AN ADDICTION

An exercise that complements the previous one is to deliberately frustrate an addiction. This is a common exercise in the world religions. When taken to extremes and when all cravings are frustrated, it becomes asceticism. However, it can also be done far more gently by selecting one attachment at a time.

To do this, choose something you are attached to—perhaps cigarettes, certain foods, or television—and decide to go without one for a specific time period, such as a day. Be sure to select realistic goals that you can be reasonably certain of accomplishing. It is better by far to decide to go without cigarettes for a morning and succeed than rashly to decide to quit forever and fail miserably. Of course, it is again crucial to ensure that the addiction frustration you choose does no significant harm to you or anyone else.

During the exercise, bring as much awareness to your experience as possible. You may find it helpful to stop whatever you are doing periodically so you can explore your experience more deeply. Carefully observe the sensations, feelings, and thoughts that arise as you frustrate your cravings. Jotting some notes down in a diary can be useful. In the evening, take time to reflect on the day and what you learned from it. What feelings did you have, what fears arose? What new insights and understandings emerged, what surprised you? Many people start this exercise feeling fearful about being deprived but are pleasantly surprised to find that they manage better than expected. This is why the exercise not only helps understand and weaken addictions but can also strengthen willpower and self-esteem.

The exercise can also be done in ways that strengthen additional capacities. For example, going without food by fasting for a day is an ancient and widely used technique. I find that its benefits are enhanced if I try to use each feeling of hunger to remind me of the many hungry people around the world. That way, each hunger pang not only reduces craving but also elicits concern and compassion for the hungry. The exercise then both reduces attachment and redirects motivation, the two key elements of the practice of transforming motivation. By redirecting motivation we can focus on what we *really* want and find our soul's desire.

CHAPTER 7

FIND YOUR
SOUL'S DESIRE

REDIRECT MOTIVATION

Where your treasure is, there will your heart be also.
—Jesus

Our attachments are unnecessary psychological and spiritual baggage. Yet many people worry that relinquishing their attachments will leave them apathetic and joyless. This utterly false fear assumes we need attachments in order to motivate ourselves; for example, we must be attached to money in order to work, or we need to crave fame in order to practice a sport or art.

I once believed this. Consequently, my first psychotherapy session proved to be a shock. At the time I had just begun my psychiatry training, and as I walked into my therapist's office and settled into the chair I was eagerly looking forward to learning more about the mind and myself. For the first twenty minutes I felt fascinated and excited as we explored my life patterns and goals. But as we probed more deeply, I began to feel increasingly anxious. Suddenly I was shocked to hear myself blurt out the words, "If you cure me, I'll never amount to anything."

It was a moment of terror, and the beginning of freedom. I deeply believed that I desperately needed my fears and attachments in order to goad and motivate myself, and that without them I would be reduced to an apathetic slob, unmotivated to do or achieve anything of consequence. Later, as the release of each attachment resulted not in a deadening apathy, but in a delightful sense of freedom and energy, I would look back and laugh at this belief. But at the time it seemed very real.

This kind of belief comes from confusing desires with attachments. Desires are a necessary and natural part of life; attachments are an unnecessary source of suffering. Since they are different, desires remain when attachments are relinquished, so we are still motivated to live our lives fully and well. In fact, we are better able to do so, since we are no longer helpless puppets dancing on the strings of compulsive cravings that distort our priorities and lives. Relinquishing attachments leaves us not apathetic but calm, not joyless but content, not indifferent to others but more concerned and caring. According to Patañjali, who wrote the classic text on yoga two thousand years ago, "When we are established in nonattachment, the nature and purpose of existence is understood."

Consider the great saints and sages. They may be free of attachments, but they devote their lives to the welfare of all people and even all creatures. Freed from ceaselessly chasing after the physical foursome, they are able to follow their higher motives.

HIGHER MOTIVES

When the mind is less tossed about by the storms of competing cravings, it feels the gentle pull of subtler, more mature motives, which are healthier, more refined, and ultimately far more satisfying than the desires that usually preoccupy us. The more mature motives include desires for truth and justice, kindness and altruism, beauty and the sacred, or as Plato, the founding father of Western philosophy, famously summarized them: the good, the true, and the beautiful.

These desires are called "higher motives" or "metamotives" and are tremendously honored by the great religions. Though conceived of in quite different ways—for example, the higher chakras of Hinduism or the *yezer tov* ("good inclination") of Judaism—these higher motives are recognized, revered, and cultivated by each tradition. Cultivating them is a central goal of spiritual practice.

Curing Divine Homesickness

At the summit of higher motives is the pull to self-transcendence. This is the desire to transcend our usual false, constricted identity, to awaken to the fullness of our being, and to recognize our true nature and our true relationship with the sacred. It is the compelling call to remember who we really are and to know, even unite with, our Source. Whether described as the yearning for God, the *moksha* drive, or the desire to align with Tao, this pull to enlightenment is a supreme motive; the only one, say the great religions, capable of ultimately offering true satisfaction and bliss. No matter what other desires we satisfy, no matter how much money, sex, and power we obtain, no matter even how much good we do in the world, as long as the yearning for enlightenment goes unfulfilled, we will suffer from "divine homesickness" and "divine discontent": the sense of somehow being incomplete, unfulfilled, and not fully at home. As St. Augustine, one of the most influential of Christian theologians, summarized it, "Our hearts are restless till they rest in Thee." Rumi echoed him, saying, "The only real rest comes when you're alone with God."

The Costs of Failing to Recognize Higher Motives

By contrast with the great religions, Western culture and psychology remain spellbound by lower motives—desires for money, sex, and power, for example—and are largely blind to the existence of higher motives. This is one of humankind's greatest tragedies. But there are further costs to our metamotive blindness. The higher motives seem to be part of our very nature. Therefore, to deny them is to suffer from a shallow and distorted view of human nature. Harvard psychologist Gordon Allport wrote:

> Theories of human nature...have the power of elevating or degrading that same nature. Debasing assumptions debase human beings; generous assumptions exalt them.

To ignore metamotives means that we are starving ourselves of something essential to our well-being. We may need the good, the true, and the beautiful if we are to thrive; we may need to work for peace and justice if we are to find meaning in life; and we may need to express kindness and compassion if we are to live and love fully. In fact, if we do not honor and express our meta-motives, we may well stunt our growth and suffer from "meta-pathologies." So suggest the great religions.

A growing number of psychologists agree, including Abra-ham Maslow, who spent much of his life studying exceptionally healthy people. Maslow combed both religious and psychologi-cal literature and found over a dozen specific metapathologies. These include a sense of meaninglessness and nihilism about life, an attitude of cynicism and distrust of others, a lack of values and guiding principles, a feeling of alienation from society, and hope-lessness about the future.

Maslow was quick to point out that many of these meta-pathologies are now rampant in Western society and represent a major threat to our culture. That is exactly what one would expect given that our culture has so denied and starved higher motives. The recognition and cultivation of metamotives may be essential, not only for individuals, but also for cultures and civilization.

Fortunately, the great religions not only describe higher mo-tives, but also offer techniques for developing them.

Cultivating Higher Motives

The great religions call us to redirect our desires and enjoy the rewards of mature motives. They beg us to stop looking outside ourselves for satisfactions that can only be found within. They urge us to realize the limitations of physical delights, pleasant as they are, and to appreciate the unspeakable delights of the spirit; to reduce our craving for temporary satisfactions, and to seek in-stead the source of all satisfaction.

Traditionally this reorientation of desires has been described as "purification." Today we call it the maturing of motivation. But whatever name we give it, the great traditions are unani-mous in emphasizing its importance.

An exquisite description of this maturation comes from Ra-makrishna, a nineteenth-century Indian saint who was one of the most remarkable spiritual practitioners of all time. Born in 1836, he started having spontaneous spiritual experiences while still a child, and by his early twenties was already far advanced in one branch of Hinduism. Not content with this, he began practicing other branches as well, and then Buddhism, Islam, and Christianity. He quickly had profound awakenings in each, which gave him a direct experience of the truths of each tradition. Ramakrishna was speaking from his own direct experience when he described the maturing of motivation:

> As hunger and thirst arise spontaneously, so does longing for God. It is simply a matter of time. Yearning for God-realization cannot arise until one has to some extent satisfied the desires of social existence or has seen through them and been freed from them.... The constant quest for egocentric pleasure not only defrauds you of your birthright, which is infinitely blissful awareness, but mere pleasure-seeking inevitably produces suffering, both for yourself and for others.... Like the swan flying north in its yearly migration, the true human being moves powerfully forward in one direction, toward Truth alone.

Initially we have to work, and sometimes even struggle, to redirect motives hardened by a lifetime of habit. However, with practice they eventually soften, and higher motives become increasingly effortless habits that guide us gently to the highest good. Confucius left us a superb example of the way in which motives can mature when cultivated over a lifetime:

> At fifteen, I set my heart upon learning.
> At thirty, I had planted my feet firm upon the ground.
> At forty, I no longer suffered from perplexities.
> At fifty, I knew what were the biddings of Heaven.
> At sixty, I heard them with a docile ear.
> At seventy, I could follow the dictates of my own heart; for what I desired no longer overstepped the boundaries of right.

This is one of the most exquisite accounts ever written about the maturing of motivation.

- Confucius began by making a commitment to learning.
- By thirty his commitment was firmly grounded.

- At forty he was free of doubts and conflicts created by competing cravings.
- By fifty his mind was calm and clear enough to know the pull of metamotives.
- By sixty he was so free of competing compulsions that he felt no resistance to following these higher motives.
- Finally, at seventy, his heart and mind had been so transformed that he desired only the good and could follow his heart's desire without hesitation or concern.

Hidden in Confucius's account is a crucial, little-recognized secret: the relinquishment of attachments and the maturing of motives that accompany spiritual growth are not a sacrifice. Rather, they reflect a simple outgrowing of less mature and less satisfying pleasures. Just as the desires of childhood, such as wanting dolls or toys, naturally fall away as we begin to enjoy adult pleasures, so too do ordinary adult desires, such as those for fame and recognition, grow pale and less interesting as we taste the delights of more mature motives.

❋

We don't need to give up ordinary pleasures and pastimes. What we do need to give up is our attachment to them. Freed from craving and fear, we may even be able to enjoy them more. "Strive first for the kingdom of God," said Jesus, "and all these things will be given to you as well."

CHAPTER 8

EXERCISES TO
REDIRECT DESIRES

Ecstasy assumes the place of the scattered and external
pleasure of the mind...or rather it draws all other delight
into it and transforms by a marvelous alchemy the mind's and
heart's feelings.

—*Sri Aurobindo*

How do we strive first for the highest good? How do we lay aside
trivial pursuits and devote our lives to what really matters? How
do we redirect our hearts and minds to what truly satisfies?

Unfortunately, not by making a simple one-time decision to
do so. We all know how long New Year's resolutions last. While
the decision to change is an essential first step, other steps must
follow. We need techniques and exercises, inspiration and support, that we can call on repeatedly to shift the habits of a lifetime.
To begin, it is helpful to view our lives from a larger perspective.

EXERCISE 7: THINK OF A LONG TIME

Usually we are so preoccupied by the events of the day that we
lose sight of the big picture. The great religions repeatedly urge
us to look at our lives and the issues we face from a larger perspective. That perspective can be very large indeed. The traditions encourage us to keep our whole lives and inevitable deaths
in mind when making major choices. Buddhism and Hinduism
speak of countless lifetimes, while Christianity urges us to view

our lives *sub specie aeternitatas* (under the aspect of eternity). This exercise offers a taste of such a perception.

Find a quiet, comfortable place to sit where you won't be disturbed. When settled, relax by following the instructions in the next paragraph.

Begin by taking a few minutes to breathe slowly and deeply. Allow yourself to relax more and more with each breath. Notice an interesting thing about breathing: there is no effort required to breathe out. You breathe in and then simply let go. As you do, the air falls out by itself, and the muscles around the chest and shoulders relax automatically.

Allow that sense of relaxation to deepen and spread through the body with each breath. Let it flow up into the neck, out into the arms, and down through the abdomen and into the legs. If you notice any areas of muscle tightness, see if you can relax them. Continue to breathe slowly and deeply throughout the exercise. The ability to relax like this is a valuable skill for dealing with stress and tension of any kind. It will deepen many of the exercises and meditations presented throughout this book. When you are calm, read through the rest of the exercise carefully so you know what to do, then close your eyes.

Begin by thinking of a long time, perhaps a period of many years. Then think of a longer time. Then think of a still longer time. When you are ready, double the time. Then double it yet again. Now think of eternity.

From this all-encompassing, eternal perspective, look back at your life and ponder the following questions. You do not need to analyze or try to figure out answers. Rather, simply allow the intuitive wisdom within you to bring answers into awareness.

- What is really important in your life?
- What really matters?
- What would you be better off doing more of?
- What would you be better off doing less of?

Then take a moment to see if there is any other vital information this eternal perspective can offer you.

When you feel complete, open your eyes and bring your attention back to your environment. As with so many exercises, it is helpful to write down your insights in a journal immediately and then to take a few minutes to reflect. As you reflect on your life, think of the advice from the eighteenth-century Jewish sage Rabbi Nachman, who was famous for his wisdom and teaching stories: "Consider what you are doing and ponder whether it is worthy that you devote your life to it."

In the light of eternity, many of the things and much of the busyness in our lives seem rather insignificant. Though this discovery can be difficult at first, it can also be extremely freeing. It allows us to forgo the time-consuming trivia of worthless pastimes and possessions and to focus our lives on what really matters.

Choices for men and women on the spiritual path are very simple. They happily choose those friends, activities, and possessions that foster spiritual qualities in their lives, qualities such as love, generosity, joy, and wisdom. At the same time, they relinquish whatever inhibits these qualities and distracts them from their goal. Thus their lives gradually become less scattered and frenetic, more simple and peaceful.

EXERCISE 8: DEDICATE AN ACTIVITY TO A HIGHER GOAL

In Tibetan Buddhism each major activity—whether it be meditation, eating, or cleaning—starts and ends with a dedication. Before beginning meditation, a practitioner will repeat words such as, "I dedicate this practice to my awakening in order that I may serve and awaken all beings." At the end of the meditation, the practitioner will close by dedicating the benefits to others with words such as, "I offer the benefits of this practice to the welfare and awakening of all beings." These dedications take less than a minute, yet can profoundly deepen the motivation and experience of any activity.

This Tibetan practice provides a beautiful example of the way in which dedications can transform motivation. While changing what we do is essential for spiritual growth, changing the underlying motives may be even more vital. The same act can be done with dramatically different motives and results. Cutting a person open may be a hate-driven act of horrifying violence, yet in the hands of a doctor it might be a life-saving surgery. Fortunately, we have the power to choose the motives that direct our acts and lives. The following story, which I have expanded from an anonymous tale, shows how dramatically different these motives can be.

> For several weeks strange sounds had drifted over the mountains from the neighboring valley. There was much talk in the village about what these noises could be, but no one could make sense of them. Even the village elders had never heard anything like them. Finally one of the young men of the village was chosen to cross the mountains and see what was going on.
>
> After two days of hiking, he reached the mountaintop and saw in the valley far below him a hive of activity with dozens of people working. As he drew closer, he saw a line of people, each with a huge stone in front of them that they were hammering and chiseling.
>
> When he finally reached the valley floor he approached a young man at one end of the line and asked, "What are you doing?"
>
> "Huh!" grunted the young man. "I'm killing time until I get off work."
>
> Puzzled, the hiker turned to the second person in the line, a young woman, and asked, "Excuse me, but what are you doing?"
>
> "I'm earning a living to support my family," she responded.
>
> Scratching his head, the hiker moved on to the third person and asked again, "What are you doing?"
>
> "I'm creating a beautiful statue," came the reply. Turning to the next person, the hiker repeated his question.
>
> "I'm helping to build a cathedral," came the answer.
>
> "Ah!" said the hiker. "I think I'm beginning to understand." Approaching the woman who was next in line he asked, "And what are you doing?"
>
> "I am helping the people in this town and the generations that follow them, by helping to build this cathedral."
>
> "Wonderful," exclaimed the hiker. "And you, sir?" he called to the man beside her.
>
> "I am helping to build this cathedral in order to serve all those who use it and to awaken myself in the process. I am seeking my salvation through service to others."

Finally the hiker turned to the last stone worker, an old, lively person whose eyes twinkled and whose mouth formed a perpetual smile. "And what are you doing?" he inquired.

"Me?" smiled the elder. "Doing?" The elder roared with laughter."This ego dissolved into God many years ago. There is no 'I' left to 'do' anything. God works through this body to help and awaken all people and draw them to Him."

Seven people cutting stones. What a world of difference in their motives and lives.

We too have an equally wide array of motives from which to choose. A central principle of both spiritual practice and psychology is that the more often we choose a particular motivation, the stronger it becomes. Taking a moment before an activity to choose our motive can therefore transform the activity and ourselves.

A good way to begin is by selecting one activity to dedicate each time you do it. For example, each time I sit down to write this book I try to remember to dedicate it to the welfare of all the people who read it. In this way I hope that my selfish motives, such as the desire for fame and recognition, are reduced, while care and concern for others are enhanced.

Choose an activity that you do regularly and would like to dedicate. It could be anything from meditation to housework to reading this book. Think about the motive you would like to cultivate and find your own words to express this motivation and to dedicate the activity.

You might dedicate it to your learning, your awakening, or the welfare of everyone who will be affected by your activity. The choice is yours. Then each time you begin or end the activity, simply pause to dedicate it.

Exercise 9: Discover Your Future Self

In the previous exercises we explored principles and techniques helpful to anyone. But the great religions recognize that although there are universal practices all of us need to do, each of us is an individual and walks a path uniquely our own. Mohammad suggested, "There are as many ways to God as there are created souls," while Jewish wisdom holds, "Each and every human being has a specific task to perform in the world, a task that no one else can accomplish." Fortunately, the task we are called to perform is one that, in the depths of our heart, we truly *want* to do.

This point was expressed beautifully by Rumi, one of Islam's great mystics and its most revered poet. Born in Afghanistan in 1207, he spent much of his teenage years wandering through Iran and Syria with his family until at last his father found a teaching position in a theological college in Turkey. When his father died, Rumi, though only twenty-three, succeeded him, and for the next fourteen years lived a more or less conventional life as a religious teacher.

When he was thirty-seven, everything changed. He was approached by a wandering mystic who challenged him to answer a question. We do not know what the question was, but we do know its effect. Rumi fell to the ground. The religious scholar recognized the spiritual depth of the question and the questioner and was literally floored.

The questioner was Shams al-Din, "Sun of Religion," of Tabriz, who recognized Rumi's latent spiritual genius. The two men became inseparable, spending whole days together without food or drink, lost in ecstatic conversation and mystical love. The effect on Rumi was to catalyze his spiritual growth. The effect on his neglected students was to sow jealousy and intrigue. Sensing the problem, Shams disappeared.

Rumi was now a very different man. The former scholar spent hours listening to music, singing, and whirling around. From his lips and pen flowed a torrent of spontaneous ecstatic poetry of exquisite beauty and profundity.

Then Shams suddenly reappeared. According to Rumi's son, the two men "fell at each other's feet, and no one knew who was the lover and who the beloved." Again the two mystics spent hours lost in ecstasy, and again jealousy erupted among Rumi's students. One evening, while the two were talking, Shams was called to the door. He went out and was never seen again, apparently murdered.

Rumi was desolate. He left home and searched the country. Finally in Damascus his search succeeded, not physically but spiritually. He realized that his true nature and Shams's were identical, and he exclaimed:

> Why should I seek? I am the same as he.
> His essence speaks through me.
> I have been looking for myself.

The mystical union was complete. Shams was the source and inspiration of the ever-flowing stream of poems, and Rumi titled one huge collection *The Works of Shams of Tabriz*. Seven hundred years later these and Rumi's other poems are still regarded as among Islam's greatest literary treasures, and in the 1990s he was one of the best-selling poets in North America.

Rumi encouraged each of us to find our unique path with its specific goals and gifts. He wrote:

> Everyone has been made for some particular work, and the desire for that work has been put in our heart.

The following exercise is designed to help you see where your heart is drawn.

We spend enormous amounts of time lost in fantasies of having specific desires satisfied, of getting this new toy, that new car, and on and on. But rarely do we take time to imagine what we would *most* like to have and to *be*. This is an exercise to help you recognize these deeper, more meaningful, and ultimately more satisfying desires.

This exercise has more parts and questions than most. There are several ways of doing this and other long exercises. The simplest way is to read it through, then do it from memory, perhaps peeking at the book occasionally if necessary. Alternately, you can have someone slowly read the instructions and questions to you, or you can tape them and play them back.

Begin by giving yourself time to relax. Take some slow, deep breaths to let go any tensions you may be experiencing.

When you are ready, imagine yourself as you would most like to be at some future time, perhaps a few years from now. There is no need to struggle or force an image or idea to appear; let it arise spontaneously and effortlessly. With these kinds of exercises, some people see a clear image while others have more of a felt sense. Either is fine.

Imagine yourself living where you would most like to live and having done the things you most want to do. See yourself having achieved what you want, having learned what you want to learn, having made significant contributions to others, and having healed old relationships and established satisfying new ones.

As you visualize your future self, look to see where you are and what type of environment you are in. Does your future self look different in any way? What is your posture like? How do you feel? What emotions are predominant? What fears are gone? What strengths are obvious? What new capacities are evident?

Now imagine being your future self and ask, "Of all the things I have done, what makes me most happy?" Allow a moment or two for an answer to arise from the wisdom in your mind, and take time to savor and reflect on the answer. When you are ready, move on to the following questions and repeat the same process for each one. Ask yourself:

- Of all the things that I have done, what makes me most satisfied?
- What is the most valuable thing I have learned?
- What is the best thing I have done to help other people?
- What are my most satisfying relationships like?

When you have responses to these questions, then ask:

- In order to achieve these goals, what strengths and capacities do I need to recognize in myself?
- In order to achieve these goals, in what ways do I need to stop underestimating myself?
- Finally, ask yourself: What could I do now to begin achieving these goals?

When you are ready, open your eyes and take a moment to reflect on what you have experienced and learned. Writing down any insights immediately is helpful and will make the details of your future vision more vibrant and compelling.

CHAPTER 9

THE HIGHER REACHES OF DESIRE

No drives, no compulsions
No needs, no attractions:
Then your affairs
Are under control.
You are a free person.
—*Chuang Tzu, Taoist sage*

As we grow and change, so do our pleasures and the source of our pleasures. As infants, our desires are determined largely by our bodies, in conventional adulthood, largely by society. But as we mature further we begin to seek those people and pastimes that are more nourishing for the soul. In using the word *soul* I do not mean to imply any particular theological view; I am using the term metaphorically to point to the deeper aspects of the mind and self.

At transpersonal levels, conventional norms and guidelines become less helpful. Spiritual practitioners begin to realize that they must rely more on their own judgment and sense of what is appropriate and pleasurable. They increasingly turn inward to contact their own feelings to see what they truly want and what will bring true satisfaction. The source of motivation shifts from the infant's body to the adult's society to the postconventional person's inner world.

By following these deeper desires, we come to a wonderfully liberating realization: What we most truly and deeply want is what is best for us and the world. We discover that our deepest desires are healthy and altruistic, and that to do what is most deeply satisfying is to follow, and ultimately to find, our bliss.

"Follow your bliss," a phrase made famous by the mythologist Joseph Campbell, is therefore excellent advice *if* it is properly understood. It does not mean doing whatever happens to feel good at the moment; it does not mean merely pursuing fleeting pleasures and sensations; and it certainly does not mean doing whatever you want regardless of the cost to others. To do these things is to confuse temporary pleasure with timeless bliss and to hurt ourselves and others as a result. This is why the Buddha advised:

> There is pleasure
> And there is bliss.
> Forgo the first to possess the second.

Bliss is infinitely more than the feeling of pleasure. Bliss is a taste of our spiritual nature. To follow our bliss is therefore to do what best expresses and opens us to our true nature and its Source. For some this might be painting or poetry, for others being in nature, for still others helping the poor or sick. All of us face the pleasant challenge of finding out what gives us most profound satisfaction and making this a larger part of our lives.

THE DELIGHT OF EFFORTLESS BEING

At first, reducing attachments and redirecting motives is a struggle. The inertia of a lifetime is not undone in a day. It is a slow process, but it is also a cumulative one. Gradually the old cravings lose their compulsive pull, deeper desires become dominant, and the new life direction feels increasingly natural and unconflicted.

With advanced practitioners, struggle and conflict largely drop away. Living and growth become increasingly spontaneous, a condition Buddhism calls "effortless effort." Such people continue to practice—to meditate, pray, and serve—but these are experienced as natural, spontaneous activities. Finally, as awakening dawns and the separate self dissolves, any sense of personal striving or doing drops away. The seeker has become a sage. Rumi summarized the process in verse:

> All humankind are children except those who are drunk with God.
> No one is mature who is not free of self-will.

The sage continues to act and serve, but such actions are experienced paradoxically as spontaneous, unmotivated responses to each situation, free of personal needs or motives. Free of craving, conflict, or compulsion, the sage can respond easily and appropriately in all circumstances. This is the condition of "effortless being," which Meister Eckhart described as "acting without why," and which Taoism calls "nondoing" or "nonaction." Buddhism claims that "Not to act is the vital point of great action," while according to the *Tao Te Ching:*

> Less and less do you need to force things,
> until finally you arrive at non-action
> Where nothing is done, nothing is left undone....
> The Master does nothing
> yet...leaves nothing undone

We have all had times when we danced for joy and gave to others to share our joy. We didn't dance or give to acquire happiness; we danced to express happiness. The translator of *The Yoga Sutras*, the classic text of yoga, describes the difference as follows:

> Most desires arise from a feeling of lack,
> but the mind that is infinite lacks nothing.
> As the practice of yoga matures,
> desires cease to be the expressions of need
> and become instead the spontaneous unfolding of love.

The sages, immersed in the joy of their true nature, no longer act to find happiness or the sacred. Rather, their actions *express* happiness and the sacred, and are part of what Hinduism calls *lila:* the play of the divine. These sages are now able, as Ramakrishna exclaimed, "to experience Divine Bliss flowing through every action, every perception." "Follow your bliss" has become "express your bliss."

✳

Transforming motivation by reducing craving and finding your soul's desire is an essential spiritual practice. Among its many benefits, it reduces painful emotions such as fear and anger and fosters positive emotions such as love and compassion. It provides a foundation for transforming emotions and healing the heart, the second of the seven practices common to world religions.

CULTIVATE EMOTIONAL WISDOM

HEAL YOUR HEART AND LEARN TO LOVE

Love all people and draw near to humanity.
—*Confucius*

CHAPTER 10

THE GIFT OF LOVE

> It is well known that emotions of the soul affect the body and produce great, significant and wide-ranging changes in the state of health. Emotions of the soul should be watched, regularly examined, and kept well balanced.
>
> —*Maimonides, twelfth-century Jewish sage*

Our emotions rule our lives. The feelings we repeatedly invite into our minds eventually seduce and dominate our minds. Then these emotions color our perceptions, mold our motives, and direct our lives. What we feel within ourselves we find reflected in our world. If we feel angry, we look out on a hostile world; if fearful, we find threats everywhere. But when love fills our minds, we see a world that yearns to love and be loved.

Transforming our emotions is an absolutely essential practice, and the great religions offer three central approaches:

- to reduce painful feelings such as fear and anger
- to foster helpful attitudes such as gratitude and generosity
- to cultivate positive emotions such as love and compassion

This part offers exercises to do all three. Before beginning them, though, it is essential to understand the nature of love.

THE NATURE OF LOVE

Numerous emotions sweep through our minds each day: anxiety and anger, jealousy and joy, love and compassion, and many, many more. But one emotion has long been praised as supreme by the great religions: love.

The Search for Love

To experience and express love has been one of humankind's greatest quests. Love has been the subject of countless myths and poems and the object of study by philosophers, psychologists, and sages. Love is a source of meaning for countless people, a goal for which millions live and die, and a force that shapes countries and cultures. After surveying the world's societies and religions, the *Encyclopedia of Religion* concluded:

> the idea of love has left a wider and more indelible imprint upon the development of human culture in all its aspects than any other single notion. Indeed, many notable figures... have argued that love is the single most potent force in the universe, a cosmic impulse that creates, maintains, directs, informs, and brings to its proper end every living thing.

Though love is much sought, it is little understood; though universally desired, it is rarely wholly fulfilled. Most people feel like helpless victims of love, which seems to overwhelm us like epilepsy and then vanish, leaving us dazed and abandoned.

Where and how do we find love? Most people assume it is something they get from outside themselves, from a few special individuals. They hurl themselves into a desperate lifelong search for the perfect person, relationship, or community who will give them the love they crave.

The Pain of False Love

Yet this desperate search is based on the same tragic error that underlies all craving; it is driven by an unexamined sense of inadequacy, deficiency, and fear. This error leads to the futile search for something or someone outside ourselves to compensate for what seems to be lacking within.

This is a recipe for disaster. Another lover, a new spouse, or the wild cheers of an adoring crowd may offer temporary satisfaction. Yet as long as the inner fears and insecurities remain unrecognized and unhealed, outside rewards bring temporary relief at best.

This deficiency-based craving for love brings a plague of further problems. When our sense of well-being seems dependent on the approval and love of other people, we naturally become dependent on, or even addicted to, them. We cling, demand their exclusive attention, and love them *conditionally*, offering love when they behave as we want and withholding it when they do not.

If you turn on a radio almost anywhere in the Western world, you stand a good chance of being bombarded by an endless series of popular "love songs," fascinating examples of pleasure and pain, pathos and pathology. They wail such mournful lines as, "I can't live without you," "I can't stop thinking about you," or "I get chills thinking about you."

To a doctor such cries feel painfully familiar: These are the symptoms of heroin addiction! One of the great tragedies of our times is that our culture has confused love with addiction. Of course, there are also more mature forms of love, and healthy relationships and families depend on them. Mature love is based more on sufficiency and wholeness than on deficiency and fear. But fear-based infatuation and craving for affection are so common and fill so much of the media that we sometimes assume this is all that love can be.

The Bliss of True Love

The great religions disagree. While they honor romantic love, and in many cases regard it as a sacred gift, they also feel that it can deepen and mature enormously. For them, many popular forms of love are merely immature reflections of a love infinitely greater, purer, and more profound. Though they differ on details—for example, Islam and Christianity regard love as central to salvation, whereas Buddhism places more value on wisdom— the world's religions have celebrated and sought this greater love for thousands of years.

At the heart of Jewish tradition lie the two commandments "Love God with all your heart and with all your soul and with all your might" and "Love your neighbor as yourself." Jesus agreed that "there is no other commandment greater than these" and begged us to "love one another just as I have loved you." For

Jesus, true love excluded no one, and the challenge he set for us was to love even our enemies.

No one ever lived up to their own words better. Not surprisingly, Jesus's profound transconventional teachings were much misunderstood and proved enormously threatening to the convention-enslaved rulers of his time. Religious leaders regarded his recognition that "the Father and I are one" as utterly blasphemous. The Romans regarded talk of his "kingdom" as dangerously rebellious, even though Jesus was crystal-clear that "my kingdom is not of this world." He was sentenced to death by crucifixion, an inconceivably painful form of torture. Dying in agony on a cross, mocked by his executioners, and jeered by a hostile crowd, he breathed a prayer for them all: "Father, forgive them, for they know not what they do."

The Indian traditions of Hinduism and Buddhism echo the call for an all-encompassing love. They expand the embrace of love still further to include not only all people but all creatures. In Hinduism, Gandhi added to the command "Love your neighbor as yourself" the statement "and every living being is your neighbor." Likewise, the Buddha pleaded:

> As a mother watches over her child,
> willing to risk her own life to protect
> her only child, so with a boundless heart
> should one cherish all living beings,
> suffusing the whole world with unobstructed lovingkindness.
> Standing or walking, sitting or lying down,
> during all one's waking hours,
> may one remain mindful of this heart
> and this way of living that is the best in the world.

If the great religions sing the praise of love so highly, it must be something very different from our usual addictive experience of love, something far more profound and powerful, boundless and beneficial. And indeed it is. The love that the great religions offer—Christianity's *agape*, Buddhism's *metta*, and Hinduism's *bhakti*—is far more than the fleeting infatuations praised in popular songs.

Whereas addictive love is based on a painful sense of lack and need, this greater love is based on overflowing fullness and joy.

Spiritual love has no desire to get but only to give, no goal except to awaken itself within others, no need except to share itself. Being unconditional, it never fails or falters; being boundless, it embraces everyone.

Best of all, say several religions, this boundless love is already within us, hidden behind petty barriers such as fear and anger, yet eager to fill our hearts, to flood us with unspeakable joy, and to overflow into our lives and relationships. No wonder so many saints have lauded love as the most important of all human capacities. St. Paul sang its praises in some of the most poetic lines of the Christian bible:

> If I speak in the tongues of mortals and angels,
> but do not have love,
> I am a noisy gong or a clanging cymbal.
> And if I have prophetic powers,
> and understand all mysteries and all knowledge,
> and if I have all faith, so as to remove mountains,
> but do not have love, I am nothing....
> Love is patient; love is kind;
> love is not envious or boastful or arrogant or rude.
> It does not insist on its own way;
> it is not irritable or resentful;
> it does not rejoice in wrongdoing,
> but rejoices in the truth.
> It bears all things, believes all things,
> hopes all things, endures all things.
> Love never ends.

But love does even more than this because love has the power to awaken us. According to Ramakrishna, "The sublime and ineffable state of samadhi, total absorption in Divine presence, is reached most directly and naturally through selfless love," while the neo-Confucian sage Wang Yang-ming said:

> Everything from ruler, minister, husband, wife and friends to mountains, rivers, spiritual beings, birds, animals, and plants should be truly loved in order to realize my humanity that forms one body with them, and then my clear character will be completely manifested, and I will really form one body with Heaven, Earth and the myriad things.

CHAPTER 11

THE CHALLENGE OF DIFFICULT EMOTIONS

Never let the sun go down upon your anger.
—*St. Paul*

Challenging emotions such as fear, anger, jealousy, and despair are among the most difficult, sometimes most destructive, of all experiences. None of us escape them. But some people learn how to live with them, learn from them, and grow through them, while other people inflame them, wallow in them, and kill or die for them. Learning how to respond skillfully to painful emotions is one of life's most crucial challenges.

The first step is to recognize that difficult emotions are a natural part of life and not to be automatically condemned as bad or evil. Some are appropriate responses to reality and, at least in our early years, may be essential to survival: hard-wired responses that draw attention to vital issues and galvanize reactions in threatening situations.

UNSKILLFUL RESPONSES

However, if we respond to them unskillfully, difficult emotions can all too easily torment and devastate us and those around us. The stakes are very high. It is a tragedy so few people know how to work effectively with their emotions and so few are masters of emotional wisdom.

We suffer from three major errors:

1) judging or condemning difficult emotions as bad or evil
2) ignoring or defensively pushing painful emotions out of awareness
3) indulging or inflaming them, for example, by nursing feelings of resentment toward someone who hurt us and gleefully plotting revenge

In these cases we become what Shakespeare so eloquently called "passion's slave."

When we condemn painful emotions, and ourselves for having them, we set up an unwinnable inner war. The emotions will continue to arise as life throws up its inevitable challenges, but now we add an unnecessary and painful burden. We become angry that painful emotions have arisen, fearful of being overwhelmed by them, and depressed that we have to battle them yet again. The battle can never be won, but fortunately it can be stopped: by declaring a truce and by learning to accept painful emotions as a natural and normal part of life.

When we ignore or repress difficult emotions we also suffer, though more subtly. The emotions remain, of course, but now they lie hidden in the depths of the psyche, where they furtively seek expression as symptoms and defenses. For example, if we repress anger we may be unaware of it in ourselves but defensively project it onto others. Now "I am not angry, but people around me are," and symptoms such as anxiety may occur for no apparent reason. We are out of touch with our emotions—a condition called *dyslexathymia*—and thereby alienated from a crucial source of information and vitality.

The third major error is to deliberately indulge and inflame difficult emotions. The ideal is neither indulgence nor repression but rather appropriateness, balance and equanimity. Daniel Goleman summarized the ideals of balance and appropriateness in his book *Emotional Intelligence*:

> The goal is balance, not emotional suppression: every feeling has its value and significance. A life without passion would be a dull wasteland of neutrality, cut off and isolated from the richness of life itself. But, as Aristotle observed, what is wanted is *appropriate* emotion.

The great religions place great emphasis on *equanimity:* the capacity to experience the inevitable ups and downs of life without being thrown into wild emotional swings. The early Christians spoke of divine *apatheia* and *temperantia* or temperance, freedom from emotional excess. Likewise Jews speak of serenity, Taoists about "the principle of the equality of things," and Hindus about *vairaga* or dispassion.

How are we to work with and relate to difficult emotions? The challenge is to neither suppress nor indulge, but rather to explore and learn. In this way we come to understand our emotions. We learn how to release and transform them and use them appropriately. This is the basis of emotional wisdom.

Two of the most powerful and difficult of all emotions are fear and anger.

THE FANTASY OF FEAR

We all know the sensations that signal fear—the tightness in the chest, the dry throat, the racing heart. It is a natural and valuable emotion that plays a vital role in warning us of danger. Yet we also fear many things that are not really dangerous, and we can even become fearful of fear itself. Fear can become so painful that we are willing to do almost anything—to sacrifice almost anything—in order to avoid it. Much of our lives is spent avoiding fear and paying the price for the avoidance. What we are unwilling to experience runs our lives. When we are unwilling to experience fear, if we fear planes, we don't fly; if we fear failure we don't take risks; if we fear love we live without love. Our lives are constricted by the fears we are unwilling to face.

President Franklin Roosevelt made the famous claim, "The only thing we have to fear is fear itself." But do we really have to fear fear, or is this only a trick we play on ourselves? What is it we really fear?

Take a moment to think of the things you fear: Perhaps a car crash, the loss of a loved one, or losing your job? Now reflect for a moment. Is it the actual crash, the actual death, or the actual loss of your job that terrifies you? Or is it what you imagine will happen as a result? For example, is it the actual moment of the crash, or is it your fantasies of the pain and injury you fear might follow it?

Notice that we don't fear what is happening now. Rather, we fear our thoughts and fantasies about what may happen in the future. Fear is *always* about the future. But the future does not exist; it lives only in our fantasies. Only this moment right now exists. Everything else is our imagination. Mark Twain made the point: "My life has been filled with many misfortunes, most of which never happened."

This leads to a remarkable conclusion: *We do not usually fear reality, what is actually happening, but rather our own thoughts and fantasies about what may happen.* We fear what is going on in our own minds. Rabbi Nachman explained, "In truth, the one thing man is afraid of is within himself, and the one thing he craves is within himself." Once we really understand this, we also understand that we do not have to feel so helpless in the face of fear and craving. This is why fear has been described as "*F*alse *E*xperience *A*ppearing *R*eal."

Of course, there are some things in life that naturally evoke fear, even terror. But recognizing the falsity of so many of our daily fears and worries can be a crucial first step in freeing ourselves from them.

THE AGONY OF ANGER

Anger is an emotion of enormous power. Surveys show that most people find it the hardest of all emotions to master, while spiritual traditions regard uncontrolled rage as one of the greatest causes of suffering and barriers to awakening. Of course, anger is natural, and sometimes we can use it for good. More often, it uses us. Once anger arises, it can overwhelm even the best of motives and obliterate clear thinking. This is a condition psychologists call "cognitive incapacitation."

When anger becomes a way of life, it can devastate not only the mind but also the body. Research suggests that anger plays a lethal role in two of the deadliest medical disorders: heart disease and cancer. The harried person who is constantly busy and irritable may be particularly prone to heart attacks, while people who carry an enormous residue of rage but stuff it out of awareness may increase their risk of cancer. Not surprisingly, people who have had a heart attack and then go through stress management programs where they learn to release anger through relaxation, forgiveness, and open communication are much less likely to suffer a recurrence than people who continue to wallow in their old aggressive ways. Reducing anger can literally be life-saving.

Granted, it may temporarily feel good to nurse rage, to plot revenge, even to lash out in anger and deliberately hurt someone. But the long-term costs are severe. In rare cases it may be essential to express anger in order to right a wrong or to stop someone from doing harm. However, the great religions usually counsel forgiveness, and psychologists have discovered why. Study after study has found that ventilation and vengeance leave people feeling more enraged, not less.

The great religions warn again and again of the dangers of uncontrolled anger. Jewish sages warn that anger "can prevent enlightenment," while Christians view it as one of the seven deadly sins. Buddhists compare it to a forest fire roaring through the mind, consuming what is good. A famous Zen story makes the point dramatically.

A Japanese warrior approached a Zen master to request answers to some questions that had been troubling him.

"What is it you want to know?" queried the Zen master.

"Tell me, sir, do heaven and hell exist?"

"Ha!" snorted the Zen master in a tone that was half-laugh, half-sneer. "What makes you think that you could understand such things? You are only an uneducated, brutish soldier. Don't waste my time with your silly questions."

For an instant the warrior froze in shock. No one, but no one, ever spoke to a Japanese warrior like that. It meant instant death. "Are you too stupid to understand what I said?" roared the Zen master. "Stop wasting my time and get out of here."

The warrior exploded with rage. His hand flew like lightning to his sword and swept it aloft for the kill. But in the split second before the sword descended to crush the monk's skull, he heard the words:

"This is the gate to hell."

Again the warrior froze in astonishment. His own rage brought hell to him and those he attacked. And the master had risked his life to make this fact inescapably clear. Breathing deeply, he slowly replaced his sword and bowed humbly in awe and respect.

"And this," smiled the Zen master, "is the gate to heaven."

How do we free ourselves from the emotional hell unbridled fear and rage create, and how do we open the gates of heaven? The great religions offer three approaches:

- mastering and reducing difficult emotions, especially fear and anger
- cultivating attitudes such as gratitude and generosity that foster love
- cultivating love itself

CHAPTER 12

EXERCISES TO REDUCE FEAR AND ANGER

There are no chains like hate....
Dwelling on your brother's faults
Multiplies your own.
You are far from the end of your journey.
—*The Buddha*

Fear and anger are both responses to threat. One is a passive contraction and the other an active explosion. Since the two are closely linked, reducing one helps reduce the other, and the following exercises help to master both. But before working on these two specific emotions, it is important to recognize our capacity to transform emotions in general.

EXERCISE 1: MOVE FROM VICTIM TO CREATOR

Most people live spellbound by the belief that they are helpless victims of their emotions. If we are to transform our emotions, we first need to recognize our role in creating them. This exercise gives an immediate taste of this possibility.

Take a moment to be aware of how you feel. Notice the emotions you are experiencing. Next, think of or visualize someone you like. Then notice any emotions that arise. Now think of or visualize someone you dislike and watch the play of corresponding emotions.

82

Next, simply draw the corners of your mouth up and put a smile on your face. Observe that a gentle wave of happiness follows immediately. This exercise takes only a few seconds, but those seconds are sufficient to give a taste of your power.

HEALING PAINFUL EMOTIONS

I do not mean to suggest that we can transform all our emotions immediately or effortlessly. Chronic emotional habits, built up over a lifetime, develop formidable mental momentum. Yet with consistent spiritual practice it is possible to gradually transform our emotional responses into more life- and love-affirming ways.

This does not happen overnight. Although painful emotions such as fear and anger diminish with practice, only in the very highest reaches of spiritual maturity do they begin to disappear. A vital challenge of psychological and spiritual growth involves learning to experience difficult emotions consciously while continuing to live life fully and appropriately. We don't have to eradicate fear, but we do need to learn to act appropriately in spite of it. Taoism and Confucianism summarize this goal by pointing out that the sage "has emotions but no ensnarement" and "responds to things, yet is not ensnared by them." This is a specific example of the general principle that "The superior person is the master of things; the small person is their slave."

When we think of mastering fear and anger, we often imagine battling them and wrestling them into submission. This can sometimes be valuable, but also tricky. For example, if we attack anger and ourselves for having it, we can easily pile anger upon more anger. As the Buddha made clear:

Hate never yet dispelled hate.
Only love dispels hate.
This is the law,
Ancient and inexhaustible.

Spiritual traditions usually recommend more gentle approaches. They suggest understanding and undermining difficult emotions by carefully experiencing and exploring them—or by counteracting them with kindness and generosity.

EXPLORING FEAR

EXERCISE 2: EXPLORE FEAR

We devote enormous amounts of time and energy to avoiding fear. What would it be like to consciously explore fear and learn from it? It is less painful and more valuable than we might assume. Fear thrives in darkness and ignorance, but when we turn the light of awareness on it, it shrivels and transforms, as in this powerful story of a woman whose two-year-old daughter, Esther, fell and faced possible paralysis:

> I found myself in the grip of an overwhelming fear. Emotions this strong compel us to seek distraction, comfort, or oblivion, but in my case the sheer power of emotion seemed to render these options useless. I decided instead to face the fear and let it be, to make fear my "meditation."
>
> All night I lay awake, experiencing a succession of bodily and mental states: numbing cold in my extremities, my gut churning, hot dry ice radiating from my chest. I watched my mind tell a succession of tragic tales about Esther and the whole family. I tried to approach this experience in the way that had worked for me in giving birth to my three children: Instead of moving away from the pain, I opened myself up to it and let it pass through me. After a seemingly endless ordeal, I noticed a shift: It no longer felt like *my* fear—it was just fear. At four in the morning, the fear broke, like a fever. Suddenly I was lifted into a state of inexplicable ecstasy, my face awash with tears of gratitude. Energy coursed through me, moving and concentrating itself in my hands. I heard an inner voice say, "Go to your child." In Esther's room, I stood at her bedside and instinctively extended my hands over her sleeping form. I felt the warm energy streaming out of my hands toward her body. After some time, the guiding voice said, "She is all right." I returned to my bed and slept soundly. When I awoke a short time

later, I felt rested and calm. Monday, we returned to the orthopedist, who told us, with obvious befuddlement, that the CT scan was normal. Was Esther's physical healing some kind of shamanic magic I had stumbled onto or simply a doctor's mistaken diagnosis? In either case, I found healing in facing my fear.

Facing and exploring fear is a powerful means for healing it that can be tested in this exercise.

Begin by sitting comfortably. Take some time to relax. Remember to breathe slowly and deeply, relaxing more with each breath.

When you feel calm and comfortable, think of something that makes you afraid. For this exercise, it is best to choose a fear that is troubling but not overwhelming. For example, a mild fear of spiders would be better than an overwhelming terror of heights.

Allow yourself to feel the fear and then begin to explore it. Notice that the actual sensations of fear seem to be located in a particular part of your body. Where is the fear located? How large is it? What shape does it have? What does it feel like? Is it a tingling, vibrating sensation or more like a hard, solid lump?

Now turn your attention to other aspects of the experience. Is there an image associated with the fear? If so, what is it? What is your posture like, and are there particular muscles that are tense? Can you relax some of these muscles as you continue to breathe slowly and deeply? What thoughts run through your mind?

Take a few really slow, deep breaths. Now explore the experience of fear again. Notice its location right now. What size and shape does it have *now*? What does it feel like *now*? Be careful to explore it carefully this second time, because the experience of fear, like all experiences, changes constantly. It probably has a somewhat different size, shape, and feel from those of a few minutes ago. What about the posture and muscle tension? And the thoughts and images—are they different, too?

Now notice something fascinating and freeing about the experience of fear. When you look closely, none of the sensations, thoughts, and images that make it up are terribly distressing in themselves. Perhaps the muscle tension or an image is a little uncomfortable. However, when we actually *experience* it, fear is usually nowhere near as devastating as we imagine it to be. Rather, it is our unexamined beliefs and fantasies about it—and our unexplored reactions to it—that lock us into the painful unconscious cycle of automatic contraction and withdrawal.

Notice something else: When you breathe slowly and consciously, the body and then the mind tend to relax, and as they do the fear begins to diminish. You have uncovered an important healing principle discovered centuries ago by meditators and recently by psychologists: you can't be relaxed and fearful at the same time. To the extent you can relax—through breathing, yoga, or any other method—fear dissolves.

Now sit in a firm, erect posture with the back straight and shoulders back. What happens to the fear? The mind and body are so closely linked that to change one is to change the other. If you sit firm and erect, a posture associated with strength and courage, you tend to elicit these feelings and to diminish those of fear. This is one reason a strong posture is encouraged in meditation.

Notice also that as you continue to explore it, the fear tends to decrease. This is a very important psychological and spiritual principle: Simply bringing conscious awareness to dark states of mind tends to heal them. *The conscious mind is a self-healing mind.* If you experience and explore a painful state with as much awareness as you can, the mind will do the rest. Awareness, or mindfulness, as the Buddha called it, is healing. This is why the Buddha claimed that mindfulness is always helpful and why, 2,500 years later, psychologists recognize that "awareness per se—by and of itself—can be curative." It is also why meditation, which is the cultivation and training of awareness, plays such a vital role in spiritual life.

Our unexamined experience and fantasies of fear lock us into the painful cycle of contraction and withdrawal. Meditators say we are like an artist who paints a picture of a tiger and then flees in terror. We paint thoughts and fantasies of pain and disaster and then recoil in horror. However, when we look carefully, we recognize that the mental tiger or disaster is not real, and in that recognition we are free.

EXERCISE 3: STAY WITH FEAR

Once you understand how freeing it is to experience and explore fear consciously, a further exercise becomes possible. This one was recommended by the Buddha, who was not one to give in to fear—or anything else, for that matter. Determined to overcome fear, he decided that whenever it arose, he would remain absolutely unmoving until he had explored it carefully and it passed. He reported: "While I sat, the fear and dread came upon me; I neither walked nor stood nor lay down till I had subdued that fear and dread." Likewise, "While I stood, the fear and dread came upon me; I neither walked nor sat nor lay down till I had subdued that fear and dread."

This exercise involves exploring fear, as in the previous exercise. Now, instead of deliberately evoking it, wait until fear arises spontaneously during daily life. Then remain in the same posture exploring it until it subsides. Obviously there are times (such as when you're crossing the street and see a large bus racing towards you) when this exercise might be unwise. It's better to choose a time when you are unlikely to be interrupted by a bus or anything else.

When asked to do this exercise, some people worry that if they remain in the same posture exploring a fear until it subsides, they risk spending the rest of their life frozen like a statue. However, one of the benefits of exploring fear is that awareness speeds its disappearance.

EXERCISE 4: DO WHAT YOU FEAR AND FEAR WILL DISAPPEAR

We pour an enormous amount of energy into avoiding people and places we fear. Unfortunately, when we avoid what we fear, the fear tends to grow. But, as a popular saying puts it, "Do what you fear and fear will disappear."

This exercise consists of choosing to do something that is fearful to you. Again, it's best to choose fears that are manageable. You probably don't want to follow the Buddha's suggestion of meditating alone in a cemetery or jungle at midnight. Better to begin by choosing to speak up at a meeting, or perhaps by saying "no" to someone who asks you for something you don't want to do.

The exercise is very simple. Start by selecting something that you would like to do but find a little scary. Then make a commitment to do it during a particular time period—perhaps a day or a week—each time you have the opportunity. Keeping a diary, telling a friend what you plan to do, and later reporting your experience can be helpful in gathering your courage.

HEALING THE HOSTILE HEART AND RELEASING ANGER

The greatest victor wins without a battle....
But as long as there be a foe, value him,
Respect him, measure him, be humble toward him:
let him not strip from you, however strong he be,
compassion, the one wealth that can afford him.

—*Lao Tsu*

Releasing anger is a crucial but challenging part of fostering love. Forgive and forget: it sounds so simple until we try it. Then we come face to face with the raw power of anger and its insatiable thirst for vengeance and violence. No wonder Mohammad told his followers:

Who do you imagine to be strong or powerful?
It is he who masters himself when angry.

An eye for an eye and a tooth for a tooth is anger's fiery logic. To escape anger's vicious cycle, we need a very different kind of logic and a variety of exercises.

EXERCISE 5: RECOGNIZE THE COSTS OF ANGER

The first step is to recognize the many costs of anger for yourself and those around you. The exercise is very simple.

When you next find yourself bristling with anger, find a place where you won't be disturbed. Then take time to explore your experience.

First, turn your attention to the body and observe the sensations that make up anger. Are there burning sensations, perhaps over your face? Is there a contraction in the stomach? Examine the tensions that tighten the body. In this way you can identify the range of body experiences that make up anger.

Then turn attention to your mind. What is going on there? Is your mind racing with thoughts of vengeance? Are there violent fantasies scurrying through?

When you observe anger carefully in this way, its costs become painfully apparent. You can see how it overwhelms and obliterates positive feelings and consumes the mind with thoughts of vengeance. Physically, you can observe how the body goes into overdrive preparing to attack: your blood pressure rises and your heart races. It's not a pretty sight and the more clearly you see it, the less attractive holding on to anger becomes.

EXERCISE 6: COMMUNICATE ABOUT ANGER

The second step in relinquishing anger is to talk to someone about it. Simply talking about one's anger, not in order to complain or attack, but rather to forgive and release, is a surprisingly helpful process. Many of the benefits of both Christian confession and modern psychotherapy flow directly from it. Of course, you can also communicate to a trusted friend or, if you can do so without attack, directly to the person who caused your pain.

A related approach is to write a letter to the offending person. Here you describe the things that made you angry as honestly and gently as you can. Many people find that simply writing this letter is sufficient and that there is no need actually to send it.

EXERCISE 7:
RECALL YOUR OWN MISTAKES

It is so much easier to recognize the mistakes of others than our own. Jesus made this painfully clear with one of his startling, graphic images:

> Why do you see the speck in your neighbor's eye,
> but do not notice the log in your own eye?
> Or how can you say to your neighbor,
> "Let me take the speck out of your eye,"
> while the log is in your own eye?
> You hypocrite, first take the log out of your own eye,
> and then you will see clearly
> to take the speck out of your neighbor's eye.

Focusing on other people's mistakes and overlooking our own makes it easy to become enraged at others. A useful antidote to rage is to recall our own mistakes, especially those similar to the one made by the person who hurt us.

To do this, first recall something you feel angry about. Next, reflect on exactly what the offending person did that hurt you. Perhaps he or she forgot to thank you for a gift you gave or snapped at you when you made a mistake. When you are clear about the offensive action, try to recall times when you made similar mistakes. All of us have said or done countless foolish things and can usually recall several times when we were just as foolish as the person who hurt us.

EXERCISE 8: RECALL THE GOOD

There is another method for reducing fault-finding and anger. This exercise involves recalling or learning about the good things that people have done.

When you find yourself angry, stop what you are doing. Then think of the person or people who hurt you. Recall any good deeds they have done, especially any that may have benefited you. Everyone has done some good in their lifetime, and this exercise involves bringing as many of those good deeds to mind as you can. They don't have to be dramatic; some could be as simple as a smile. Simply recalling people's good deeds—especially those that have benefited you—fosters gratitude, and gratitude undermines anger.

EXERCISE 9: THINK OF LOVING PEOPLE

Simply thinking of loving, forgiving people can begin to loosen anger's stranglehold. If, when your temper flares, you bring to mind the image of a loving friend or a kind spiritual teacher, their love and kindness may partly replace your rage. Sometimes a great religious teacher can be used. An angry Buddhist, for example, may think of the Buddha and his unwavering kindness to all people; a Christian may recall the love of Christ. At other times a loving person you know personally may be more helpful. It can be particularly valuable to visualize a loving person in your situation and to imagine how he or she would respond.

EXERCISE 10: GIVE TO FORGIVE

During the fourth century, the deserts of Palestine, Egypt, and Arabia, long avoided because of their drastic and difficult conditions, became the dwelling place of a new type of man. These were the Christian Desert Fathers, men who fled the comforts and security of conventional society in order to devote themselves to the single-minded quest for salvation. Living simple, spartan, and largely solitary lives, they gave themselves to prayer, meditation, and fasting, striving to purge the barriers that stood between them and the all-consuming love of God and humanity they sought above all else. They left us short, pithy stories of their struggles and the lengths they would go to in order to achieve their goals. One goes:

> There was a certain elder who, if anyone maligned him, would go in person to offer him presents, if he lived nearby. And if he lived at a distance he would send presents by the hand of another.

This is an elegant technique for forgiveness recommended by several religions: If you are having difficulty forgiving someone, give them a gift. It doesn't have to be big or expensive. What matters is that you want to let the anger go and that your gift is intended to help you do so. It is hard to feel angry at people when you give them a gift. It is also hard for them to remain angry at you when they receive it.

Exercise 11:
A Forgiveness Meditation

Jack Kornfield is a well-known Buddhist meditation teacher and psychologist. He says:

> For most people forgiveness is a process. When you have been deeply wounded, the work of forgiveness can take years. It will go through many stages—grief, rage, sorrow, fear, and confusion—and in the end, if you let yourself feel the pain you carry, it will come as a relief, as a release for your heart. You will see that forgiveness is fundamentally for your own sake, a way to carry the pain of the past no longer. The fate of the person who harmed you, whether they be alive or dead, does not matter nearly as much as what you carry in your heart. And if the forgiveness is for yourself, for your own guilt, for the harm you've done to yourself or to another, the process is the same. You will come to realize that you can carry it no longer.

Forgiveness is most powerful and encompassing if it extends in three directions:

- the request for forgiveness from those you have hurt
- forgiveness for yourself
- forgiveness for those who have hurt you

Sit comfortably and allow the breath to come slowly and easily. Let your body and mind relax. You may wish to imagine that you are breathing in and out through the center of your chest.

Turn your attention to any memories or areas of your life where you have not forgiven or been forgiven. Become aware of the associated feelings, of any barriers to forgiveness, and any holding of past pain or resentments. Simply allow the experiences to float through awareness without judging them. When you are ready, begin the process of forgiveness:

FORGIVENESS FROM OTHERS

Acknowledge the ways in which you have hurt others. To whatever extent you can do so without contracting, allow images and memories of times when you hurt others to come to awareness. Notice that at these times you often felt fearful, defensive, or confused. There is no need to condemn yourself for your mistakes; that only adds further fear and defensiveness. Open to the regret you now feel and also to the possibility that you can now release your guilt and pain. Gently and slowly repeat several times, "I ask for forgiveness, I ask for forgiveness."

FORGIVENESS FOR YOURSELF

We have all hurt, embarrassed and belittled ourselves in countless ways and probably still carry much of the pain. Now you can begin to let it go.

Allow memories of times when you hurt yourself to come into awareness. As each one arises, regard it and yourself gently and lovingly and repeat several times, "I forgive myself."

FORGIVENESS FOR OTHERS

All of us have been hurt many times by others in ways large and small. In addition, we have all added to those hurts by holding onto resentments, closing our hearts, and seeking revenge. Now you can begin to relinquish these old hurts and additional self-inflicted pains.

Continue to breathe slowly and deeply. Allow memories of times when you were hurt to come to awareness. You might wish to begin with some of the smaller, more manageable pains. See if you can recognize the fear, defensiveness, or confusion in the person who hurt you that produced their hurtful behavior. Then repeat to yourself several times, "I forgive you."

Sometimes old hurts dissolve rapidly doing this forgiveness meditation. More often they weaken slowly and the exercise must be repeated several or even many times. Be gentle and patient with yourself. If you find yourself getting impatient and irritated with yourself, forgive that, too. Forgiveness cannot be forced, but it can be practiced.

The Value of Patience

> At the end of the way is freedom.
> Till then, patience.
>
> —*The Buddha*

Sometimes forgiveness heals both ourselves and the person we forgive; in other cases the other person may seem unchanged. We can't force another person to change. Our task is simply to forgive as fully as we can.

Sometimes it may take years before the full benefits of forgiveness become obvious. I once experienced this when visiting my family. My father and I had a difficult relationship distorted by years of chronic anger and resentment. It was only when I understood myself better that I could recognize the many ways in which I was like him and could begin to appreciate the pain behind my father's rage. The French have a saying, "To understand is to forgive." As I began to understand both him and myself better, anger melted, and my love for him emerged.

I began writing to him, expressing appreciation for the many things he had done for me, from teaching me to drive to funding my medical school education. I wrote regularly for several years and received not a single reply. Yet years later when I returned home and happened to open a drawer in his desk, there I found every one of my letters, carefully folded and obviously read many times.

The Higher Reaches of Forgiveness

> Only pursue an offender to show him the way.
>
> —*Lao Tsu*

Reducing anger and resentment is no small achievement, but mature forgiveness extends still further to helping and even loving those who hurt us. From this advanced perspective, vengeance is a mutually destructive dead end. The only truly worthwhile motive for pursuing those who hurt us is to help and teach them. The Desert Fathers recommended:

> Malice will never drive out malice.
> But if someone does evil to you,
> you should do good to him,
> so that by your good work you may destroy his malice.

Likewise, Mohammad urged:

> Forgive those who wrong you;
> join those who cut you off;
> do good to those who do evil to you.

It is important to remember that forgiving does not mean condoning harmful behavior. Forgiveness is a relinquishment of one's resentment, not a relinquishment of one's ethics. Mature spiritual practitioners may be able to forgive, even love, someone who has hurt them while simultaneously insisting that the person cease doing any further harm.

Wise people the world over agree that forgiveness is a tool of extraordinary power and benefit. These benefits are portrayed exquisitely in the following lines from a Christian text:

> What could you want forgiveness cannot give?
> Do you want peace? Forgiveness offers it.
> Do you want happiness, a quiet mind,
> a certainty of purpose,
> and a sense of worth and beauty
> that transcends the world?
> Do you want care and safety,
> and the warmth of sure protection always?
> Do you want a quietness that cannot be disturbed,
> a gentleness that never can be hurt, a deep,
>   abiding comfort,
> and a rest so perfect it can never be upset?
> All this forgiveness offers you, and more.

Masters of emotional wisdom are able to forgive because they see below the mask of anger to recognize the fear and insecurity that power it. Such masters are therefore less likely to react defensively and can respond in ways that are helpful and healing. The following story by an Aikido student offers an example:

The train clanked and rattled through the suburbs of Tokyo on a drowsy spring afternoon.... At one station the doors opened, and suddenly the afternoon quiet was shattered by a man bellowing violent, incomprehensible curses. The man staggered into our car. He wore laborer's clothing, and he was big, drunk, and dirty. Screaming, he swung at a woman holding a baby. The blow sent her spinning into the laps of an elderly couple. It was a miracle the baby was unharmed.

Terrified, the couple jumped up and scrambled toward the other end of the car. The laborer aimed a kick at the retreating back of the old woman but missed as she scuttled to safety. This so enraged the drunk that he grabbed the metal pole in the center of the car and tried to wrench it out of its stanchion. I could see that one of his hands was cut and bleeding. The train lurched ahead, the passengers frozen with fear. I stood up.

I was young then, some twenty years ago, and in pretty good shape. I'd been putting in a solid eight hours of Aikido training nearly every day for the past three years. I liked to throw and grapple. I thought I was tough. The trouble was, my martial skill was untested in actual combat. As students of Aikido, we were not allowed to fight.

"Aikido," my teacher had said again and again, "is the art of reconciliation. Whoever has the mind to fight has broken his connection with the universe. If you try to dominate people, you are already defeated. We study how to resolve conflict, not how to start it."

I listened to his words. I tried hard. I even went so far as to cross the street to avoid the *chimpira*, the pinball punks who lounged around the train stations. My forbearance exalted me. I felt both tough and holy. In my heart, however, I wanted an absolutely legitimate opportunity whereby I might save the innocent by destroying the guilty.

"This is it!" I said to myself as I got to my feet. "People are in danger. If I don't do something fast, somebody will probably get hurt."

Seeing me stand up, the drunk recognized a chance to focus his rage. "Aha!" he roared. "A foreigner! You need a lesson in Japanese manners!"

I held on lightly to the commuter strap overhead and gave him a slow look of disgust and dismissal. I planned to take this turkey apart, but he had to make the first move. I wanted him mad, so I pursed my lips and blew him an insolent kiss.

"All right!" he hollered. "You're gonna get a lesson." He gathered himself for a rush at me.

A fraction of a second before he could move, someone shouted "Hey!" It was earsplitting. I remember the strangely joyous, lilting quality of it—as though you and a friend have been searching diligently for something, and he had suddenly stumbled upon it. "Hey!"

I wheeled to my left; the drunk spun to his right. We both stared down at a little old Japanese man. He must have been well into his seventies, this tiny gentleman, sitting there immaculate in his kimono. He took no notice of me, but beamed delightedly at the laborer, as though he had a most important, most welcome secret to share.

"C'mere," the old man said in an easy vernacular, beckoning to the drunk. "C'mere and talk with me." He waved his hand lightly.

The big man followed, as if on a string. He planted his feet belligerently in front of the old gentleman, and roared above the clacking wheels, "Why the hell should I talk to you?" The drunk now had his back to me. If his elbow moved so much as a millimeter, I'd drop him in his socks.

The old man continued to beam at the laborer. "What'cha been drinking?" he asked, his eyes sparkling with interest. "I been drinkin' sake," the laborer bellowed back, "and it's none of your business!" Flecks of spittle spattered the old man.

"Oh, that's wonderful," the old man said, "absolutely wonderful! You see, I love sake too. Every night, me and my wife (she's seventy-six, you know), we warm up a little bottle of sake and take it out into the garden, and we sit on an old wooden bench. We watch the sun go down, and we look to see how our persimmon tree is doing. My great-grandfather planted that tree, and we worry about whether it will recover from those ice storms we had last winter. Our tree has done better than I expected, though, especially when you consider the poor quality of the soil. It is gratifying to watch when we take our sake and go out to enjoy the evening—even when it rains!" He looked up at the laborer, eyes twinkling.

As he struggled to follow the old man's conversation, the drunk's face began to soften. His fists slowly unclenched. "Yeah," he said. "I love persimmons, too...." His voice trailed off.

"Yes," said the old man, smiling, "and I'm sure you have a wonderful wife."

"No," replied the laborer. "My wife died." Very gently, swaying with the motion of the train, the big man began to sob. "I don't got no wife, I don't got no home, I don't got no job. I'm so ashamed of myself." Tears rolled down his cheeks; a spasm of despair rippled through his body.

Now it was my turn. Standing there in my well-scrubbed youthful innocence, my make-this-world-safe-for-democracy righteousness, I suddenly felt dirtier than he was.

Then the train arrived at my stop. As the doors opened, I heard the old man cluck sympathetically. "My, my," he said, "that is a difficult predicament, indeed. Sit down here and tell me about it."

I turned my head for one last look. The laborer was sprawled on the seat, his head in the old man's lap. The old man was softly stroking the filthy, matted hair.

As the train pulled away, I sat down on a bench. What I had wanted to do with muscle had been accomplished with kind words. I had just seen Aikido tried in combat, and the essence of it was love.

Love is also the essence of emotional wisdom.

CHAPTER 13

CULTIVATE LOVE AND GRATITUDE

Wherever you are,
Whatever your condition is,
Always try to be a lover.

—*Rumi*

Love does not flower in a vacuum, but rather is nourished by supportive attitudes such as generosity and gratitude. Generosity is so important, not only to love but to all spiritual life, that it is one of the seven central practices and is discussed separately. We explore gratitude here.

GRATITUDE: THE DOORWAY TO LOVE

While forgiveness heals the heart of old hurts, gratitude opens it to present love. Gratitude bestows many benefits. It dissolves negative feelings: anger and jealousy melt in its embrace, fear and defensiveness shrink. Gratitude deflates the barriers to love.

Gratitude also evokes happiness, which is itself a powerfully healing and beneficial emotion. The great Taoist sage Chuang Tzu even went so far as to say that "When one reaches happiness, one is close to perfection." When we are happy, we like to make others happy, and this fosters kindness and generosity.

Gratitude is a gift to everyone. No wonder Saint Paul urged us to "Rejoice always" and to "Give thanks in all circumstances."

Like other attitudes, gratitude can be cultivated. We don't have to wait for our fairy godmother to shower us with gifts before feeling thankful. We can develop gratitude by reflecting on the gifts that are already ours. This reflection can be done for a minute, a day, or throughout a lifetime. Most people celebrate their birthday and holidays, but those who cultivate gratitude celebrate every day. We can be grateful because we are happy, but we can also be happy because we are grateful.

EXERCISE 12: SAY GRACE

One ancient and time-tested approach is to say grace: that is, to offer thanks before each meal. As with all techniques, much depends on the spirit in which it is done. If grace is merely a mindless ritual to be endured before grabbing for the food, it is not likely to be of much help. If the minute or two of grace, however, is used for reflecting on the gifts that have been given us, it can foster thankfulness very effectively.

Grace can also be done in ways that help us appreciate our relationships with other people and the world. For example, if we think of how a simple vegetable came to our plate, we realize that hundreds of people—farmers, harvesters, truck drivers, cashiers, and many more—all worked to get this food to us. This is why, before they eat, Zen practitioners recite:

> Innumerable labors brought us this food,
> We should recall how it came to us.

The vegetable was born in the earth's soil, watered by summer rains, warmed by the sun, and pollinated by bees. Without nature's miracles and many people's labor, we would go hungry. This simple vegetable mirrors the world and its gifts, and reflecting on these gifts is a wonderful way to develop gratitude.

EXERCISE 13: RECALL HELPFUL PEOPLE

> As we recall the compassion
> shown us by our parents,
> so may we dedicate ourselves

to turning that compassion
toward all the inhabitants of the earth.
—*Jewish prayer*

Recalling the help we have received from others—especially from
our parents—is a common practice in many religions. To do this
as a specific exercise, begin by getting comfortable and relaxed.

When you are settled, think of two or three people who have
been particularly helpful to you. Recall some of the ways they
helped. Perhaps they came to your rescue in a time of need; perhaps they introduced you to a new friend. Large or small, simple
or complicated, it doesn't really matter. What does matter is that
you take a few minutes to remember their kindness and to allow
feelings of gratitude to arise.

EXERCISE 14: A DAY OF
THANKFULNESS

When you are ready to extend this exercise, commit to doing it
for a longer time, perhaps an hour, a morning, or a day. There
are two steps to this exercise:

1) Think of the people you will meet during this time.
These might include family members or friends who love you,
the bus drivers who get you to and from work, or the janitor
who cleans your room. See if you can find a reason to feel
grateful to each person you meet.

2) Continue this recollection of gratitude throughout the
day. Try to bring to mind a reason for feeling grateful to each
person you meet. This need not take long; a few seconds may
be enough to recall some quality or gift of theirs that you appreciate. In this way each person becomes a bearer of good feelings and each meeting is a cause for gratitude.

At the completion of the exercise period, take time to reflect
on the people you met and your feelings about them. After a day
like this, you may understand why gratitude is called the heart of
love.

THE DIRECT CULTIVATION OF LOVE

Fan Ch'ih asked about benevolence.
[Confucius] said, "Love your fellow men."

Reducing the barriers to love and cultivating attitudes that support it smooth the way for our hearts to open. The next step is to cultivate love directly with the following exercises.

EXERCISE 15: RECALL LOVING PEOPLE

Make yourself comfortable in a place where you can sit quietly without interruption for several minutes. Take time to relax and breathe slowly and deeply. You might wish to imagine that you are breathing in and out through the center of your chest, since this fosters feelings of warmth and love.

Then bring to mind people you know or know of who are exceptionally loving. They might include family members, friends, wise people you have met, or saints and sages you have heard of. Take a moment to think of each person. As you do so, bring to mind the gifts they give. Consider their personalities and behavior. What qualities make them so kind and loving?

Notice your state of mind as you reflect on these people. You may find yourself feeling grateful and loving because, simply by directing attention to specific people, we begin to feel the qualities they express. This is an important lesson: those people we give attention to have powerful effects on us. Associate with angry people and anger surges up within us; think of loving people and love arises. The Buddha warned:

Do not look for bad company
or live with people who do not care.
Find friends who love the truth.

To Give Is to Receive

We tend to forget how very different the laws that govern the mind are from the laws that operate in the physical world. In the world, if we give a physical thing to another person, whether it be a toy or a diamond, we lose it. Yet in the mind, the opposite is true. Whatever we intend for another person we experience ourselves, whatever we give we gain, whatever we offer flowers in our own minds.

If you feel hatred toward someone, that hate boomerangs back and scorches your own mind. On the other hand, if you offer love to someone, that love first fills and heals your mind. Once this is understood, the desire to hate and hurt starts to shrink, while the desire to love and help begins to flourish. The words "As you give so shall you receive" are a profound statement about the way our minds work. This is the basis of the prayer of St. Francis, one of the most beloved of Christian saints:

> Grant that I may not so much seek....
> To be loved as to love.
> For it is in giving that we receive.

This crucial psychological fact is the basis of the next two exercises.

EXERCISE 16: I WILL RECEIVE WHAT I OFFER NOW

Find a quiet, comfortable place where you won't be disturbed. Take time to relax. Breathe slowly and deeply until you feel calm. Then say to yourself:

> As I give, so shall I receive.
> I will receive what I offer now.

Now think of those experiences and qualities of mind that you would like to give to others and thereby enjoy for yourself. You might, for example, wish to offer and receive love. You might wish to offer and receive happiness, healing, peace, and rest. To do this, quietly say to yourself phrases such as:

> I offer love to everyone.
> I offer happiness to everyone.
> I offer peace to everyone.

To everyone I offer healing.
I offer rest to everyone.

Each sentence should be said slowly and gently while you explore and feel its meaning. You might also visualize some or many people receiving and enjoying these gifts. As you do so, continue to repeat the sentences. If your mind wanders away and you become lost in fantasies, simply return attention to the sentences and begin repeating them again. Continue for several minutes, or longer if you wish. Sooner or later the gifts you offer will begin to arise in your own mind automatically, so there is no need to try to force them to appear. As with any exercise, the effects become more powerful with practice, so it is valuable to repeat it regularly.

This exercise can easily be extended into other parts of the day and can even be done while you are busy with repetitive tasks such as gardening or washing dishes. Simply pause, take a couple of slow, relaxing breaths, and then begin to repeat the sentences for as long as you wish. This is a wonderful way to relieve stress or other unpleasant feelings. For example, imagine that you are in a meeting where tension is high and tempers are hot. Taking a moment to quietly recite these sentences, wishing happiness and peace to everyone in the room, can transform your feelings and make you a calming, healing influence for others.

EXERCISE 17: ALL-ENCOMPASSING LOVE

Put away all hindrances,
let your mind full of love pervade...
the whole wide world,
above, below, around and everywhere,
altogether continue to pervade with love-filled thought,
abounding, sublime, beyond measure.

—*The Buddha*

The following meditation is a simple yet effective way of expanding the scope of love to encompass more and more people. Elements of this meditation can be found in several traditions.

In Judaism it is said that commandments such as "'Love your neighbor like yourself'... actually mandate such a meditation."

As with most meditations, it is best to sit comfortably and upright. Take time to relax. Breathe slowly and deeply. It can be useful to imagine yourself breathing in and out through the center of your chest. As you do, notice any sensations and feelings of warmth that arise in your chest.

When you feel ready, think of someone you love dearly. If you can, visualize this person clearly in your mind's eye. Be aware of any feelings of warmth and love that arise as you see this person.

When you are aware of warm feelings, expand your awareness to include people around you. If you are in a building, you might think of people in adjacent rooms. Try to let your feelings of love and warmth embrace them. Continue to breathe slowly and deeply.

When you are ready, expand your awareness further to encompass more distant people. You might now include all the people in your building or in neighboring buildings. Include these people in your feelings of love.

If at any stage you notice the feelings of love begin to disappear, return attention to the person you love deeply whom you began with. Then, when feelings of love arise again, again expand to include others.

Now extend your awareness throughout your neighborhood and city. Accept all these people as worthy of your love and include them in the scope of your care. Remember to keep breathing slowly and deeply.

Now expand the scope of your love still further to encompass the entire country. Then, when you feel ready, expand your awareness to include the entire world. Touch all people with your love—all ages, all races, all countries—without exception or reservation.

Take one final step. Include all creatures within the boundless circle of your love. Embrace all life so your love knows no limits or boundaries and includes everyone and every creature. Simply rest in this experience for as long as you are able and then gently return your attention to your surroundings.

EXERCISE 18:
LOVINGKINDNESS MEDITATION

Twenty-five hundred years ago a group of Buddhist monks walked into the dark depths of the Indian jungle. There they planned to live in solitude and devote themselves to intensive meditation. This was no small commitment, considering that the jungle teemed with tigers and other dangers. Before long they fled. Rushing to the Buddha, they complained of overwhelming fear and begged for help. The Buddha answered their plea by promising to teach them the most potent of all antidotes to fear.

The Buddha did not teach sword fighting or other martial arts, for the Buddha and his followers were committed to never hurting anyone. He also did not teach the men to grit their teeth and fight the fear.

Rather, the Buddha taught the monks a meditation for cultivating feelings of love and kindness. Smart psychologist that he was, the Buddha realized that fear and love displace each other, and that if the mind is filled with love, fear is swept away. We all know from painful, personal experience that fear can overwhelm love. What is not so well known is that when love has been practiced and strengthened, it can overwhelm fear. In the words of the Christian bible, "Perfect love casts out fear."

Gentle yet powerful, the lovingkindness meditation taught by the Buddha has flourished for two and a half thousand years and has helped countless millions of people. Like many profound techniques, it is deceptively simple. It consists of the repetition of short phrases designed to evoke emotional qualities such as happiness, peace, gentleness, and of course love.

A word of caution about this meditation. I said that with the exception of three meditations, all the exercises in this book were chosen because they are easy and can produce significant benefits relatively quickly, often even the first time they are done. While the lovingkindness meditation may be helpful the first time, many people find that it takes considerable practice.

The meditation begins in a way that surprises many people: by cultivating loving feelings towards yourself. This is not a recipe for selfishness, but rather for selflessness, since the ego and selfishness thrive on fear but dissolve in love. In addition, the meditation gradually extends its scope to encompass friends, strangers, enemies, and ultimately all people and all life.

Some people feel uncomfortable starting with themselves and prefer to begin by focusing on someone who has been kind and helpful to them. It is fine to start in this way, but it is important to include yourself at some stage.

The phrases are very simple. They traditionally include four desired qualities such as "May I be happy, kind, loving, and peaceful" or "May I be joyful, gentle, calm, and loving." As the meditation progresses, these phrases will be modified—for example, "May you be happy, kind, loving, and peaceful"; then "May all people be happy, kind, loving, and peaceful." Finally, when the meditation becomes all-encompassing, the sentence becomes, "May all beings be happy, kind, loving, and peaceful."

To do the meditation, first decide how long you want to devote to it, perhaps ten to twenty minutes the first time. Find a place where you won't be disturbed and sit comfortably with your back straight and your body relaxed. Take a few slow, deep breaths to relax and settle both body and mind. You can close your eyes or leave them open.

Begin to repeat a phrase such as "May I be happy, joyful, loving, and peaceful." Repeat the phrase slowly and gently to yourself. If you wish, you can begin by speaking the words, then gradually let them become softer and softer until you are repeating them mentally. Don't struggle or force an emotion to arise. Merely allow the words to sink into your mind. Your task is to relax, repeat the phrases, and be aware of whatever experiences and emotions arise. Whenever the mind strays to irrelevant thoughts or fantasies, return it gently to the phrases.

As you continue, you may be surprised to find yourself gripped by emotions such as anger or jealousy that are very different from those you hoped for. There is no need for alarm. Their appearance is a natural and helpful part of the process. These are the barriers blocking your experience of love, and they naturally surface when you attempt to cultivate love. There is no need to condemn these barriers or yourself for having them. There is no need to fight or even resist them at all. If you remember the healing power of awareness and simply observe them without condemning or fighting, they will gradually weaken and unravel by themselves. This is one of the ways in which meditation heals the mind and opens the heart.

During the first sitting it may be quite appropriate to continue to direct the thoughts of lovingkindness toward yourself. However, sooner or later, perhaps during the first sitting or in a subsequent one, you will want to begin directing your good wishes towards a dear friend or someone who has helped you. As you do, change the phrase to, "May you be happy, joyful, loving, and peaceful." It may help to visualize or look at a picture of the person as you do so.

Generally it is a good idea to avoid choosing someone who is sexually attractive to you. Otherwise love and kindness may become tinged with sexual feelings. This can limit the scope of the meditation, which aims to develop an all-embracing love that encompasses all people equally.

In subsequent sittings you can gradually expand the scope of your love. You may find it helpful to begin each sitting with loving thoughts for yourself, and then for your friend. Feelings of love and happiness are an excellent signal that you are ready to expand the meditation. At that time think of and visualize a group of people and direct your loving thoughts to them all. As always, if the mind wanders and you become lost in thoughts or fantasies, there is no need for regret or guilt. Everyone becomes distracted many times. Just begin the phrases again.

At some later stage you may want to expand your meditation still further to include all people. Now the appropriate phrase becomes, "May all people be happy, joyous, loving, and peaceful." You might wish to visualize the earth and imagine all people in all places receiving your love.

The final step in the progression is to extend your love to embrace all creatures as well as all people. At this stage a useful phrase is, "May all beings be happy, joyous, loving, and peaceful." You are now developing feelings of love and kindness for all life, without exception or reservation.

Continue for as long as you wish. When you end the meditation session, get up slowly so as not to disrupt the calm and emotions you have cultivated.

There is one further step in this meditation that can be very rewarding but also initially very difficult. This involves cultivating positive feelings toward a person or group of people whom you dislike or even hate. Even anger, perhaps the toughest of all emotions, melts in the embrace of mature love. This does not mean that you accept a person's behavior if it is harmful to others. It does mean that you free yourself from the self-made torture of uncontrollable rage.

To heal hatred, begin by generating feelings of love and kindness towards yourself or someone you love. When the positive feelings are strong, bring the person you dislike into awareness and begin repeating the phrase with him or her in mind. If you start to feel overwhelmed by anger, stop and return your attention and loving thoughts towards people who are easier to work with. When your feelings of love are again strong, you can then return attention to your enemy.

If the negative feelings this person evokes are too strong to work with successfully, simply stop. Don't strain or struggle or try to force the mind to feel something it is not ready for. Remember that part of the lovingkindness meditation involves accepting and loving yourself (and your mind) exactly the way you are. You can always return to the person you're angry with at some future time.

Sometimes people beginning this meditation are disappointed because they expect to dissolve into an ocean of love immediately. If you could do that, you wouldn't need the meditation. Remember that this meditation is an exercise and, like all exercises, it takes time to blossom. At first the effects may be subtle and hard to detect, but over time they accumulate and grow.

A delightful thing about the lovingkindness meditation is that it can be done at almost any time and place. Feeling bored during a meeting? Look at the people in the room and recite loving phrases towards them. Feeling weary during a long drive? Intend love and happiness for everyone you pass. This can transform your feelings and the situation dramatically. Some people find it easier to do the meditation this way than when sitting alone with eyes closed, so it is valuable to experiment with both approaches.

I first learned how dramatically this meditation can transform situations when I was trying to get to a conference near a little town on the California coast. When I got off the plane at the small airport I still had forty miles to go. It was a beautiful spring day and the drive along the coast promised to be spectacular. But the next bus was not due for five hours, so I decided to hitchhike. *After all, it shouldn't be hard to get a ride here*, I thought. I was very wrong. Car after car roared past without even bothering to slow down, and I became increasingly hot and angry.

Finally I remembered the lovingkindness meditation. As people swept past, instead of grumbling and complaining I wished them happiness, joy, love, and peace. What a difference it made. As each car roared by I felt happier and happier. I don't think it got me more rides, but it certainly transformed the afternoon! It also reminded me that the goal is to bring this meditation and attitude into more and more of life until love touches and transforms all our attitudes and relationships.

CHAPTER 14

THE HIGHER REACHES OF LOVE

The supreme purpose and goal for human life... is to cultivate love.

—Ramakrishna

A person who radiates love becomes a force and inspiration of extraordinary power. Mother Teresa, whose lifelong dedication to serving the poor earned her a Nobel Prize and a reputation as one of the great saints of the 20th century, saved thousands of lives and inspired millions more. Beginning in 1948 when she felt called to serve the poorest of the poor, she left the security of her convent and lived and worked in the slums of Calcutta. There she tended the sick, fed the hungry, and ministered to the dying. Her life was a whirlwind of loving service, and for years she stopped only to pray and to sleep three hours a night.

By the time of her death in 1997, she had established centers in Calcutta for the sick, dying, mentally disturbed, lepers, and abandoned children, as well as hundreds of other centers around the world staffed by thousands of followers. She was very clear that the task was not only to offer food and medicine but above all to offer love. "God loves the world through us," she exclaimed, and she regarded herself as "a pencil in the hand of God writing a love letter to the world."

Sometimes she took her role as a love scribe quite literally. Whenever she boarded a plane she carried a sack containing some of the thousands of letters she regularly received from around the world. Seating herself, she reached into the sack, took out a letter, and began writing, treating each person with equal love and respect.

Dear Johnny. Thank you for your letter. I will pray for you and your school friends.

Dear Mrs. Smith. Thank you for your letter and donation. I will pray for you and your family.

Dear Queen Elizabeth. Thank you for your letter. I will pray for you and your family.

On and on she wrote until the plane landed. Then Mother Teresa would hand the sack to one of her sisters and race off to her next task, leaving the sister to mail her love letters to the world.

One of her letter-writing sprees took place on the plane taking her to the United Nations' fortieth-anniversary celebration. Mother Teresa had been invited to address the General Assembly. There was one problem: the United Nations has a rule that there are no prayers said there. A mere rule was not going to stop Mother Teresa. She marched to the podium, prayed, and delivered the following love letter to the assembled world leaders:

You and I must come forward and share the joy of loving.
But we cannot give what we don't have.
That's why we need to pray.
And prayer will give us a clean heart,
and a clean heart can see God in each other.
And if we see God in each other
we will be able to live in peace.

This is a beautiful summary of Mother Teresa's path of love, and her life demonstrates the impact a life dedicated to love can have.

LOVE: PERSONAL AND TRANSPERSONAL

Spiritual practices can expand and deepen love so it becomes both more intense and more frequent. In advanced practitioners this intense love may mature from what psychologists call a transitory "peak experience" into a longer-lasting "plateau experience." That is, it becomes more continuous, gracing more and more activities and relationships and imbuing all life with its fragrance.

Even at this stage we think of love as only an emotion generated by and limited to our own minds. Yet many of the great religions paint a very different picture of love because at its deepest, love becomes so profound, so awesome, that it seems as much divine as human. This love is not personal but transpersonal, not only part of us but also part of the cosmos, not limited to our individual minds but part of the universal Mind, Spirit, or God. In fact, love may be a fundamental aspect of the very nature of reality, perhaps even, as the *Encyclopedia of Religion* summarizes it, "the single most potent force in the universe, a cosmic impulse that creates, maintains, directs, informs, and brings to its proper end every living thing."

There are two major exceptions to this view. Both Judaism and Taoism do not describe ultimate reality at all. This approach is the *via negativa*, which recognizes that the ultimate lies far beyond the power of words to embrace. Judaism recommends, "You shall love the Lord your God with all your heart," but regards God's essential nature as inscrutable. Likewise, Taoism emphasizes that the Tao is beyond words and that "The tao that can be told is not the eternal Tao."

Other traditions are more outspoken. Two of Hinduism's greatest sages, Ramana Maharshi and Ramakrishna, both announced that "God is love," echoing the words of the Christian Bible. In Islam, Allah is "the all-merciful, the all-compassionate"; in neo-Confucianism, love "both forms and proceeds from the basic principle of all things"; while in Buddhism ultimate reality is tinged with love's close cousin, compassion.

According to these traditions, we partake of this love; it is part of us and we are part of it. "There is no boundary whatsoever to pure love—it embraces humanity and Divinity," cried Ramakrishna. Likewise, Ramana Maharshi claimed that "Love is not different from the Self...the Self is love."

Sufis seek to taste this love so fully that the ego dissolves. Then only Love and the divine Beloved remain. This is the source of the apparently paradoxical cry:

When the lover is annihilated in Love
his love becomes one with the Love of the Beloved.

Likewise, Christians trust that "If we love one another, God lives in us, and his love is perfected in us."

Over the centuries, saint after saint has sung love's praises. Yet even as they sang they confessed that their words could give no more than the faintest hint of love's limitless bliss, its heart-melting tenderness, and its boundless concern for all beings. Rumi sang:

Ecstatic love is an ocean.
And the Milky Way is a flake of foam
floating on that ocean.

Ramakrishna begged us to "become mad with love in order to realize God-consciousness, which is ten million times more blissful than sexual experience." With these words he pointed to the magnificent recognition that love not only heals and delights us, but also awakens and unites us with the Divine. In the words of the Christian Bible, "God is love, and those who abide in love abide in God, and God abides in them."

Being boundless, love spontaneously overflows as care and concern for others. This care is expressed in an ethical lifestyle that seeks to avoid doing harm and to enhance the well-being of others. Ethical living both expresses love and further refines it.

LIVE ETHICALLY

FEEL GOOD BY DOING GOOD

Regard your neighbor's gain as your gain,
and your neighbor's loss as your own loss.
                                        —*Taoism*

CHAPTER 15

THE VALUE OF VIRTUE

[A wise person] is good to people
who are good.
She is also good to people who
are not good.
This is true goodness.

—*Lao Tsu*

The practice of ethics is terribly misunderstood. The costs of this misunderstanding are enormous. Indeed, ethical living is one of the most powerful yet most misunderstood of all religious practices. "Rare are those who understand virtue," sighed Confucius.

Many people regard the ethical guidelines of the great religions as just one more set of burdensome rules to be either blithely ignored or blindly obeyed. Unfortunately, this superficial understanding of ethics completely overlooks their remarkable spiritual potential. When rightly understood and practiced, ethical living—being kind, compassionate, and truthful—is a gift to everyone, and an essential means for awakening. This is why ethics hold such an honored place in each of the great religions.

The central message is very simple. It may be stated as the Golden Rule of Christianity: "Do to others as you would have them do to you," or its mirror image, the Silver Rule, in traditions such as Confucianism: "Do not do to others what you would not have them do to you." But whatever the words, the basic ethical message is the same: treat others as you wish to be treated. This principle is so crucial that when a Jewish sage was challenged to explain the essence of Judaism in the time he could remain standing on one foot, he immediately responded: "That which is hurtful to you, do not do to your neighbor. This is the whole doctrine."

These are fine words, but the question still remains: "Why should we bother?" Unfortunately, some ancient answers are based more on fear and guilt than on deep understanding of the benefits of ethical living. Tales of hideous demons or fire-breathing gods, whose idea of a good time is barbecuing us if we're not good, imply that the main reason for being ethical is to avoid punishment. Likewise, being called a miserable sinner and feeling torn by guilt if you make a mistake is hardly an inspiring reason to be kind and loving. There has to be a better reason for living ethically than fleeing guilt and hellfire. Fortunately, there is.

BENEFITS OF VIRTUE

At the spiritual heart of the great religions is a far deeper, post-conventional understanding of ethics. This perspective is based more on love than on fear, more on kindness than on guilt. At its center is a profound understanding of the way our minds work, which makes clear that unethical living is destructive to both oneself and others, whereas ethical living can bring happiness and also awakening.

The Costs of Unethical Living

Acting unethically exacts both immediate and long-term costs. When we deliberately lie, steal, or hurt someone, even ourselves, our minds are convulsed by painful emotions such as anger, fear, and jealousy. Such emotions can be destructive to others and also intensely painful and damaging to us. After all, if we attack because we're boiling with anger, it is we who burn in the flames of our own resentment. Unethical actions inflict an immediate emotional cost.

There are also long-term costs. Both ancient sages and modern psychologists agree that unethical behavior tends to be self-perpetuating because it not only springs from destructive states of mind but also strengthens them. When we attack in anger or lie from fear, we drive these emotions deeper into our minds and carve their traces further into our brains. In psychological terms, we condition our minds; in Asian terms, we imprint destructive karmic patterns on our souls. What we do, we become.

It is all too easy to see the hideous costs to everyone in extreme cases, such as when power-crazed leaders plunge whole countries into war. What is harder is to appreciate the costs of the seemingly minor infractions all of us commit: deliberately hurting someone's feelings, lying a little here, taking more than our fair share there.

❈

My first meditation retreat, which I described in an earlier chapter, made these costs painfully apparent. I had hoped for peace and insight, and in fact these occurred eventually. But as I first settled into the routine of continuous silence and meditation, I experienced anything but peace. I was unaccustomed to hours of silence and reflection each day and initially found the experience very difficult. My mind desperately sought distractions, but in the silent, secluded retreat setting there were few to be found.

Finally I discovered that showers could be a wonderful way to avoid self-awareness. Under the rush of warm water I could happily drift off in daydreams and forget the self-examination and reflection I had traveled five hundred miles to Oregon to learn.

But there was a problem with my solution: the showers were directly under the meditation hall. Naturally they proved a noisy distraction to the people who were actually doing what I was supposed to be doing: meditating. Consequently, we were requested to shower only between meditation sessions.

This request for fairness was no match for my greed. I continued to take long showers whenever I wanted to, whether between meditation sessions or not. Yet over the next few days the pleasure from the showers shriveled because, as the retreat continued, my mind became increasingly sensitive and I could no longer block from awareness the discomfort I was causing others.

I recognized that to justify my actions I was engaging in destructive mental exercises. First, I was deliberately suppressing my awareness of the irritation I was causing other people. Worse, I was trying to convince myself I was more important than they were and my comfort more important than theirs. I was exaggerating my own worth and belittling theirs and thereby alienating myself from everyone. Quite a price to pay for an extra shower.

It was a painful, life-changing lesson. Most importantly, I learned that until I look carefully, I remain blind to the deeper costs of unethical behavior. I simply don't see how it can fog awareness, muddy the mind, and poison relationships.

The toxic effects of emotions such as anger, guilt, and fear, which are inflamed by unethical acts, are not limited to the mind alone. The central recognition of psychosomatic medicine is that mental distress can lead to physical distress, and the distress of unethical actions is no exception.

> A woman with heart disease...had suffered frequent chest pain from her disease. Over the years she modified her diet, learned to meditate, and had been successful in controlling most of her pain. Yet some of her pain had been resistant to her efforts. Paying very careful attention to this, she had been shocked to notice that she experienced pain when she was about to do or say something that lacked integrity, that really wasn't true to her values. These were usually small things like not telling her husband something that he did not seem to want to hear, or stretching her values a bit in order to go along with others. Times when she allowed who she really was to become invisible. Even more surprising, sometimes she would know this was happening but sometimes the chest pain would come first, and then, examining the circumstances which provoked it, she would realize for the first time that she had been betraying her integrity.... Stress may be as much a question of a compromise of values as it is a matter of external time pressure and fear of failure.

Once the toxic costs of unkindly, unethical behavior are recognized, life is never quite the same. After all, who wants to continue hurting themselves once they see this is exactly what they are doing? For thousands of years the great religions have warned about the costs of unethical living, and now we see that these costs are not only spiritual, but also psychological and physical, and may even be life-threatening.

The Benefits of Ethical Living

Ethical behavior—when we try to foster people's well-being, including our own—is far more beneficial to both ourselves and others than we usually recognize. When we act ethically—when we forgive instead of retaliate, help instead of attack—we become a source of healing rather than pain.

Ethical living heals our minds. Acts of forgiveness and helping are incompatible with feelings such as overwhelming anger and jealousy, so these emotions begin to lose their compulsive power. In addition, ethical acts foster qualities such as love and generosity, so these qualities blossom. For example, when we give someone our love, that same love first flowers within our minds and then overflows into others, leaving its healing imprint on both. This is the basis of the lovingkindness meditation I described earlier, in which you cultivate feelings of love and happiness by wishing that others may have these feelings.

This general psychological and spiritual principle—what we intend for others we create for ourselves—is one of the most powerful and important, yet, sadly, also one of the least understood and appreciated, of all spiritual principles. Once it is understood, it transforms the basis of all relationships. The great secret of ethics is as the Buddha pointed out: "Whatever you do, you do to yourself."

Ethical living is absolutely crucial for advanced spiritual work, and without it, progress is difficult. Unethical acts create deep deposits of fear and guilt, paranoia and defensiveness. Though perhaps hidden from awareness by our defenses, they nevertheless agitate and cloud our minds, making it difficult to achieve calm and clarity. As Jack Kornfield put it, "It's hard to sit down and meditate after a day of lying, cheating and hurting people."

All the great religions regard ethical living as a foundation practice, one on which all the other practices depend. Each of the great religious founders both praised and embodied impeccable ethical living, and thereby provided moral beacons that have shone across cultures and centuries and illuminated the world. The great religious scholar Huston Smith, author of the superb book *The World's Religions*, summarized their impact:

> In the final analysis, goodness becomes embodied in society neither through might nor through law but through the impress of a great personality.

Perhaps the religious founder who focused most on ethics was Confucius. One of the most influential men ever, he shaped Chinese culture for 2,500 years. Born of humble origins, he loved learning and devoted every moment and encounter to it. Always modest, he was loath to claim any special virtue for himself, but he did acknowledge:

> There are bound to be those who are my equal in doing their best for others and in being trustworthy in what they say, but they are unlikely to be as eager to learn as I am.... Perhaps it might be said of me that I learn without flagging and teach without growing weary.

When a governor asked what kind of man Confucius was, one of his students was at a loss for words. Confucius suggested:

> Why did you not simply say something to this effect: he is the sort of man who forgets to eat when he tries to solve a problem that has driven him to distraction, who is so full of joy that he forgets his worries and who does not notice the onset of old age.

Confucius became the most learned man of his time, a veritable one-man university. But he was interested in learning more than mere facts.

Whether we recognize it or not, each one of us has a central sacred question around which our lives circle. It may be apparently abstract, such as, "What is truth?" or "What is wisdom?" Or it may be eminently practical, such as, "How can I learn to love?" "How can I best contribute to others?" "What is my gift to the world?" Whatever the question, how passionately we pursue and live it in large part determines how fully and wholeheartedly we live and how peacefully and contentedly we die.

"How do we live wisely and well?" was Confucius's sacred question, and he threw himself into answering it with a passion rarely matched in human history. The meaningless pastimes and pursuits that fill, then devour, most people's lives held little interest for him. He found profound joy by following his heart in an outwardly simple life. For him:

> In the eating of coarse rice and the drinking of water, the using of one's elbow for a pillow, joy is to be found. Wealth and rank attained through immoral means have as much to do with me as passing clouds.

Learning, personal integrity, and helping others were what mattered to him, and he devoted his life to practicing and teaching these ideals. Always humble, he never pretended to have perfected them. "How dare I claim to be a sage or a benevolent man?" he asked. Yet in his old age he did acknowledge that ethical living had become so natural to him that:

> At seventy, I could follow the dictates of my own heart; for what I desired no longer overstepped the boundaries of right.

The China of his day was wracked with conflict and oppression, and Confucius yearned for an official position so he could help and bring relief. He walked from one province to another until at long last he found an appointment. But he was far too uncompromisingly ethical to last long amidst the trickery and backstabbing of political life. Like the great Greek philosopher Plato, who a century later also took a government position, he soon resigned in disgust.

Because of his lack of political success, Confucius was often regarded by his contemporaries as a failure. But, undeterred, he gathered students around him without regard for their rank or finances and became the first person to make learning available to people not born to nobility. So deep was his wisdom, so inspiring his example, and so powerful his impact on students, and they in turn on others, that this political failure inspired Chinese culture for 2,500 years and came to be regarded as the greatest moral teacher of East Asia. The path he pointed out was not yet a full spiritual path—it lacked concentration practices, among other things—but it provided the foundation from which the full tradition of neo-Confucianism would flower and transform millions of lives.

After a lifetime of pondering the sacred question "How do we live wisely and well?" he concluded that of all the crucial elements, "It is morality that is supreme." He concluded, "If...I had to take one phrase to cover all my teaching, I would say, 'Let there be no evil in your thoughts.'"

Confucius recognized, as do all the great religions, that the person who becomes more ethical gradually unearths a treasure house of life-altering gifts in the depths of the heart, mind, and soul. According to the great religions, these many gifts include:

- reduced anxiety, guilt, and fear
- less cause for worry, defensiveness, and denial
- fewer bouts of self-doubt, depression, and despair
- growing confidence, courage, and strength
- deepening relaxation, calm, and peace
- greater capacity for openness, honesty, and intimacy
- a sense of integrity, trust, and wholeness
- relationships of closeness, consideration, and care
- emotions of happiness, joy, and delight
- a heart that is more open, kind, and loving
- and a mind that is more open, sensitive, and awake

In the words of the Buddha:

Speak and act with a pure mind
And happiness will follow you
As your shadow, unshakable....
Set your heart on doing good.
Do it over and over again,
And you will be filled with joy.

CHAPTER 16

WHAT IS AN ETHICAL LIFE?

We are visitors on this planet. We are here for ninety, a hundred years at the very most. During that period we must try to do something good, something useful with our lives. Try to be at peace with yourself and help others share that peace. If you contribute to others' happiness, you will find the true goal, the meaning of life.

—*The Dalai Lama*

What does it mean to live ethically? There are three aspects of our lives we need to attend to if we are to live more consciously and kindly. The first two are our speech and our actions, and the third is the emotional residue left over from past unethical behavior.

RIGHT SPEECH AND RIGHT ACTION

Right Speech

In the 3,000-year-old Hindu Vedas, sacred speech is seen as a primal creative force, while the Christian gospel of St. John opens with, "In the beginning was the Word." These texts imply that the power of speech is awesome. And so it is. A truthful statement can end years of misunderstanding, an apology can heal, while a few kind words can leave heartwarming memories that last a lifetime, as the following story by a young teacher makes clear.

Faced with a difficult class of students who were not getting on well, she asked them to list the names of the other students on a piece of paper and then to write the nicest thing they could say about each person. Taking the lists home, she wrote the name of each student on a separate piece of paper and then listed all the things each person had said about that student. The next morning she handed each student his or her list. Soon everyone was smiling, and she heard whispers such as "Really?" "I didn't know anyone liked me that much." "I never knew that meant so much to anyone."

The assignment was never mentioned again until years later when one of the students, Mark, was killed in the Vietnam War. After the funeral service the teacher and some of Mark's former classmates were invited to Mark's parents' house. The parents approached her and said: "We want to show you something. Mark was carrying this when he was killed." His father pulled something from a wallet. It was the list of all the good things Mark's classmates had said about him. "Thank you so much for doing that," Mark's mother said. "As you can see, Mark treasured it."

A group of Mark's classmates overheard the exchange. One smiled sheepishly and said, "I still have my list. It's in my top desk drawer at home." Another said, "I have mine, too. It's in my diary." "I put mine in our wedding album," said a third. "I bet we all saved them," said a fourth. "I carry mine with me at all times. I think we all saved our lists!"

That's when I finally sat down and cried. The lesson my former students taught me that day became a standard in every class I taught for the rest of my career.

Just a few warm words, but their impact lasted a lifetime and demonstrated the truth of the saying, "Good words are worth much and cost little."

While warm words can heal, unethical speech can destroy. A harsh word can hurt; a lie, especially by someone with power, can cause untold suffering. The Bible's advice is to be wary of:

the gossips and double-tongued,
for they destroy the peace of many....

Many have fallen by the edge of the sword,
but not as many as have fallen because of the tongue.

One would think our words, so fleeting and insubstantial, would be easy to change. In practice, it is quite a challenge. Most of us have grown careless with our speech: saying what people want to hear rather than what is true, spouting little lies to protect our egos, big lies to protect our little lies. All too quickly, this becomes a vicious cycle.

In light of this, it is no wonder the great religions urge us to choose our words with care and compassion and to say only what is true and helpful. Buddhists call it *right speech*. Right speech requires sensitivity to other people and to our own motives and emotions. Only then can we see what is both true to our experience and likely to be helpful. We are never completely certain what will be most helpful, but the more sensitive we are in choosing our words, the better our chances of helping rather than harming.

Right speech, like all components of the seven practices, is a skill that improves with practice. Over time it becomes increasingly effortless and produces a growing sense of peace. Gradually it becomes apparent that Jesus was not exaggerating when he claimed, "The truth will make you free." According to the Buddha, those who master right speech:

offend no one.
Yet they speak the truth.
Their words are clear
But never harsh....
They do not take offense
And they do not give it.

Right Action

Like right speech, right action focuses on doing what is beneficial to everyone, *including yourself.* Including yourself is vital. Otherwise, it is all too easy to fall into the painful trap of thinking right action is the same as sacrifice. In fact, when practiced wisely, right action is anything but a sacrifice. Like all components of the seven practices, right action is a kind of enlightened self-interest. In other words, it serves our well-being and self-interest, but those of others, too. With right action we serve ourselves by serving others; the result is that everyone gains.

The Trap of Ritualism

The emphasis of mature ethical speech and action is not on a complex code of do's and don'ts, of rules and regulations that attempt to lay down the law on what is right and wrong in every conceivable circumstance. Such rigid codes rapidly degenerate into compulsive ritualism. Of course, rituals can be wonderful, heartfelt spiritual techniques. But they can also easily degenerate into mindless, repetitive obligations. Then people obsess more about surface details, such as not eating this particular food on that day of the week, than on caring about their motives for acting and what effects their actions have on others. At this stage people follow rules rather than their hearts and concern themselves with surface appearances rather than deeper motivations. The *Tao Te Ching*, the central book of Taoism, points out the result and the remedy:

> When goodness is lost, there is morality.
> When morality is lost, there is ritual.
> Ritual is the husk of true faith....
> Therefore the masters concern themselves
> with the depths and not the surface.

This ritualization of religion is an absolutely lethal problem for every tradition. Not one of the great religions has escaped it. In each, the process of decay is the same. The religious founders break through into a fresh, ecstatic realization and pour forth a white-hot torrent of transformative spiritual energy, describing their realizations and the practices by which others can also attain them. But if followers fail to take up these practices and do not transform themselves, they cannot hear and preserve the deeper wisdom in the founders' teachings. "Let anyone with ears to hear listen!" cried Jesus.

The result is a process of "truth decay," whereby effective spiritual practices fade into ineffective rituals that fall into mere ritualism. Likewise, descriptions of direct experience solidify into theoretical doctrines that in turn ossify into rigid dogma. Compassionate ethics degrade into conventional moralism, then harden into formal legalism. The result is an archaic collection of mindless, deadening, formal rules and rituals that neither enliven nor enlighten.

How to replace merely ritual activities with truly transformative practices and legalistic hair-splitting with genuinely compassionate ethics is one of the greatest challenges every religion and each generation must repeatedly face. Numerous religious revivals and whole new religions have been born from these concerns. Calls for heartfelt ethical actions and criticisms of purely ritual practices were hallmarks of the Jewish prophetic tradition. Amos cried:

> I hate, I despise your festivals,
> and I take no delight in your solemn assemblies.
> Even though you offer me your burnt offerings and
> grain offerings I will not accept them....
> But let justice roll down like waters,
> and righteousness like an everflowing stream.

Confucius took to task the Chinese elite who believed that merely outward displays of piety, devoid of inner sincerity and benevolence, were sufficient. "What can a person do with the rites who is not benevolent?" he asked. Centuries later, when Confucianism had ossified into elaborate formalities, Taoists would level similar critiques against it. Likewise, Buddha rejected Hindu ritual sacrifices and listed reliance on mere rituals as one of the fetters that block enlightenment. Jesus scorned the hair-splitting legalism of the Pharisees. Centuries later, though, Christianity was split when Protestants rose up in revolt against Catholic sacramentalism that emphasized orthodox rites as essential for salvation. In each protest the central concern was the same: to redirect attention away from mindless, external routines and back to effective practices and the inner condition of heartfelt spiritual sincerity.

A similar process is now at work in our own time. In the West, there is a growing recognition that the spirit has died in much of conventional religion. Many conventional churches and synagogues offer social support and the comfort of centuries-old rituals, but the authentic transformative practices that truly awaken people have been long forgotten.

This has led to several responses. Revival movements have attempted to ignite a new fervor, and many do in fact produce powerful, though not necessarily growth-inducing, emotional experiences. A further response, one probably characteristic of readers of this book, is to seek authentic practices capable of fostering real spiritual growth and awakening. Ethical action is central to these practices.

Ethical Motives

The underlying motive is crucial in spiritual life and ethical action, which is why Mohammad claimed that "all actions are judged by the motives prompting them." The central motive underlying mature ethics is kindness, which has two aims: to be both harmless and helpful.

First Do No Harm

Like physicians, whose 2,400-year-old oath is, "First do no harm," many religions place enormous emphasis on not causing harm or suffering to any person, or even any conscious living creature. Jain priests go to the extremes of sweeping the ground in front of them as they walk and filtering their drinking water to avoid accidentally injuring any creature. Perhaps the greatest and most inspiring example of nonharming in modern times was Mahatma (meaning "great soul") Gandhi, who led India to independence.

Gandhi began his career as a timid, rather ineffectual lawyer, too shy to hold his own in court. But all that began to change when he worked in South Africa and was exposed to the horrors of racial discrimination. At one point he was thrown violently off a train when he attempted to sit in a whites-only carriage. He began his life's work of social reform, first in South Africa and then in his native India.

Gandhi could easily have become an angry, embittered man and an apostle of violence. Instead he became an apostle of peace and forged a new revolutionary movement that combined social action with spiritual values. Instead of regarding his opponents as inhuman enemies, he viewed them as potential friends; instead of slandering them, he relied on *satyagraha* (holding fast to truth); and instead of crushing them physically, he sought to uplift them morally. With these ethical weapons he attracted millions of Indians into a social movement of such moral force that it shook the mighty British empire, won India its freedom, and inspired similar leaders and movements around the world, including Martin Luther King, Jr., who wrote:

> The nonviolent approach does not immediately change the heart of the oppressor. It first does something to the hearts and souls of those committed to it. It gives them a new self-respect; it calls up resources of strength and courage that they did not know they had. Finally, it reaches the opponent and so stirs his conscience that reconciliation becomes a reality.

A commitment to do no harm is a gift to others and also a powerful, purifying discipline for the person practicing it. In trying to be harmless, we are forced to become more sensitive to the feelings of others, more alert to our own emotions such as anger or fear, more careful in our actions, and more willing to relinquish selfish motives. Being harmless, like other ethical exercises, is a superb method for self-awareness, self-healing, and purification. Sri Nisargadatta Maharaj described it as follows:

> Harmlessness is a most powerful form of yoga and will take you speedily to your goal. This is what I call...the Natural yoga. It is the art of living in peace and harmony, in friendliness and love.

Of course, the great religions advocate being not only harmless but also helpful. The ultimate goal is what Tibetans call "all-embracing kindness," which excludes no one from our concern. Indeed, the final stage on the awakened sages' path involves single-minded devotion to the welfare of all creation. But before we can develop all-embracing kindness, we must begin to heal the wounds of the past.

HEALING THE PAST

Not to mend one's ways when one has erred
is to err indeed.

—*Confucius*

When we sit down to reflect or meditate, we soon discover that our minds are a jumble of activity. Thoughts, fantasies, memories, and emotions jostle one another in a ceaseless whirlwind of mental motion. Many of the most disruptive emotions and attention-grabbing fantasies echo a common theme: They erupt from disturbing memories of unethical behavior, times when we either hurt others or were hurt by others. These memories may be years or even decades old, but they can still hold our minds prisoner. This imprisonment to the past is what Indian religions call *karma*, the psychological and spiritual residue of our previous actions.

Sometimes it feels as though we are forever doomed to be our own jailers and will never free our minds from the past. The great religions argue that it is not only possible to set our minds free, it is essential. Only when we are free of the past can we be fully alive to the present.

The way to free yourself from the past is to resolve or complete it, because the events that haunt you are ones that remain unresolved and unhealed. Perhaps someone hurt you long ago but you still burn with rage; perhaps you cheated or stole and feel wracked with remorse; perhaps you lament that you never told your parents you loved them before they died. Whatever the issue, if it continues to hurt you, it probably remains incomplete and unhealed.

How do we heal ourselves? While the precise steps depend on the specific nature of the problem, the great religions offer valuable general guidelines.

Guidelines for Healing the Past

• *Undo any damage.* If you caused pain or harm, it is wise to undo it wherever possible. For example, if you hurt someone's feelings, you may want to apologize; if you stole something, it may be appropriate and healing to replace it or pay for it.

• *Aim for solutions in which everyone wins.* The ideal solution is one in which everyone involved gains and learns from the process. For example, if someone hurt you, it is far better to gently explain that the behavior was hurtful than it is to attack. Ideally, both of you will then learn from and be healed by the interaction.

• *Avoid attack.* It is terribly tempting to retaliate when someone hurts you. The painful result, however, is usually only a dizzying spiral of ever-increasing anger, attack, and counterattack. The Buddha lamented:

> Alas for the man
> who raises his hand against another,
> and even more for him
> who returns the blow.

• *Communicate.* Simply telling someone honestly and openly about your pain can be remarkably healing. The pain may be guilt and embarrassment over something unethical you did, or anger at someone else's lack of ethics. This kind of communication is so effective that it forms the basis of the healing offered by religious confession, psychotherapy, and self-help groups such as Alcoholics Anonymous.

• *Learn.* As always, learn as much as possible from your experience. For example, when you have resolved a dilemma, see what worked and what didn't, so you can proceed more effectively in the future.

Examples of Healing the Past

Insurance companies can be a nightmare of torturous rules and regulations. Negotiating them is a test of patience, a test I failed. I had been suffering from a curious stomach disorder that defied diagnosis. After numerous fruitless tests and several specialist consultations, my insurance company suddenly announced they would not reimburse my expenses. I was stuck with hundreds of dollars' worth of bills. Gritting my teeth in anger, I called the company to complain. After being shuttled from one clerk to another, I finally found someone who had my file. The more the clerk explained the bizarre complexities of the company's rules, the more my anger spilled over us both like a cloud of toxic waste. It was not a happy interaction for either of us.

Afterward, I grumbled and tried to go back to work. But unpleasant memories of the conversation kept bubbling into awareness. As they did, I had a blinding insight into the obvious: the clerk was not responsible for the company's policies, and it was inappropriate for me to blame her. After a moment's hesitation, I picked up the telephone, called her back and apologized. It was an immediate relief for both of us. She was happy and I was freed of my anger. I had undone the damage, communicated honestly, and learned from the experience. The whole process took less than five minutes.

❈

When grievances have been allowed to boil and fester over long periods, they usually require more time and effort. Yet healing is still possible, as a friend of mine demonstrated beautifully.

Bill was a successful psychologist at a major East Coast university. Like many prestigious universities, his was an enormously competitive institution where rivalry flourished and faculty members fought over limited funding. Bill and his coworker, Peter, were caught up in one of these nasty turf battles, became bitter rivals, and eventually refused to speak or even look at one another.

Some three years after their rivalry began, Bill found himself increasingly drawn towards spiritual practice. As his practice deepened, he realized just how destructive his hatred of Peter was and that he desperately needed to heal the relationship. After years of mutual disdain, this was not going to be an easy task.

Bill began by waiting in the coffee room one morning until Peter came for his coffee. When Peter walked in Bill simply smiled. After several days of this Bill made sure he had the coffee pot in his hand when he saw Peter approaching. "Peter, can I pour you a cup of coffee?" Bill asked, smiling from ear to ear. Peter's response was something close to a grunt, but since Bill had the coffee and Peter wanted some, he had no choice but to accept. The next morning Bill was there again, coffee pot in hand and a smile on his face, saying, "Hi, Peter, how are you? Can I pour you some coffee?" A few days later Bill was waiting in the coffee room with an article relevant to Peter's research saying, "Hi, Peter, good to see you. I thought you might be interested in this article."

It's hard to stay angry with someone when, day after day, they smile at you and do things for you. Gradually Peter's resistance melted. It took many months of gentle, patient effort by Bill, but eventually the relationship was healed. In time they even became close friends.

The vital importance of completing the past and healing relationships can be judged from the words of Jesus:

> So when you are offering your gift at the altar,
> if you remember that your brother or sister
> has something against you,
> leave your gift there before the altar and go;
> first be reconciled to your brother or sister,
> and then come and offer your gift.

One area where many people are sorely tempted to set ethics aside is their taxes. Unfortunately, I was no exception. It's not that I forged documents or stole money, but for several years I was certainly generous in giving myself the benefit of the doubt in any gray areas. Not surprisingly, when I was audited the tax authorities were delighted to find some dubious deductions and fined me accordingly.

The first few times this happened, I was indignant. Finally I had another blinding insight: The tax authorities were giving me feedback about my ethics. I was making dubious deductions and was not being careful with my record-keeping. Yet I kept blaming the tax system instead of taking responsibility myself. I had been slow in getting the lesson from a Christian text:

> Trials are but lessons that you failed to learn
> presented once again,
> so where you made a faulty choice before
> you now can make a better one.

It was time for me to make a better choice. I decided to try to view my tax preparation not as a loathsome necessity, but rather as an interesting exercise in ethical training. I first committed to doing my taxes completely honestly (practice 3), then tried to be as aware as possible (practice 5) and to see where I was tempted to cheat. Whenever temptations arose, I checked to see what motives and emotions, such as greed or fear, were seducing me and worked to transform them (practices 1 and 2).

I learned a lot and also received several rewards. My taxes became a lesson rather than a trial and, in a curious twist of events, the tax agents became my teachers, showing me where I was being careless, unconscious, or unethical. This is an example of the principle that anyone can become our teacher if we consciously decide to view them in this way. The result is that I no longer feel so anxious when doing my taxes and don't cringe whenever a letter from the tax agency arrives. And in the last two audits, every single claim I made was approved.

❋

These stories demonstrate several things. They suggest ways of healing and learning from past mistakes, and they illustrate some of the resulting benefits. They also demonstrate a crucial distinction: the difference between mature ethics and immature guilt.

Guilt-ridden people see their mistakes as unforgivable sins and punish themselves unmercifully. They do not heal or learn from the past; rather, they continue to punish themselves for it and thereby remain tied to it.

Ethical people, on the other hand, recognize their mistakes as simply mistakes. They heal the past and themselves by correcting their errors, forgiving themselves, and learning as much as they can from the process. In this way they gradually become free of the past, their minds cease to be junkyards of painful memories and guilty secrets, and they come fresh and clean to each new moment of experience.

CHAPTER 17

EXERCISES IN ETHICAL LIVING

Know that moral virtues and vices are acquired and firmly established in the soul by frequently repeating the actions pertaining to a particular moral habit over a long period of time and by our becoming accustomed to them.

—*Maimonides, twelfth-century Jewish sage*

Ethical living is vital for spiritual life, but as we all know, it isn't always easy. If it were, the world would be a different place, without wars or weapons, police or prisons. If we could simply decide to be forever kind and honest, that would be wonderful, but at one time or another we have all shared St. Paul's lament:

I can will what is right, but I cannot do it.
For I do not do the good I want,
but the evil I do not want is what I do.

Obviously, ethical transformation is a demanding process. Old habits, seductive cravings, and powerful fears are deeply ingrained and require time and techniques to change them. Having specific exercises to practice helps enormously.

EXERCISE 1: REFLECT ON YOUR GOOD DEEDS

When advanced practitioners feel despondent about their progress or themselves, their teacher may suggest they reflect on their good deeds. The reason is that advanced practitioners have a firm ethical foundation, so reflecting on the good they have done elicits feelings of happiness and inspiration. We may not be advanced practitioners, but we have all done some good and can benefit from reflecting on it. It is easy to belittle our contributions, but the Buddha advised:

> Do not belittle your virtues,
> Saying, "They are nothing."
> A jug fills drop by drop
> So the wise person becomes brimful of virtue.

Begin this exercise by relaxing. When you are ready, recall three contributions or things you have done that you feel good about. As the memories rise into awareness, allow yourself to savor each one and reflect on them. Notice the feelings they evoke.

Many people are surprised by the memories that emerge. They expect dramatic events, but often the things that stand out are quite simple and apparently unremarkable. These may include such things as taking time to be with a friend who was in pain, speaking the truth in a meeting when no one else seemed willing to, or helping a lost child find his parents. These are not the stuff of Hollywood movies but are the kinds of actions that benefit others and also leave an enduring glow in our minds.

EXERCISE 2: TELL THE TRUTH FOR A DAY

Truth is so very precious, man is naturally economical in its use.
—*Mark Twain*

The great religions all agree on the importance of telling the truth. But most people have unfortunate ideas about truth-telling. They believe it means compulsively blurting out their deepest, darkest secrets to strangers or saying anything truthful to others, no matter how hurtful. Truth-telling doesn't require we say everything that comes to mind, and it certainly doesn't imply being insensitive to people's feelings. Rather, it means carefully assessing each situation to find what we can say that is true to our experience and, if possible, also helpful to others. In some situations we don't know what the truth is, and then it is appropriate and truthful to say we don't know.

Begin by selecting a time period—a day is good to begin with—for this exercise. Then make a commitment to say only what is true and, when possible, helpful during that time. Note that you have two goals: to speak both as truthfully and as kindly as you can.

As with many exercises, it is useful to keep a diary or notebook handy. If you notice yourself lying, or even tempted to lie, record the situation, the fear or attachment that triggered it, and what you learned from the experience.

At the end of the day, take a few minutes to reflect and read any notes you took. How often were you tempted to lie and how often did you succumb? What were the seductions that tempted you to lie? What did you gain from truth-telling? Less guilt? Perhaps a sense of strength and integrity? This truth-telling exercise takes only a few minutes during a day but can offer insights that endure for years.

EXERCISE 3: GIVE UP GOSSIP

> Curb your tongue and senses
> And you are beyond trouble,
> Let them loose
> And you are beyond help.
> —*Lao Tsu*

We love to talk about other people. Sometimes this can be helpful, but often it is mere gossip: a way of uniting a group in the dubious delight of telling tales about anyone not present to defend themselves. These tales are rarely true and helpful. Avoiding gossip is another powerful exercise in truth-telling.

To begin, choose a time period of perhaps a day or a week. Then commit to not saying anything during this time about people unless you have already said, or would be willing to say, it to them directly. Whenever you find yourself tempted to gossip, try to recognize the underlying motive.

It can be hard not to be sucked into the gossip game, but it can also be rewarding. To begin with, you will be fostering harmony rather than antagonism, and you will no longer have to worry that someone you maligned will learn of your gossipy put-downs. Just as important are the internal rewards. A sense of integrity and strength comes from holding to the truth, treating people with respect, and refusing to succumb to hurtful talk. "Better than a thousand hollow words," said the Buddha, "is one word that brings peace."

EXERCISE 4: DO NO HARM

Being harmless is a wonderful gift. It means that we are not acting from, and therefore reinforcing, anger in ourselves, and that people are safe in our presence. This allows them to let down their guard, set aside their defenses and pretenses, and feel at peace.

To give this gift, decide on a time period—perhaps a day—and try the best you can not to harm anyone. Of course this means not causing physical harm—but it also has more subtle implications, such as practicing right speech in order not to hurt people's feelings or self-esteem. As with most exercises, it is helpful to write down your experiences and insights and to reflect on them at the end of the day.

If you want to take the exercise further, try not to hurt any conscious creature. Yes, this includes even insects. If a mosquito bites you, do as the Dalai Lama does; gently blow it away. This may seem to be taking things to extremes but is actually a very valuable exercise. As one of my meditation teachers taught, and as I've since learned myself, even killing an insect exacts a palpable toll on me (let alone the insect). If I am aware when I swat a mosquito, I notice my mind is filled with anger and aversion towards it, and I have temporarily lost touch with compassion and any appreciation of the sacredness of life. These are not states of mind I want to reinforce, so not harming any conscious creature makes more and more sense.

EXERCISE 5: COMMUNICATE TO HEAL

Right speech can be remarkably healing. There is something about sharing a painful experience that can detoxify it and give new insights and perspectives on it. This is particularly true of pain resulting from unethical behavior.

Of course, the communication needs to be done with the intention of healing. Spewing anger over people with the aim of making them angry too is not going to heal anyone. Talking about anger in order to release it is another, far more pleasant story.

To do this exercise, select an unethical behavior, either yours or someone else's, that still disturbs you. It should be one you would like to resolve and would be willing to communicate. Then select someone you trust to communicate with. Ideally this will be someone wise enough to listen carefully and sympathetically and, of course, able to keep a secret. This person might be a professional counselor or priest but, except with complex or overwhelming psychological or spiritual problems, might just as well be a friend. It is helpful to select a time and place where you won't be disturbed.

Your job is to talk as openly and honestly as you can about your pain. It's better not to give long explanations, theoretical interpretations, or justifications. Simply talk about your personal experience and especially your feelings. "I feel..." is a good way to start sentences. The listener doesn't have to provide answers or solve the problem. His or her job is simply to listen. Continue until you feel some sense of completion. At that point, you can tell your friend you are complete, and then you can both reflect together on what can be learned from the experience.

EXERCISE 6: RIGHT A WRONG

Unethical behavior tends to produce a black cloud of guilt and discomfort that hangs over our heads and sometimes subtly, sometimes all too obviously robs us of joy and vitality. The surest way of healing this is to attempt to undo any damage our behavior caused. This might involve apologizing for a hurtful remark, replacing a stolen item, compensating people for their loss, or making amends the best way you can.

For this exercise, reflect on unethical things you have done that remain unresolved. Choose one you would like to resolve and decide how to do it. It is useful to decide on a time by which to complete the task, because guilt has a tricky habit of helping us procrastinate and forget. The Buddha provided a warning about all ethical acts:

> Be quick to do good.
> If you are slow,
> The mind, delighting in mischief,
> Will catch you.

CHAPTER 18

THE HIGHER REACHES
OF ETHICAL LIVING

Wish for others whatever you wish for yourself.
—*Mohammad*

As the practice of ethics deepens, its benefits flow into more and more aspects of life, dissolving old pains, releasing fear and anger, healing damaged relationships, and freeing us from the past. Even death—the greatest mystery and source of anguish in life—begins to lose some of its terror. This shift is portrayed exquisitely in *Everyman*, one of the most popular plays of all medieval literature.

Everyman receives a most unwelcome visitor, the angel of death, who informs him that his time has come. Needless to say, Everyman is far from happy. He pleads for more time and offers bribes, but to no avail. Everyman then begs a variety of symbolic characters—such as Beauty, Knowledge, Fellowship and Worldly Goods—to accompany him, but none of them are at all enthusiastic about the idea. Eventually Everyman finds one character—only one—willing to accompany him on his final journey. That character is Good Deeds. Good deeds, or ethical living, the play tells us, ease both life and death.

As ethical living becomes a deep and natural way of life, it offers increasingly profound gifts. As the mental fog unethical behavior creates begins to lift, we can see ourselves more clearly and realize we are not who we thought we were. We recognize how unnecessary and illusory so many fears and defenses were, because who we really are needs no defense. We understand that the self-image we lied to protect or stole to satisfy is merely an illusion, a frightened fragment of the mind. Ethical living helps us see through this illusion, recognize our true Self, and see beyond our Self to our Source. This is the ultimate gift of ethics: to know in our own ecstatic experience the truth of Jesus's words, "Blessed are the pure in heart, for they will see God."

When we recognize our own Self, we also recognize that same Self in others. Then we look out on the world and see our Self in all people. There are no "others" to lie to, cheat, or mistreat. In the words of the Buddha:

> See yourself in others.
> Then whom can you hurt?
> What harm can you do?

At this stage ethical living is no longer a struggle; it is a natural, effortless, and ecstatic expression of our true nature, of who we really are. Jack Kornfield summarized the growth of ethics as follows:

> At first, precepts [ethics] are a practice. Then they become a necessity, and finally they become a joy. When our heart is awakened they spontaneously illuminate our way in the world. This is called Shining Virtue. The light around someone who speaks truth, who consistently acts with compassion for all, even in great difficulty, is visible to all around them.

Ethical living offers a further benefit. By loosening the grip of jarring emotions such as guilt and anger, it leaves the mind less vulnerable to upset and agitation. This helps concentrate and calm the mind.

CONCENTRATE AND CALM YOUR MIND

Control the mind.
Attain one-pointedness.
Then the harmony of heaven
Will come down and dwell in you.
You will be radiant with life.
You will rest in Tao.
            —*Chuang Tzu, Taoist sage*

CHAPTER 19

YOUR MEANDERING MIND

May you develop mental concentration...
for whosoever is mentally concentrated,
sees things according to reality.

—The Buddha

Our minds are restless creatures. Always on the move, they wander ceaselessly, jumping from past memories to future fantasies, constantly plotting and planning, pursuing pleasures and fleeing fears. While driving down the road we plan our day, refight yesterday's argument, worry about our finances, and listen to the radio.

No wonder so many people feel frazzled during the day and exhausted by the end of it. No wonder also that so many people try to shut their minds off with television, alcohol, or drugs. Even more remarkable than the perpetual agitation of our minds is the fact that we recognize only a fraction of this frenzy, though it is not hard to recognize. You can get a taste of it in just a couple of minutes by doing the following brief experiment.

Read the following instructions. When you are clear about them, put the book down and close your eyes.

Visualize a white ring with a white dot in the middle, on a black background. Try to focus your attention undistractedly on the image and to keep it clear and steady in your mind for one to two minutes. Do the visualization now.

It is astounding to find how dramatically the image shifts and changes despite your best efforts to hold it steady. Not only does the image change, but attention wanders away to passing thoughts and fantasies.

This brief glimpse of the mind's agitation and limited concentration surprises most people. The mind has a mind of its own.

CAN YOU TAME YOUR MIND?

The recognition of just how extraordinarily out of control our minds are was one of the greatest shocks of my life. None of my training in medicine, neuroscience, or psychology had given me more than a hint of it. I was utterly unprepared for the realization of the extent of the mind's wanderlust that my first retreat revealed.

Each hour I would sit down determined to remain alert and aware and to focus on the sensations of the breath. Yet within seconds my attention would zoom off into pleasant memories or fearful fantasies and all thought of the breath, or even that I was meant to be focusing on it, was totally forgotten. Time and again I would awaken from my fantasies and vow that this time I would *really* focus on the breath, and yet, seconds later, both breath and vow would be forgotten. It was a humbling experience, and afterward I wrote:

> I was forced to recognize that what I had formerly believed to be my rational mind, preoccupied with planning and problem solving, actually comprised a frantic torrent of forceful, demanding, loud and often unrelated thoughts and fantasies.... It became clear that I had little more than the faintest inkling of self-control of either thoughts or feelings.

Psychology Gives Up on the Problem

Sigmund Freud, the father of psychoanalysis, glimpsed part of this issue. Freud went on to scandalize the Western world with his claim that we are not the fully conscious, rational creatures we fondly imagine ourselves to be. Rather, said Freud, we are driven by powerful unconscious forces deep within us. Freud summed up our dilemma with his famous lament that "man is not even master in his own house...in his own mind."

America's greatest psychologist, William James, reached the same insight as early as 1899. James recognized the tragic implications of this lack of mental mastery and concluded that an education for developing sustained attention "would be the education par excellence." Unfortunately, James could not find such an education and at last resigned himself to the idea that "Attention cannot be continuously sustained." For almost the entire twentieth century Western psychology wrongly accepted James's dismal conclusion, thereby severely underestimating our capacities.

The Great Religions Solved the Problem

Although they did not know it, Freud and James were echoing the cries of centuries of novice meditators who discovered for themselves how distractable attention is. Buddhists have long compared the mind, lurching from thought to thought, to a crazy monkey leaping erratically from branch to branch. Likewise, two thousand years ago the *Bhagavad Gita*, the "Hindu Bible," lamented:

Restless the mind is....
Truly I think
The wind is no wilder.

But whereas Western psychology threw up its hands at the problem, the great religions solved it. Western psychologists say attention *cannot* be sustained, but the great religions say that it can and *must* be sustained. Ramana Maharshi, one of the twentieth century's greatest Hindu sages, emphasized: "All scriptures without any exception proclaim that for attaining salvation mind should be subdued." When a student asked him, "What stands in the way of my knowing myself or God?" he shot back, "Your wandering mind." The vital importance of this problem is captured by a Zen story:

A student of Zen purchased a spiritual text. Bringing it to the monastery, the student asked if the teacher would write some words of inspiration in it.

"Certainly," replied the teacher, who wrote for a second and then handed the book back. There the student found only a single word: "Attention!"

"Will you not write more?" pleaded the disappointed student, again offering the book to the teacher.

"All right," said the teacher, who this time wrote for several seconds. Inside the book the student now found three words: **Attention! Attention! Attention!**

Some practitioners have been willing to go to any lengths to master attention. Wang Yang-ming lived in sixteenth-century China and was one of the greatest neo-Confucian philosopher-sages. During his quest for enlightenment, he and his friend Ch'ien decided to focus undistractedly on a piece of bamboo in an attempt to hone their awareness to the point where they could recognize the sacred principle within it. He wrote:

> Day and night Ch'ien meticulously investigated the principle of the bamboo. For three days he exhausted his mind, until his mental energy was overtaxed and he became ill. At first I said that this was because his strength was insufficient. I took up the task myself, and investigated the bamboo early and late, but still could not uncover its principle. After seven days I too became ill because of having worn out my mind. So we sighed together and said, "The reason we cannot be sages or worthy men is that we lack the great strength that is needed."

Fortunately, Wang Yang-ming eventually had two realizations:

1) He recognized that such arduous mental marathons were not necessary.
2) He realized that the sacred principle he sought was to be found within his own mind. With this realization, he finally attained enlightenment and subsequently went on to become one of China's greatest philosophers and statesmen.

WHY CONCENTRATE?

Why is training your attention so vital? Why bother learning to concentrate? Because our untrained minds take an enormous toll on our psychological and spiritual well-being, and because, once tamed, a concentrated mind offers enormous benefits. The Dalai Lama claimed, "Religion is at best a tool to help you train your mind." In the words of the Buddha:

> More than those who hate you,
> more than all your enemies,
> an untrained mind does greater harm.
> More than your mother,
> more than your father,
> more than all your family
> a well-trained mind does greater good.

Costs of Poor Concentration

If our minds are out of control, our lives are out of control. The root of our problem is that we allow ourselves to become slaves rather than masters of our own minds. Ram Dass summarized our dilemma:

> We are all prisoners of our minds. This realization is the first step on the journey to freedom.

A Sufi teacher put it succinctly by saying, "The bind is in the mind."

As long as we cannot focus our attention and it leaps unbidden from one thing to another, we are doomed to agitation and distraction. Just how costly this can be is evident from an extreme case.

> Mark was a seven-year-old whirlwind. From the moment he raced into the conference room at our child psychiatry clinic, there was no stopping him. He darted from one corner to another, clambered onto a chair, and then immediately jumped off it when he spied a toy on the floor. Even the toy couldn't hold his attention, and within seconds he was exploring something else. No amount of cajoling by his mother was sufficient to quiet him down. The child psychiatrist tried to engage him in conversation, but Mark only half listened and then abruptly darted off to inspect the psychiatrist's bag. Asked to solve a block puzzle, he began with great gusto. Yet even before it was half done, he had lost interest. His

mother tried to coax him to finish, but the result was a furious temper tantrum. Not surprisingly, Mark had few friends, was having trouble at school, and was driving his parents crazy.

Mark was suffering from ADD, attention deficit disorder, a disorder that wreaks havoc in the lives of millions of children and many adults. Unable to maintain attention on anything for more than an instant, they career through life impulsive, irritable, fidgety, and constantly distracted. Consequently, they are unable to stick with anything, have trouble learning essential skills such as reading and writing, do poorly at school and work, and are constantly forgetting things.

Relationships are difficult for people with ADD. Whether children or adults, people with attention deficit disorder have great trouble learning social skills and developing close relationships. Much of the art of relationships involves paying close attention to subtle cues such as emotions and facial expressions. A person with poor attention can easily miss these cues, seem insensitive and inappropriate, and end up a social misfit. As work and social failures mount, so too do frustration, embarrassment, and poor self-esteem. Desperate for relief, millions of these people take medication every day to control their careening attention.

Psychiatrists identified ADD only recently. Now it is apparent that it is a common disorder, affecting some 3 percent of children and many adults, exacerbated by our frenetic, deadline-driven, sound-bite culture and exacting enormous individual and social costs.

Two thousand years earlier, the great religions came to a similar, though more profound diagnosis. With the aid of the mental microscope of meditation, they were able to observe the mind and its wandering attention in minute detail. Their arresting conclusion was that we *all* suffer from attention deficit disorder. All of us suffer from a hyperactive attention which, while not as frenetic as in people with a clinically severe disorder, still careens uncontrollably from one object to another. And all of us, say the great religions, pay severe psychological, relationship, and spiritual costs.

The great religions not only came up with a diagnosis but also with a treatment program. Unlike Western psychiatry, which relies on medication to suppress the wandering of attention or therapy to compensate for it, they discovered methods for training and taming attention and learned just how beneficial these methods can be.

Benefits of a Concentrated Mind

The mind has a remarkable ability to mirror and take on the qualities of whatever we attend to. If we listen to an angry person or watch a violent scene our minds start to boil with anger. If we focus on a loving person, our minds tend to fill with love.

Once this is recognized, two things quickly become apparent:

1) If we could control attention, we could concentrate on specific people and memories in order to evoke desired qualities such as love and joy.

2) What we put into our minds is just as important as what we put into our mouths. Our mental diet affects our mental health. If we practice what Buddhists call "unwise attention" and stuff our minds with such things as an insane television diet of violence, greed, and fear, these same qualities grow and fester within us. Psychological research has made this painfully clear. The more violence people watch on television—and it is hard to watch television without watching violence—the more aggressive they tend to become.

But if we practice "wise attention" and carefully select a healthier diet of sane television programs, reading, and friends, we cultivate healthy states of mind. St. Paul was practicing not only good religion but also good psychology when he advised:

Whatever is true, whatever is honorable,
whatever is just, whatever is pure,
whatever is pleasing, whatever is commendable,
if there is anything worthy of praise
think about these things.

What we concentrate on we become, and once we can control attention, we can concentrate on anything we wish. This opens enormous possibilities.

CHAPTER 20

DEVELOP
A PEACEFUL MIND

Our essential nature is usually overshadowed
By the activity of the mind....
When the mind has settled,
we are established in our essential nature
which is unbounded consciousness.

—The Yoga Sutras of Patanjali

Though the rewards of developing a calm, concentrated mind
are enormous, it is a challenging task. Just as a powerful wild animal accustomed to roaming where it wants resists being tamed,
so too does the wild monkey mind.

Shankara was one of the greatest spiritual geniuses of all time
and the most influential of all Hindu thinkers. Born in 788, he was
a prodigy who while still a child left home in search of a teacher.
He spent years honing his mind through ascetic practices, intensive meditation, and philosophical study, and while still in his teens
he became deeply enlightened. By the time of his death at age
thirty-two, he had written some of India's most influential religious and philosophical texts, founded a monastic order, and established Hinduism's most influential school of thought.

Few people in history have been such intellectual and spiritual geniuses as Shankara, and few people could speak so author-
itatively about training the mind. When he was asked, "What is
the most difficult task?" he replied, "To keep the mind under
constant control."

Even saints have been humbled by the challenge. One of the
most beloved of Catholic saints, Teresa of Avila, cried out in frustra-

tion, "Sometimes I want to die in that I cannot cure this wandering of the intellect." Training the mind and attention is sometimes called the art of arts and science of sciences—for good reason.

The challenge of mastering attention is not so much that it is a painful process but rather that it is a slow one. It takes time and specific methods, which include meditation and contemplation, yoga, chanting, and continuous prayer.

MEDITATION: A UNIVERSAL PRACTICE

To know Tao
meditate and still the mind.
Knowledge comes with perseverance.
—*Loy Ching Yuen,*
nineteenth-century Taoist master

Many people think of meditation and contemplation—practices that train attention in order to foster spiritual growth—solely as techniques of Asian religions. Some conservative Jews and Christians have even argued that meditation has no legitimate place in their religions, citing such proverbs as "An idle mind is the devil's workplace" or "Idleness is the enemy of the soul." Yet as anyone who has done significant meditation knows, there is a huge difference between lazy idleness and profound peace. Meditation has been used for thousands of years in both the Jewish and Christian traditions.

Meditation is a worldwide practice that has an honored place in the history and heart of all the great traditions. "Meditation is the chief possession of the mystic," say Sufis, and sages from all traditions recognize its value and agree with the words of Rabbi Nachman:

> A person who does not meditate cannot have wisdom. He may occasionally be able to concentrate, but not for any length of time. His power of concentration remains weak and cannot be maintained.

Common Elements

Meditation and other concentration techniques have two key elements in common. First, they choose a focus for attention, whether it be the breath, an image, a word, or a prayer. Second, when attention wanders, they gently return it to this focus, again and again and again. This is the heart of the method: to return attention each time it wanders. Gradually the mind becomes less fickle and attention remains more focused on the chosen object.

But it takes time. Our minds have had an entire lifetime to indulge their fickle wanderlust. If we expect them to relinquish the habits of a lifetime in a few minutes or even hours, we are going to be very disappointed.

TRANSFORMING THE BUSYNESS OF DAILY LIFE

Some techniques for concentration are best done during specific practice periods, such as morning meditation or prayer. Others can be incorporated into the general busyness of daily life, and we will start with these.

EXERCISE 1: DO ONE THING AT A TIME

Our frantic minds reflect our frantic lives as we try to fit more and more into each day. We constantly do two or more things at a time. We dress while listening to the radio; prepare a meal while planning our day; then eat the meal while reading the paper and watching television. We listen to the radio while driving and at work talk on the telephone while preparing a report. Our lives feel fragmented, our minds are agitated, blood pressure is raised, and our attention span is shortened. Thomas Merton, one of the twentieth century's most influential Christians, summarized the dilemma:

> The rush and pressure of modern life are a form, perhaps the most common form, of its innate violence. To allow oneself to be carried away by a multitude of conflicting concerns, to surrender to too many demands, to commit oneself to too many projects, to want to help everyone in everything is to succumb to violence. The frenzy of the activist neutralizes his or her work for peace.

Yet we can live our lives in ways that foster calm and concentration rather than frenzy and fragmentation. An excellent way to begin is to practice doing just one thing at a time and giving whatever we do our full attention. This is a very straightforward exercise, yet it can have dramatic effects. One busy doctor who had spent years living at a frenetic pace reported that he was astounded at what a difference it made and that it was one of the most beneficial exercises he had ever done.

To begin, commit a specific time—a day might be good to begin with—to doing only one thing at a time. For one day you will focus your attention on each individual activity. You may not get quite as many things done, but a lot of those undone things will probably end up seeming rather insignificant. What you do get done, you will do more efficiently and enjoy a lot more.

Such a day might include changes such as: When you get up, don't turn on the radio or television until you are ready to give them your full attention. When you shower, without the radio, focus on enjoying the sensation of the water as it caresses your body and afterward on the invigorating rub of the towel as you dry yourself. A shower can be either a mindless task or a sensuous pleasure, depending on the amount of attention you give it.

When preparing breakfast, just prepare breakfast. When you eat the breakfast, give it your full attention. Turn off the radio and television and put the newspaper aside. Simply enjoy your meal, each smell, each taste, each texture. When you have finished eating, by all means, read the newspaper.

When using the telephone, give the person at the other end the gift of your full attention. When someone is talking to you, turn off the television or put down your reading and *really* listen. If you go to a restaurant, choose a quiet one where you can save your hearing, enjoy your meal, and, if you are with someone, have a real conversation.

By the end of the day you may have listened to less radio, watched less television, and perhaps made one or two fewer phone calls. But the rewards vastly outweigh the trivial losses. Since you were really present for each activity, you may feel less agitated and fragmented, and also that your day was more enjoyable and meaningful.

As you discover these benefits, you may want to extend the exercise into more of your life, relinquishing superficial distractions in order to focus on what is most meaningful and important. This is the basis of "voluntary simplicity," a lifestyle less cluttered by excess activities and possessions, a life outwardly simple yet inwardly rich. It takes practice to resist the fragmenting seductions of modern life, but the rewards are more than worth it.

EXERCISE 2: TRANSFORM DAILY ACTIVITIES INTO SACRED RITUALS

In addition to doing one thing at a time, it is possible to give special attention to specific activities, such as opening a door, answering a telephone, or driving a car. By deciding to use these activities for spiritual awakening, seemingly insignificant routines become sacred rituals dedicated to developing calm and concentration.

To begin, select a particular activity, such as opening doors, and commit to doing it for a period, perhaps a day, with as much awareness as possible. Thus, during the day, you will no longer hurl doors open and barge through them mindlessly. Rather, you might stop before each one just long enough to take a deep breath. Reach carefully for the door handle, feel its touch on your hand, turn it, and open the door gently. Then step through and gently close the door behind you. For the trivial cost of a few seconds you have calmed yourself, brought your attention into the present moment, and transformed a mindless routine into a mindful sacred ritual.

Likewise with driving: Instead of jumping into the car and roaring off with the radio blaring, try the following. Leave a few minutes early so you won't feel hurried. Seat yourself behind the steering wheel and take three slow, deep breaths. Remind yourself that you want to use this ride as part of your spiritual practice. Then drive calmly and mindfully, enjoying the scenery and the knowledge that the ride is contributing to your awakening. Many people report that when they do this their drives become more restful, enjoyable, and safe.

With exercises like these it soon becomes apparent that any normal activity can be transformed into a sacred ritual and a moment of awakening. As Jewish wisdom emphasizes: "Any natural act, if hallowed, leads to God."

Those who devote their acts to awakening to the present moment may relate to the words of Brother Lawrence, a simple seventeenth-century French monk whose writing about using daily activities as spiritual practice has inspired millions of readers. We know very little about his life except that he entered the monastery after years spent as a foot soldier. He described himself as a "clumsy fellow who used to break everything," and apparently his superiors agreed. Clumsy and seemingly untalented, he was exiled to the monastery kitchen to wash pots and pans.

But Brother Lawrence did not regard his job as a distraction from spiritual life, or as something to be quickly finished so he could get on with his prayers. Instead he decided to use washing, and every other activity, as an opportunity for remembering God, and constantly brought his attention back to this focus.

> I renounced for [God's] love everything that was not Himself... [keeping] my mind in His holy preserve, and recalling it whenever I found it had become distracted from Him.... I continued in spite of all the difficulties I found in practicing it, not becoming troubled or worried when I was involuntarily distracted. I maintained this practice no less during the day than during my times set aside for prayer.

After several years, the results of his practice became so evident that even the abbot of the monastery went to him for advice, and Brother Lawrence was able to make the remarkable statement:

> The time of business does not with me
> differ from the time of prayer,
> and in the noise and clutter of my kitchen
> while several people are at the same time
> calling for different things,
> I possess God in as great tranquility
> as if I were upon my knees at the blessed sacrament.

EXERCISE 3: TRANSFORM
INTERRUPTIONS INTO WAKEUP CALLS

A normal day is filled with numerous interruptions and minor irritations. We are having a conversation when the phone rings, enjoying a good book when a child starts crying, immersed in a project when the boss intervenes. Often we respond automatically and semiconsciously, perhaps with a twinge of annoyance or anxiety, and treat the interruption as merely a distraction.

Interruptions can also be used as wakeup calls. Taking a moment to relax and let go of any annoyance when a child starts crying allows you to be calm and comforting. Letting the telephone ring slightly longer while taking a deep breath allows you to be fully present for the conversation.

Thich Nhat Hanh is a Vietnamese monk who was nominated for a Nobel Prize for his remarkable peace work. At his center in France, the staff take two breaths before picking up the telephone. When you call the center there is a slight pause, and then you are speaking with someone offering you their full attention and calm, clear awareness.

For this exercise, select one or two common interruptions and a period of time, perhaps a day or a week, during which to use them as wakeup calls. Decide how you will respond to each of these wakeup calls. If you decide that the telephone will be your spiritual alarm, you might decide, like the people in Thich Nhat Hanh's monastery, to take a deep breath before answering. I find it helpful to put a little note to myself on the telephone to serve as a reminder. There are still many times when I answer mindlessly as soon as it rings, but sometimes I see the note and remember to take a moment of calm first. After working with a particular wakeup call for a while, you may wish to switch to or, better, add another one.

Stop to Breathe

Numerous traditions say that the breath is intimately connected to our spirit and life force. Paying attention to the breath is perhaps the world's most common contemplative exercise and a central element of yoga. Some of these meditations are so delightfully simple and easy they can be done at almost any time.

EXERCISE 4: THREE BREATHS

Turn your attention to your breath right now. Take three long, slow breaths, breathing in slowly and deeply and then relaxing and letting go as the air falls out. Feel better? Probably so!

Adding a few simple words, similar to those suggested by Thich Nhat Hanh below, can make the experience even more relaxing and delightful. Take a few breaths now and think to yourself with each one:

> Breathing in I smile,
> breathing out I relax.
> This is a wonderful moment.

Or you might like a variation in which you accompany each inhalation and exhalation with one of the following lines:

> In, out,
> slow, deep,
> smile, release.

Of course, you may prefer different words. Part of the pleasure of simple meditations such as these is experimenting to find out what works best for you. Even after years of practice, I continue to be amazed at how helpful a few conscious breaths can be.

EXERCISE 5: TAKE REGULAR BREATH MEDITATIONS

Scheduling some brief breath meditations into the day can transform it. They can be scheduled either at regular intervals or at times of transition or difficulty. A few mindful breaths before the kids come home from school or before an interview with your boss can be sanity-saving. Likewise, some calming breaths can also be a wonderful way to start each hour. In just a minute or two you can release tensions accumulated in the last hour and bring a clear, fresh mind to the hour ahead. For myself, I find that even a couple of minutes each hour makes an enormous difference to the quality of my day.

EXERCISE 6: SUSTAINED CONCENTRATION ON THE BREATH

With regard to internal factors, I do not envision
any other single factor so helpful as appropriate attention.
—*The Buddha*

The previous two exercises were hit-and-run meditations that are over in seconds, great refreshers and stress-busters. However, concentration benefits from more sustained practice and the following exercise, one of the world's most common meditations, extends these exercises. This is one of the three exercises I mentioned that usually require extended practice over a period of weeks or more in order to make significant progress. There is, however, benefit to anyone in trying this meditation at least once.

Begin by finding a quiet, comfortable place to sit where you won't be disturbed. It is helpful to decide beforehand how long you will sit. Ten to twenty minutes is a reasonable goal at first.

Turn your attention to your body and posture. Sit with your back straight and your head erect. If you are sitting in a chair, you may find it helpful to place a pillow behind the lower part of your back. This will relieve the strain on these muscles and keep you upright. With your back straight, turn your attention to the rest of your body. Simply relax it as much as you can.

Take a few slow, deep breaths to assist the relaxation process. As you breathe, notice that when you inhale you actively pull air in. However, to breathe out and release the air, all you need do is relax. With each breath you simply let go of any tension and become increasingly relaxed.

Now turn your attention to the actual experience of breathing. Notice that the two most prominent sensations are probably at the nostrils, where the air pours in and out, and at the stomach, where you can feel the rising and falling of the abdomen. Select one of these areas and give it your full attention. Follow the sensations of breathing as they shift and change as the air moves in and out and then comes to rest in the brief pause before the next cycle begins.

Sooner or later you will suddenly awaken with a little gasp of surprise as you realize that you have been lost in thoughts or fantasies, unaware of the breath or even that you were meditating. This is a natural process, just another reminder of how much our untrained minds roam away from reality. The treatment is very simple. Just return your attention, gently and lovingly, back to the sensations of the breath. You will fall into fantasies a hundred times. The task is to awaken one hundred and one times.

This is the essence of the exercise: the mind wanders unconsciously and you return it consciously. Don't judge yourself or the mind for its wandering ways. Rather, treat it and yourself with gentle love and respect and keep returning attention to the breath.

This is all that is required. You don't have to struggle or fight with the mind; you don't have to worry about how well you are doing. Simply relax, allow attention to rest on the sensations of the breath, and when it strays, bring it back. Meditation is a process of making friends with the mind. According to Aurobindo, the secret is:

> To try and try again, patiently, persistently
> and above all not to commit the mistake
> of struggling with the mind.

At the end of the session, gently open your eyes and look around you. Perhaps you will notice your vision seems a little clearer, colors a little brighter. Be careful not to leap out of the chair and rush back into your usual busyness. Get up slowly and see if you can bring whatever clarity and calm you have cultivated into your activities and interactions.

EXERCISE 7: FIRST BREATH, LAST BREATH

After you have practiced the sustained breath meditation several times, you may find the following two variations interesting.

Imagine that you are an infant and have just been born into the world. Freed from the womb, you are about to take your first breath. Each breath is a new, life-giving experience. Take time to experience and enjoy it to the full.

Now imagine you are at the end of your life. You are dying and any breath, this breath now, may be the last. Give it your full attention and use it to relax and release any fear, clinging, or concern. With each out breath, simply let go.

This is an excellent general exercise and also an excellent practice for death. One day we will be breathing our last breaths, and the peace and stability of mind developed from meditations such as this will be one factor that determines how peacefully and easily we die.

SACRED SOUNDS

Meditations on sacred sounds are enormously popular across the world. In traditions such as Judaism, Christianity, and Hinduism, the sound may be a sacred verse or the name of God, and meditation thereby merges into prayer. As quickly becomes apparent, the name of God can be remarkably evocative and powerful.

EXERCISE 8: REPEAT THE NAME OF GOD

> The breath that does not repeat the name of God
> is a wasted breath.
>
> —*Kabir, sixteenth-century Sufi mystic*

Before beginning, you may wish to decide how long to do this exercise. Ten or fifteen minutes is probably a good beginning. If you continue this meditation over a period of days or weeks you can gradually lengthen these sittings as feels comfortable. Some people like to set an alarm; others prefer to place a clock where they can see it when they open their eyes.

Begin as in the sustained breath meditation, by sitting comfortably with your back straight. Relax the rest of your body. Then begin gently to repeat your favorite name of God, for example *God, Lord, Allah, Father, Divine Mother, Shiva*. At first you might whisper the name, but soon you may wish to repeat it silently.

There is no need to strain or try to make something happen. All you have to do is to repeat the name slowly and gently, again and again, and allow it to work its effects on you. In time you will discover for yourself that "God's name cannot be heard without response, nor said without an echo in the mind that calls you to remember." As Ramakrishna proclaimed from his own direct experience of practicing several religions, "every revealed Name of the One Reality possesses irresistibly sanctifying power."

The following graceful description of this type of meditation comes from a modern Christian teaching.

> Repeat God's Name slowly again and still again. Become oblivious to every name but His. Hear nothing else. Let all your thoughts become anchored on This.... And then God's Name becomes our only thought, our only word, the only thing that occupies our minds, the only wish we have, the only sound with any meaning, and the only Name of everything that we desire to see.... Sit silently, and let His Name become the all-encompassing idea that holds your mind completely. Let all thoughts be still except this one.... Turn to the name of God for your release and it is given you.

EXERCISE 9: CONTEMPLATIVE PRAYER

We usually think of prayer as a request or dialogue with God. Yet contemplative prayer has a different form. Here the focus is on the repetition of a spiritually significant word, phrase, or sentence. Almost any phrase can be used, provided only that it is spiritually meaningful and calls forth positive feelings from your heart and mind. Some people prefer a word such as *love, peace,* or *grace.* Others choose a line from a sacred text. In Christian history the most popular has been the Jesus Prayer, "Lord Jesus Christ, have mercy on me."

The technique is almost identical to the meditation on the name of God. Simply repeat a phrase softly and gently over and over again, either quietly with the lips or silently in the mind. As with other meditations, there is no need for strain or struggle. Simply keep returning attention to the phrase and allow the prayer to work its effects on your heart and mind.

As with all meditation, the experiences can vary widely. At one extreme, there may be an upwelling of undigested emotions and painful memories. At the other, there may be periods of deep calm and tranquility.

Both experiences are valuable. The release of old conflicts from the unconscious where they have been preserved in darkness brings them to the healing light of awareness. Continuing to repeat the sacred sound rather than becoming caught up in or worrying about the conflicts provides an optimal environment for healing them.

Occasionally the mind may become very calm and still, so still that all thoughts, including the sacred sound, may cease. At these times you have a choice: You can exert a slight effort of will and gently restart the sound so that it continues unceasingly throughout the practice period. This is the method of some mantra meditations and the Jesus prayer. Alternatively, with TM (Transcendental Meditation) or the Christian Centering Prayer, you make no effort whatsoever and simply rest in the silence. This silence of the mind unveils the profound experiences of the sacred that lie beyond thoughts and images, experiences TM describes as "transcendental consciousness" and the Centering Prayer as "the presence of God."

ESTABLISHING A ROUTINE

Setting time aside each day solely for meditation or prayer is invaluable. Freed of distractions and demands, the mind can come to rest, slip loose from trivial pursuits, and give full attention to what really matters.

How Much and How Often?

How much and how often should these contemplative sessions be done? In general, more is better. But it is better to start with a small, manageable commitment than with grandiose plans that soon fall by the wayside. Beginning with ten to twenty minutes for five days each week might be a reasonable goal. Over time, this amount can gradually be increased if you wish. What is most important is to make these sessions part of a daily routine. Many people find the early morning a particularly valuable time. Then the mind may be calm and receptive, and meditation or prayer can set the tone for the day.

What is most important is to find what works best for you and then to stick with it. As with all practices, it can be helpful to discuss your experience with a wise friend or teacher to guide you as you journey deeper into the mind.

Progress on the Path

Contemplation and meditation are skills; as with any skill, they take time to master. For most people the benefits develop slowly but build over time. The first days or weeks of practice may feel neither deep nor rewarding, so when starting it is helpful to make a commitment to continue for a specific period, perhaps at least a month. This ensures that you give the meditation time to work and yourself time to experience some of the benefits.

It's like learning to play a musical instrument. At first you have to learn how to make individual notes, which is not a lot of fun. Only after some weeks do you begin to combine the notes into recognizable, or partly recognizable, music. But over time the melodies become more harmonious and playing the instrument becomes a pleasure for you and, hopefully, for those who hear you.

With contemplation, over time the pleasures increase until eventually your contemplations—whether meditation or prayer— become a source of delight for you and those whose lives you touch.

CHAPTER 21

THE HIGHER REACHES OF CONCENTRATION AND CALM

> When, through the practice of yoga,
> the mind ceases its restless movements,
> and becomes still, one realizes the Atman [Self],
> It satisfies one entirely.
> Then one knows that infinite happiness
> which can be realized by the purified heart
> but is beyond the grasp of the senses.
>
> —*The Bhagavad Gita*

As spiritual practice deepens, concentration and calm increase. They yield a peace so unshakable and profound that the Buddha called it the highest form of happiness. Christians describe it as "the peace of God which surpasses all understanding." This peace is the doorway to the sacred; when the mind is focused and unperturbed, it opens effortlessly to its Source.

This was one of humankind's earliest and most important spiritual discoveries: a tranquil, concentrated mind is a mind primed for awakening. The most ancient of all Indian religious texts, the Rig Veda, was composed more than three thousand years ago, and the most venerated of its many thousands of verses states simply:

> Let us bring our minds to rest in
> The glory of the Divine Truth.

This bringing our minds to rest is the essence of yoga. Yoga is the discipline at the heart of Indian religion and combines ethics and meditation with control of body, breath, and mind. The opening lines of the classic yoga text proclaim: "Yoga is the settling of the mind into silence." Likewise, the *Bhagavad Gita* sings:

> those who have gained tranquility
> through the practice of spiritual disciplines,
> behold him [God] in their own consciousness.

Western religions have made the same discovery. The Jewish Torah urges us to "Be still and know that I am God," while Christian contemplatives claim "the path leading to heaven is that of complete stillness."

Continuous Concentration

As the capacity for concentration matures, the ability to give care and attention to each moment becomes increasingly steady and continuous. Eventually it culminates in continuous, unbroken practice in which each moment and each activity becomes a means for awakening. Such uninterrupted practice is one of the highest goals of the great religions. "Be constant in prayer," pleads the Koran, while both the Christian St. Paul and the Hindu sage Ramakrishna urged us to "pray without ceasing." Ramakrishna wrote:

> What is necessary is to pray without ceasing, to reach a state in which the sacred message . . . is being profoundly assimilated with each breath, each thought, each perception.

At this stage concentrative attention is so continuous that practice ceases to be a special activity done at special times and is now part of every activity and every time. Aurobindo says this is the art by which one transforms "the whole act of living into an uninterrupted yoga." According to Judaism, the result is that every moment is "suffused with the awareness of God."

An exquisite example of the power of continuous prayer comes from a simple Russian peasant who lived around the middle of the nineteenth century. We know very little about him, not even his name, except that he was a pious man who was startled to hear a preacher quote St. Paul's words, "Pray without ceasing." For some years he puzzled over how this could be done until, after his wife's death, he left home and set out as an itinerant pilgrim in search of a teacher. After months of fruitless seeking, walking from one town to another, he eventually found a monk who instructed him in the Jesus Prayer, and he devoted the rest of his life to practicing it ceaselessly. For years he wandered across the Russian countryside reciting the Jesus Prayer at every waking moment, eventually even in his dreams. So powerful were the effects of his continuous practice that he became an overflowing fountain of love and a source of inspiration to people who have since read his words.

> I set out again, continuously praying the Jesus prayer which had become more precious and sweeter to me than anything else in the world. There were days when I covered forty-seven miles or more, and I didn't even feel the effort of walking. The prayer alone filled my consciousness. When it was bitterly cold, I would pray more fervently and soon I'd feel warm all over. If hunger threatened to overcome me, I would call upon the name of Jesus Christ with re-newed vigor, and soon my hunger was forgotten. If I felt ill and pain wracked my back and legs, I would give myself over to the prayer and soon was deaf to the pain. If someone offended me, I needed only to remember the sweetness of the Jesus prayer and all hurt and anger vanished.... I was very much at peace and often even dreamed that I was uttering this prayer.... I thanked God! For now I understood clearly the meaning of the apostle's words that I had heard: "Pray without ceasing!"

This is the summit of concentration practice, the practice by which the wild monkey mind is gradually trained, tamed, and transformed into a mind that is increasingly focused, calm, and clear. In India the development of concentration and its calming effects on the mind have been portrayed by comparison to the evolution of a river.

At first, spiritual practitioners feel that the mind is like a waterfall, bouncing from rock to rock, roaring and turbulent, impossible to tame or control. In midcourse, it is like a great river, calm and gentle, wide and deep. At the end its boundaries expand beyond sight and its depth becomes unfathomable as it dissolves into the ocean, which is both its goal and Source.

The concentrated mind is not only calm and wide, but also clear. Just as still water becomes lucid and mirrorlike, so too a calm, clear mind accurately reflects the world. Chuang Tzu wrote:

> When water is still it is like a mirror....
> And if water thus derives lucidity from stillness,
> how much more the faculties of mind?
> The mind of the sage being in repose
> becomes the mirror of the universe.

A calm mind offers a clear mirror with which to look out at the world and in at ourselves. Less compelled by compulsive needs, less troubled by painful emotions, less perturbed by ethical lapses, and less disturbed by wandering attention, we can now begin to awaken sacred vision.

AWAKEN YOUR SPIRITUAL VISION

SEE CLEARLY AND RECOGNIZE THE SACRED IN ALL THINGS

Wherever you turn,
there is the face of God.
—*The Koran*

CHAPTER 22

THE HEALING POWER OF AWARENESS

The true person sees what the eye sees,
and does not add to it
something that is not there.

—*Chuang Tzu*

As the Jewish Talmud observes, we do not see things simply as they are, but also as we are. Everything we experience comes to us molded by our minds. Yet our untamed minds have minds of their own: What we perceive is selected by our desires, colored by our emotions, and fragmented by our wandering attention. What we see outside us reflects what is inside us. The result: we do not see ourselves or the world clearly or accurately.

Sages, philosophers, and poets have echoed this theme for thousands of years, and recently psychologists have joined in. The Buddha diagnosed our problem as "mindlessness," meaning that we live semiconsciously because our awareness is clouded and our spiritual vision asleep. Psychologists agree that "mindlessness occurs in many more situations and is much more pervasive in our lives than people realize."

THE COSTS OF UNCONSCIOUSNESS

Living mindlessly—bereft of spiritual vision—takes an enormous toll. What we get from each moment depends on the attention we give it, and the quality of our experience reflects the quality of our awareness.

Usually we bring far less than full awareness to our experience. Lost in past memories and hypnotized by future fantasies, we sleepwalk through life, and the costs include absentmindedness, alienation, automaticity, and illusion.

Absentmindedness

This moment is the only time there is. As an unknown poet put it:

> The past is history,
> The future a mystery,
> This moment is a gift.
> Which is why it is called "the present."

How sad we so rarely open to this present moment. Sometimes it's as simple as misplacing our keys. At worst, we miss much of our lives as we stumble mindlessly through our days.

We all know the symptoms. We are reading a book and suddenly realize we haven't a clue about what was on the last few pages; we get out of the car and realize we left the keys in it; we go to a talk and the only memories we leave with are fuzzy recollections of our daydreams. In social interactions, we miss parts of the conversation as well as the subtle emotional and social cues that are so vital for interpersonal skills. It's not just that we weren't concentrating. In those lost times, we are so mindless we are quite unaware of the present moment.

Self-Alienation

> What can we gain by sailing to the moon if we are not able to cross the abyss that separates us from ourselves? This is the most important of all voyages of discovery, and without it all the rest are not only useless but disastrous.
>
> —*Thomas Merton*

There is much talk of social and economic alienation, and rightly so—these are terrible problems. But a more powerful and pervasive problem is self-alienation. We are strangers to ourselves: we do not know our own minds, our inner depths, or who and what we really are. Consequently, we identify with the external and superficial aspects of ourselves, especially with the body. We believe we are egos wrapped in skin. Buddhism calls this mistaken identity "wrong view," and yoga describes it as identification with the senses, while Christianity laments that we fall into forgetfulness of the fact that our true nature is an *imago dei* (image of God). Psychologists agree that we are painfully out of touch with ourselves. My own therapist, James Bugental, wrote:

> A great deal of the distress which so many people experience may be traced in no small part to our living as exiles from our own homeland, the inner world of subjective experience.... Our homeland is within, and there we are sovereign. Until we discover that ancient fact anew and uniquely for each of us as an individual, we are condemned to wander seeking solace where it cannot be found, in the outer world.

Automaticity

According to the great religions, we have been conditioned by decades of semiconscious living, and these unfortunate habits have become deeply ingrained. In part, we are automatons meandering automatically and semiconsciously through the routines of our lives. The Buddhist economist Schumacher summarized our dilemma:

> Close observation discloses that most of us, most of the time, behave and act mechanically, like machines. The specifically human power of self-awareness is asleep and the human being, like an animal, acts—more or less intelligently—solely in response to various influences. Only when a man makes use of his power of self-awareness does he attain to the level of a person, to the level of freedom. At that moment he is living, not being lived.

Mindlessness imprints not only automatic conditioning but especially unhealthy conditioning. We all know we are often at our worst when we are tired and our awareness is weak. At such times we are particularly likely to react with fear or anger and to regress to childish patterns of behavior. Unhealthy motives and emotions erupt most during moments of mindlessness. Buddhist psychology claims it is *only* in moments of mindlessness that these unhealthy forces arise.

Life in Illusion

The net effect of these distortions is that we live in an impaired and painful state of consciousness. The great religions speak of this state as a dream, illusion, or *maya* in which, according to Christianity and Islam, our minds are veiled. St. Paul claimed "a veil lies over their minds," while Islam multiplied the metaphor to seventy thousand veils.

Similar ideas can be found among philosophers, poets, and psychologists. In the West, Plato suggested we live in a cave, mistaking shadows for reality, while William Blake saw man peering through "narrow chinks in his cavern." Likewise, the psychologist Charles Tart suggested we live in a "consensus trance" that is "a much more pervasive, powerful, and artificial state than ordinary hypnosis, and it is all too trancelike." The metaphors differ, but the message is the same.

BENEFITS OF LIVING MINDFULLY

Be always mindful of what you are doing and thinking. So that you may put the imprint of your immortality on every passing incident of your daily life.

—*Abd'l-Khaliq Ghijdewani, thirteenth-century Sufi*

Concentration allows us to direct attention to whatever experiences we wish, while mindfulness allows us to explore them sensitively. To live mindfully is to bring greater awareness to each activity, to be more present in each moment, and to catch subtle experiences that all too often go unnoticed. Mindfulness has five benefits. It enhances our awareness of relationships, the world around us, and the world within us. It also frees us from automaticity and heals the mind.

1) Interpersonal Sensitivity

Mindfulness makes us more present with each person we meet, more aware of the other person's feelings and the many messages conveyed by subtle body movements and vocal tones. This allows us to attune to their motives and emotions and to be more empathic with their feelings. These are essential social skills, vital for anyone who wants to enjoy good relationships. Empathy is an especially crucial skill, and research shows that meditation is one of the few methods known to enhance it.

2) Refining the Senses

There is much talk in spiritual circles about giving up sensory pleasures, but much of this discussion is superficial and mistaken. Two things really are necessary:

1) to give up *attachment* to sensory pleasures
2) to refine the senses

We do not necessarily need to give up sensory pleasures, but we do need to give up our attachment to them. Sooner or later any attachment causes suffering, and sensory attachments are no exception. Free of craving, we can enjoy our pleasures without fear or worry.

We also need to refine the senses by honoring each experience and bringing to it a careful, gentle, and penetrating awareness or mindfulness. Christians speak of this practice as the sacrament of the present moment, while some Sufis claim, "The best act of worship is watchfulness of the moments." Mindfulness allows us to recognize and appreciate the nuances of sensation: the subtle tastes and aromas of food, the background rhythms of music, the tapestry of colors in a natural setting. Mindfulness is the great antidote to absentmindedness, making us less prone to daily mistakes such as forgetting where we parked the car. Research on people who practice mindfulness meditation show that they recognize external stimuli more quickly and sensitively. They also report an enormously enhanced awareness of their inner worlds and the workings of their minds. Patañjali wrote:

From this [meditation] are born intuitive clarity, and finest hearing, finest touch, finest sight, finest taste and finest smell.

Refined senses offer three major gifts: 1) They enhance the appreciation and pleasure of each moment. 2) Because each experience is more rich and satisfying, there is less craving for more experiences. The appreciation of quality replaces the raw hunger for quantity; the glutton becomes a gourmet. 3) Refining the senses is an excellent mental training that fosters beneficial qualities such as concentration and calm. According to Patañjali: "Experience of the finer levels of the senses establishes the settled mind."

3) Knowing One's Mind

> O seeker, know that the path to Truth is within you.
> —*Sufi Sheikh Badrutdin*

As awareness matures, it is able to observe not only the outer but also the inner world with increasing precision. Much that was formerly unconscious becomes conscious. Making the unconscious conscious has been the essence of deep psychotherapy ever since Freud. It has been the essence of much meditation for thousands of years, and meditative awareness can penetrate far below the levels reached by psychotherapy.

Meditation is sometimes divided into two types. The first are *concentration meditations*, discussed in the last practice. These focus and calm the mind by holding attention on a single object such as the breath or a mantra. The second are *awareness meditations*, which allow attention to move from one object to another and which explore all experiences with care and precision. Concentration meditations provide a foundation for awareness meditations. Together they play a crucial role in awakening spiritual vision and are enormously helpful for understanding the depths and workings of mind.

Without awareness training, we are strangers to ourselves. We remain prisoners of our subliminal psychological dynamics: moved by unconscious motives and directed by unrecognized thoughts and beliefs. Meditative mental microscopy allows us to become aware of, and therefore free from, the unconscious dynamics that otherwise rule our lives and reduce us to semiconscious automatons. Asked about the purpose of meditation, Sri Nisargadatta answered:

> We know the outer world of sensations and actions, but of our inner world of thoughts and feelings we know very little. The primary purpose of meditation is to become conscious and familiar with our inner life. The ultimate purpose is to reach the source of life and consciousness.

4) Freedom from Automaticity

One afternoon 2,500 years ago, the man who was to become the Buddha readied himself for his final supreme effort at enlightenment. He had spent six hard years in his singleminded, unrelenting quest. He had studied philosophies, practiced yogas, calmed and concentrated his mind, and undertaken ascetic disciplines so austere he had almost lost his life. Yet nothing brought him the salvation he sought. Now he was ready for one last attempt.

He requested some grass from a farmer. Carrying it to the shade of a nearby tree, he prepared a pillow. Then he seated himself and vowed he would not get up until he attained enlightenment, even if he died in the attempt.

First he did concentration meditation and entered the *jhanas*, advanced concentrative states in which attention is focused like a laser and held unwaveringly on any desired object. Using this adamantine awareness, he investigated the nature of the mind and conditioning, seeking escape from the ceaseless chain of automatic responses that bind and blind us.

Following the chain, he noted that every sensory experience is automatically and immediately followed by a feeling: pleasant if we like the experience, unpleasant if we don't, and neutral if it has no value to us. These feelings in turn elicit immediate responses: craving for pleasant experiences, aversion to unpleasant ones, and inattention to neutral experiences.

In the next instant, these responses produce further responses. Craving, for example, hardens into more intense clinging to the experience. On and on the stimulus-response chain—what Buddhists call "the chain of dependent origination"—proceeds, with each response becoming the stimulus for the next response, until eventually craving drives us to seek the initial stimulus again. The chain becomes a cycle and each cycle imprints conditioning, craving, and karma ever more deeply into the mind.

It seemed hopeless. Perhaps his quest was in vain; perhaps humans were forever doomed to be automatons imprisoned by their own conditioning. Then, as he looked more closely, he detected a weak link in the chain. With microscopic clarity, he saw that the feelings that immediately follow a stimulus give rise to automatic craving or aversion only in moments of mindlessness. In moments of clear awareness, the automatic response is suppressed and we have a choice of how to respond.

Awareness can break the chain of dependent origination in the instant after a feeling arises. This deconditions and weakens the habits of craving and aversion, and thereby liberates us from our own conditioning. Seeing this, the Buddha knew there was a way out; liberation was possible. He exulted:

> This is the path to enlightenment that I have now reached.... My mind has now attained the unformed [nirvana] and reached the end of every kind of craving.... Such was the insight, the knowledge, the understanding, the vision, the light that arose in me.

The Buddha recognized a crucial example of what psychologists now call *deautomatization:* the possibility of breaking automatic habits by bringing awareness to them. Each moment of mindfulness weakens the chains of conditioning and brings us closer to liberation.

5) The Healing Power of Awareness

Mindfulness heals. Many of the unhealthy and self-destructive things we do spring from automatic, unconscious responses. We feel anxious and find ourselves smoking, feel lonely and suddenly realize we've finished a box of chocolates, feel hurt by a casual remark and damage a friendship by lashing back automatically. These responses are born of mindlessness and can be prevented by mindfulness. Mindfulness allows us to practice what Christians call "guarding the mind." To be mindful and guard the mind means that we are aware as we reach for a cigarette, choco-late, or harsh word and can therefore choose whether to con-tinue or to make a different response.

As mindfulness deepens, we gradually notice not only de-structive actions, but also the painful emotions such as anger, loneliness, or fear that power them. These emotions thrive and swell as long as they dwell unrecognized in the darkness of the unconscious, but they shrivel in the light of awareness.

In Buddhist psychology, mindfulness is said to have three major beneficial effects:

1) It inhibits unhealthy mental qualities such as greed and anger.
2) It cultivates and strengthens healthy qualities such as joy and love.
3) It promotes the optimal balance of healthy qualities.

Psychotherapists agree that awareness is profoundly healing. "Therapeutic progress depends upon awareness; in fact the at-tempt to become more conscious is the therapy," declared a Jungian psychiatrist, while Fritz Perls, the founder of Gestalt therapy, claimed, "Awareness—by and of itself—can be cura-tive." For Carl Rogers, one of the most influential of psycholo-gists, awareness was synonymous with psychological health:

> Fully functioning people [are] able to experience all their feelings, afraid of none of them, allowing awareness to flow freely in and through their experiences.

Laboratory research supports these claims. Dozens of studies suggest that meditative awareness can reduce both psychological and psychosomatic difficulties. Meditation can help with anxiety, stress, insomnia, addiction, and depression. It can also be useful with psychosomatic disorders such as high blood pressure, mus-cle tension, asthma, and chronic pain. Of course, meditation does more than heal pathology. Numerous studies show that it also improves psychological functioning and the sense of well-being. Meditators show, among other things, enhanced matu-rity, creativity, self-control, marital satisfaction, and actualization of their psychological potential.

CHAPTER 23

EXERCISES IN AWARENESS

Mindfulness...is helpful everywhere.
—The Buddha

What can we do to heighten awareness? If you have read this far and done the previous exercises, you have already done a great deal. You have diminished the discoloring effects of wayward emotions, attachments, and unethical actions, and reduced the frenzied wandering of your attention. You have begun to settle and clear your mind. This is enormously helpful and also shows how the seven practices interact and support one another. We can now add methods that specifically foster mindfulness.

EXERCISE 1: EAT MINDFULLY: THE JOY OF FOOD

We pay heavily for our busy, harried lives. One cost of our distracted lives is that we rarely take the time to really enjoy such daily delights as eating. We sit down to a fine meal and at the same time carry on a conversation, watch television, or read the newspaper. The next thing we know, our plate is empty. What a pity we didn't taste the food! Things have apparently not changed much in 2,000 years. Confucius's grandson observed, "Amongst people there are none who do not eat and drink, but there are few who really appreciate the taste." Because we don't really enjoy the taste, we feel unsatisfied and soon find ourselves reaching for a snack. One of the tricks of successful dieting is therefore to pay attention while eating and to really enjoy the food.

But eating mindfully has more than dietary benefits. When we bring full awareness to a meal, we are focusing attention and being mindful. Therefore, we strengthen these capacities while enjoying the food more, which is certainly a win–win situation. In fact, eating can be a deeply spiritual experience, as Jewish wisdom makes clear:

> Even the most mundane act can become an intimate experience of the Divine. This concept is manifestly more explicit in Jewish teachings regarding eating. It is taught that when a person eats, he should concentrate totally on the food and the experience of eating it, clearing the mind of all other thoughts. He should have in mind that the taste of the food is also an expression of the Divine in the food, and that by eating it, he is incorporating this spark of the Divine into his body. A person can also have in mind that he will dedicate the energy he will obtain from this food to God's service. It is taught that when a person does this, it is counted as if the food he is eating is a sacrifice on the Great Altar in Jerusalem.

For this exercise, treat yourself to a nice meal when you can eat in silence. Generally this means eating alone, unless you are with someone who is also doing the exercise.

Sit down and take time to relax. Begin by enjoying the sight and smells of the meal. How many colors are there? How many different fragrances can you detect?

Take your first bite, then put your fork or spoon down. Pay close attention to every sensation. What is the first taste like and how do the tastes change as you chew? What is the dominant flavor? What subtle background flavors can you find? What is the temperature and texture of the food? How do they change?

Be aware of the desire to chew and swallow quickly in order to get more. There is no need to hurry: This is one meal you can enjoy to the full. When you do swallow, be aware of all the sensations and of how quickly the urge to get more food leaps into awareness. Continue to eat each mouthful as carefully, consciously, and enjoyably as you can.

Periodically you will suddenly recognize that you were lost in thought or fantasies and were barely aware of the last few mouthfuls. That's the way we usually eat. Simply bring your full awareness back to the eating and start enjoying your meal again.

At the end of the meal, take a moment to experience the feelings of satisfaction. Chances are that you will recognize this is one of the few times in your life when you *really* tasted and enjoyed a meal.

Meditative eating is a valuable exercise to do regularly. Perhaps you could schedule a mindful meal once a week or even once a day. In doing so, you insert an island of peace into your day, in which you calm your mind and heighten your senses while enjoying your meal more.

EXERCISE 2: MINDFUL MUSIC

Music, with its remarkable power to evoke emotions and stir the soul, has long been a source of inspiration in religions the world over. The Bible relates that more than two thousand years ago, when the Jewish prophet Elisha sought inspiration, he cried, " 'Get me a musician.' And then, while the musician was playing, the power of the Lord came on him."

Unfortunately, we rarely give music a chance to offer its full benefits. Rather, we half listen, while also driving, eating, talking, or playing, further fragmenting our attention. Both the delights and benefits of music can be enhanced by mindful listening.

To do this exercise, choose a favorite piece of music, preferably something gentle and soothing. If you have a piece that has spiritual significance for you, all the better. Sit or lie comfortably and take a moment to relax. Then listen and enjoy as fully as you can. Periodically you will find your mind is adrift in fantasies and that you were largely oblivious during the last few minutes. When that happens, simply return your attention gently, just as with the previous meditations, but this time focus on the music instead of the breath.

In this exercise you want to develop not only concentration, but also greater sensitivity and clarity of awareness. Listen as carefully as you can. Try to catch the subtleties you may have missed before: the delicate notes, the background rhythms, and the emotions they evoke in you. Listening to music in this way can concentrate and sensitize the mind, while also stirring and awakening the soul.

EXERCISE 3: BECOME A GOOD LISTENER

Listening carefully as someone speaks is a gift. If you doubt this, notice how you feel when you talk to someone and he or she continues to read a newspaper or book without even looking at you. This lack of attention can be very irritating.

Listening carefully focuses your attention and refines your awareness. We can be more aware of the enormous amount of information people convey about themselves through subtle movements and voice tones. We can also catch our own emotional reactions, which might otherwise go unnoticed and unconsciously dictate our responses.

Milton Erickson, one of the twentieth century's most remarkable psychotherapists, was famous for being able to pick up subtle clues about patients that helped him offer effective treatment where other therapists failed. This sensitive awareness was not something he was born with, but rather something he developed.

As a child, Erickson was stricken with polio and spent many months in bed. To amuse himself he invented a game in which he tried to tell who was coming to his room by listening to the sound of their footsteps on the stairs. When he had mastered this ability, he moved on to trying to detect each person's mood. In this way he learned to catch subtle cues that most of us miss and to use this skill for the benefit of his many patients.

It takes no more time to listen fully than halfheartedly. For no extra cost, other people enjoy your full attention while you learn more about them, train your attention, and sensitize your awareness.

EXERCISE 4: FIND BEAUTY
IN THIS MOMENT

An enjoyable awareness exercise is to take a moment, two or three times each day, to look around and find something of beauty. It could be anything: a child playing, moonlight shimmering on water, a tree swaying in the wind, or even a tiny particle of dust dancing in a ray of sunlight.

Whatever it is, give it your full attention and explore it with as much sensitivity as you can. If it is a tree, notice the different colors, the sway of branches, and the movements of individual leaves. At the same time, be aware of your inner world and the feelings such as pleasure and appreciation that beauty gives birth to. Then bring these feelings with you as you return to your usual activities.

EXERCISE 5: HEIGHTEN
AWARENESS OF YOUR BODY

Attitudes towards the body vary enormously. At one extreme are hedonists who leap at every possible sensory pleasure. At the other extreme are ascetics who try to beat the body and its desires into submission. To achieve this they forsake physical pleasures, toughen the body through rigorous disciplines, even torture themselves with intense heat, cold, or starvation.

A more balanced approach is to adopt a middle way that honors but does not worship the body. If you regard your body as a temple of the spirit, your body is carefully cared for and its health is maintained with appropriate diet, exercise, and medical care. Mohammad drew the comparison between a warrior and his horse. If the warrior does not care for and train his horse, it may fail him and even cost him his life in battle. But if all he does is care for and tend his horse, he will never get anywhere.

When seen correctly, the body can become, in Shankara's words, "a vehicle of experience for the human spirit." Most of us are largely out of touch with our own bodies, though we usually remain unaware of this fact until we cultivate our awareness—or until we fall ill.

The mind–body link is highly intimate. The body suffers and stores the impact of millions of mental traumas, which are stored as areas of numbness and muscle tension but often remain hidden by psychological defenses. Heightening body awareness is therefore doubly valuable: It not only trains your awareness but also brings to light and begins to heal the somatic traumas that hold past pains and defenses.

Body awareness exercises are common in religious traditions, and extensive exercises are found in Hindu and Taoist yogas. One of the simplest body meditations is the Buddhist sweeping meditation. One systematically sweeps awareness through the body from head to toe, carefully feeling the myriad sensations that constitute our bodily life.

To begin this exercise, find a comfortable meditative posture. Take a moment to breathe, relax, and settle the mind. When your awareness is clear, turn your attention to the top of the head and explore any experiences there. Then gradually move your awareness down over the forehead, sides, and back of your head. Explore the sensations in each area as carefully as you can.

Slowly sweep your awareness down over your face and the rest of your head and then into your neck and shoulders. If you find areas of pressure, tension, or discomfort, feel into them and see if they release. Also look for areas of numbness. Emotions, memories, and images associated with these symptoms may arise. If they do, simply notice them without trying to manipulate or change them.

Continue to sweep your awareness slowly down through your arms, into your hands, and finally into the tips of your fingers. Then bring awareness down over your chest and back. Continue down into your abdomen, and then into your pelvis and genitals. Again, pay close attention to any symptomatic areas and associated mental reactions.

Now bring awareness down into your thighs, lower legs, and finally your feet. Feel the pressure of the floor on your feet and extend awareness down into the tips of your toes. Finally, open awareness to your entire body and its many sensations and rest in this global bodily experience for as long as you wish.

EXERCISE 6: MINDFULNESS MEDITATION

The meditation most specifically designed to enhance awareness is mindfulness or insight meditation. First introduced by the Buddha 2,500 years ago, it has been practiced by countless Buddhists, who cherish it as one of their most valuable disciplines. It has spread around the world and is used by people from diverse religious backgrounds, who find that the keen awareness it develops enhances the power of their own tradition. In Taoism the "method of internal observation" was influenced by Buddhism and is very similar to mindfulness meditation.

Mindfulness meditation builds on the breath meditation described in chapter 20. There the aim was to try to keep your attention focused solely on the breath in order to develop concentration. In mindfulness practice, however, the emphasis is less on concentration and more on clear awareness. You start with the breath but then go on to other experiences. Your aim is to explore the full range of mental and physical experiences.

As in the breath meditation, begin by sitting comfortably with your back straight and body relaxed. First focus on the breath, either the rising and falling of your abdomen or the sensations at your nostrils as the air moves in and out. Notice the ever-changing current of dozens of sensations that make up the experience of each breath. The more clear and sensitive awareness becomes, the more sensations you can observe in a single breath.

Before long another experience will catch your attention. It may be a sound in the environment, a tickle in the body, or a thought or image in the mind. Whatever it is, if your mind is drawn to it, allow your attention to shift to this experience and explore it carefully. If it is a sound, try to hear the vibrations. If it is a body pain, try to explore it so deeply that you can identify the individual sensations, such as tingling or pressure, that we interpret as pain.

In your mind you can catch sight of some of the most mysterious and powerful of all the forces that touch your life: the mental images, fantasies, emotions, and thoughts that mold your experiences. Notice the way an image or fantasy suddenly appears and seems so realistic that for a moment you become lost in it and mistake it for reality. Emotions such as anger, fear, and joy will parade through your awareness, each one bringing its own world of experience. What does each one feel like, how does it change as you observe it, and what body sensations accompany it?

Finally, try to catch the most subtle, fleeting, and powerful of all the mind's creations: your thoughts. Thoughts are experienced as words within the mind, but they whiz by like Stealth bombers, so swiftly and quietly they are hard to detect at first. Yet the effort is worthwhile because unrecognized thoughts exert an awesome influence on our behavior and experience. So potent is their influence that the Buddha began his teaching with the words:

> We are what we think.
> All that we are arises with our thoughts.
> With our thoughts we make the world....
> It is good to control them,
> And to master them brings happiness.
> But how subtle they are,
> How elusive!
> The task is to quieten them,
> And by ruling them to find happiness.

Thoughts, emotions, images, and fantasies all appear in the mind, linger for a moment, and then disappear. Contrary to many people's beliefs, the task in meditation is not to squelch them, nor even to struggle with them. Rather, simply observe and study them and they will change and pass away by themselves. When they do, simply return your attention to the breath and begin exploring it again.

Insight meditation is a rhythmic dance of awareness. You start by exploring the breath, then investigate whatever draws attention, and then return to the breath. The whole process is very gentle and allowing. There is no need to wrestle with your mind or force it in any way. You don't have to try to make certain experiences occur or try to stop others. Nothing is asked of you except to be as aware as you can in each moment. There are no distractions to worry about because "distractions," such as noises or itches, are simply further experiences to explore. You don't need to judge experiences as good or bad; you simply explore and learn from them. As you do so, you refine awareness, clear the mind, and learn from all things.

Mindfulness meditation is a superb daily discipline. When done daily for perhaps twenty minutes or more, it gradually deepens over time. Then you embrace each experience with a careful and healing awareness, grace more and more moments with clear awareness, and practice what Christians call "the sacrament of the present moment." This moment—right now, and now, and now—is a gift. Enjoy it!

Appreciating such gifts fully takes time and practice. The dulled awareness of a lifetime is not cleared in a day, but over weeks and months. Mindfulness meditation is the third of the three exercises in this book—along with the breath and lovingkindness meditations—that require regular practice for major benefits.

When done intensely in retreat, this meditation can be remarkably powerful and healing. A Vietnam war veteran who did full-time mindfulness meditation for a week provided an especially dramatic example:

> It had been eight years since my return when I attended my first meditation retreat. At least twice a week for all those years I had sustained the same recurring nightmares common to many combat veterans: dreaming that I was back there facing the same dangers, witnessing the same incalculable suffering, waking suddenly alert, sweating, scared. At the retreat, the nightmares did not occur during sleep, they filled the mind's eye during the day, at sittings, during walking meditations, at meals. Horrific wartime flashbacks were superimposed over a quiet redwood grove at the retreat center. Sleepy students in the dormitory became body parts strewn about a makeshift morgue.... As I relived these memories as a thirty-year-old spiritual seeker, I was also enduring for the first time the full emotional impact of experiences that as a twenty-year-old medic I was simply unprepared to withstand.

I began to realize that my mind was gradually yielding up memories so terrifying, so life-denying, and so spiritually eroding that I had ceased to be consciously aware that I was still carrying them around. I was beginning to undergo a profound catharsis by openly facing that which I had most feared and therefore most strongly suppressed.

At the retreat I was also plagued by a more current fear, that having released the inner demons of war I would be unable to control them, that they would now rule my days as well as my nights, but what I experienced instead was just the opposite....

What also arose at the retreat for the first time was a deep sense of compassion for my past and present self: compassion for the idealistic, young would-be physician forced to witness the unspeakable obscenities of which humankind is capable, and for the haunted veteran who could not let go of memories he could not acknowledge he carried.

Since the first retreat the compassion has stayed with me. Through practice and continued inner relaxation, it has grown to sometimes encompass those around me as well, when I'm not too self-conscious to let it do so. While the memories have also stayed with me, the nightmares have not.

By bringing his painful memories out of the unconscious and facing them with full awareness, this veteran was able to heal his psychological wounds and transform them into compassion. This is an example of the healing power of meditative awareness.

For most of us, our experiences are likely to be far gentler, especially if we are doing brief daily sittings. At first there are likely to be instants of mindful clarity separated by minutes of mindless fantasy. Gradually the balance shifts. According to Aurobindo's biographer, the secret is:

> to try and try again, patiently, persistently.
> And above all not to make the mistake
> of struggling mentally with the mind.

Patience and persistence are essential qualities for any deep spiritual work. The Christian Bible speaks for all the great religions when it urges, "Let us run with perseverance the race that is set before us." Mindfulness meditation, with its emphasis on simply being open to all experiences without wishing they were different or trying to change them, is a superb method for developing the patience and persistence required to run this race.

EXERCISE 7: MINDFUL SPEECH

Meditative awareness can be applied to the activities of daily life and combined with different practices. For example, you can carefully observe and refine the emotions and motives of your speech.

In this exercise, commit to a period, perhaps a day, of carefully observing your state of mind whenever you speak. What are your motives? Are you trying to look good, belittle someone, defend yourself? Or is your intention to speak born out of a desire to inform, help or heal?

If you find your intention is benign, then by all means go ahead and speak. But if you find your motivation is inappropriate, then you may want to let the difficult feelings pass. In this way you begin to integrate the practices of awareness, ethics, and emotional transformation.

CHAPTER 24

SEEING THE SACRED IN ALL THINGS

Where there is no vision
the people perish.
—*Jewish proverb*

The great religions consider our usual mindless meandering through life to be a tragedy. They also worry that we are blind to the sacred—in the world, in others, and in ourselves.

THE BLINDING POWER OF SCIENCE

This blindness is particularly dramatic in the modern Western world, largely due to the power of science. So potent is the impact of science on our lives, so often are we bombarded by its descriptions of the universe as a great, meaningless machine, that this view can easily seem the natural and only way to look at things.

The result is that we look out on what philosophers call a "disenchanted world": a world seemingly stripped of meaning, significance, and spirit, and we see ourselves as equally barren. No wonder our society seems adrift, without a higher goal or vision. No wonder so many people feel their lives are meaningless and hunger for something more sustaining. This something more is freely available to us all. The problem is that very few people see it, since it requires cultivating a different way of knowing.

Science is a superb method—the best humankind has ever found—for learning about physical objects and their properties.

But it can see and say almost nothing of nonphysical things, such as meaning and purpose, values and spirit. Thoughtful scientists readily acknowledge this, and two of the greatest, Albert Einstein and Sir Arthur Eddington, were blunt about it. Einstein insisted:

> The present fashion of applying the axioms [principles] of physical science to human life is not only entirely a mistake but has also something reprehensible in it.

Eddington, one of the greatest astronomers of all time, confessed:

> [the] mental and spiritual nature of ourselves, known in our minds by an intimate contact transcending the methods of physics, supplies just that...which science is admittedly unable to give.

A NEW MANNER OF SEEING

Reaching the "mental and spiritual nature of ourselves" is what spiritual practices are designed to do. The seven practices develop spiritual vision: the capacity to recognize the sacred in ourselves and in the world. Plotinus, an influential Western philosopher and mystic, described this vision as "a new manner of seeing...a wakefulness that is the birthright of us all, though few put it to use."

Spiritual vision has inspired sages throughout history and been called many names. Both Christians and Plato named it the "eye of the soul." For Sufis it is "the eye of the heart," and for Taoists the "eye of Tao" or the "inner eye." Whatever its name, it represents a flowering of intuitive awareness that recognizes the sacred in all people, in all things, and within ourselves.

THE SACRED WITHIN

This potent awareness penetrates far below the ego's restless turmoil to the sacred core of our being. St. Augustine described how he turned attention inward "and beheld with the eye of my soul...the Light Unchangeable." He concluded, "It is with the interior eye that truth is seen," and "Our whole business therefore in this life is to restore to health the eye of the heart whereby God may be seen."

Augustine was echoing an ancient theme that Plato and Lao Tsu sounded almost a thousand years earlier. Plato exclaimed, "There is an eye of the soul which is more precious than ten thousand bodily eyes, for by it alone is truth seen." Lao Tsu concluded, "A sensible person prefers the inner to the outer eye." Each of these sages echoed a similar theme: a "sensible person" values the eye of the soul even more than the physical eye because it is the eye of the soul that allows us to recognize the sacred.

THE SACRED WORLD

At first this recognition of the sacred within ourselves and in the world breaks through only in tantalizing glimpses, stirred perhaps by the beauty of a sunset, the touch of a lover, or the serenity of prayer. At such moments the mundane world is transfigured. What only moments before was a pleasant but familiar experience can become a vision of such ecstatic beauty and delight that it may remain the most treasured and transforming moment of a lifetime. Then, like Jacob in the Jewish Torah, we suddenly recognize that "the Lord is in this place— and I did not know it," and we begin to understand Jesus's statement that "the kingdom of the Father is spread out upon the earth, and men do not see it."

Sometimes an ecstatic experience occurs spontaneously and can be reexperienced and deepened through subsequent spiritual practice. The initial experience—particularly if it occurs during childhood—may be misunderstood and dismissed, especially by other people who have never tasted the sacred. Only years later, with the help of a spiritual practice and teacher, its significance may be appreciated. A Zen practitioner described such a sequence that began on the Massachusetts seacoast when she was nine years old.

The sun was just coming up, as on any ordinary day, but my awareness suddenly became altered. I saw the light arising from the ocean in slow-moving distinct particles, and I sat in awe as they combined in shifting patterns of many colors.

By the time the sun had completely shown itself, I was transported by feelings that were overwhelming and wordless. They involved what I might now describe as a sense that everything fit together perfectly, that the world was fine in every way—and that life itself was a thing of wonder and magic.... Being only nine years old I could find no words to explain my dazzling experience, and I decided to keep it to myself. But I also began to fear that there was something wrong with me.

Somehow, though, I trusted my intuition. I knew that I had come into contact with something that no one in my suburban life had mentioned. A few years passed, and my search for the meaning of my experience led me on a "spiritual journey" and eventually into Zen Buddhism. There my teacher convinced me that my sunrise experience might not be "wrong" but something very true and real and shared by others. Not long after, while I was practicing Zen meditation, my childhood memory returned with great intensity and I was finally able to recognize the spiritual encounter for what it was. I also felt sorrow for the little girl who had been enraptured and then made to feel such needless doubt.

But I remain thankful for the experience, especially for the seed it planted in my consciousness, which grew in silence and darkness for nearly thirty years until the present. I am forever grateful for that opening-up to the truth of the world and of reality.

Through practicing Zen, I have come to realize that my mystical episode can return with every moment: in a drop of water, a dirty dish...a smile.

TRANSFORMED RELATIONSHIPS

An old woman sitting by the roadside outside her town was approached by a traveler who asked, "What kind of people live in this town?"

"What were the people like in your home town?" queried the old woman.

"Oh, they were terrible!" fumed the traveler. "Liars, cheats, incompetents, you couldn't trust any of them. I was glad to leave."

"You'll find the people in this town just the same," responded the old woman.

Not long afterwards, she was approached by a second traveler who also questioned her about the people in the town.

"What were the people like in your home town?" she asked.

"Oh, they were wonderful!" exclaimed the traveler. "Fine, honest, hard-working, it was a privilege to be with them. I was so sorry to leave."

"You'll find the people in this town just the same," responded the old woman.

As this story illustrates, our personalities and expectations determine the quality of our relationships and how we see people. As the eye of the soul begins to recognize the sacred in all things, it also awakens to the sacred in all people. Where before we saw strangers or competitors, enemies or friends, we now begin to recognize Buddhas or children of God.

Needless to say, this makes for dramatically different relationships. In place of suspicion and fear arise feelings such as openness and love. If we see people enjoying good fortune and joy, we naturally feel happiness at their happiness. Buddhists call this "sympathetic joy." On the other hand, if we see people in pain, care and compassion naturally arise and we are spontaneously moved to help. As Lao Tsu pointed out:

Those who are open-eyed are open-minded,
Those who are open-minded are open-hearted.

Whenever a sick or dying person staggered into Mother Teresa's center, she saw "Christ in his begging disguise." These poor people lived like dogs, but here they were seen and treated like saints. Such is the transforming power of awakened vision.

When we recognize the sacred in others, we are reminded of it in ourselves. Then we begin to understand and answer the ancient plea that we "see Christ in each other, and be Christ to each other." The Christian contemplative Thomas Merton left a wonderful description of how other people appeared to him when his own vision awoke.

> Then it was as if I suddenly saw the secret beauty of their hearts, the depths where neither sin nor desire can reach, the person that each one is in God's eyes. If only they could see themselves as they really are. If only we could see each other that way there would be no reason for war, for hatred, for cruelty...we would fall down and worship each other.

Perception is not a passive process but rather is an active creation, and the state of the world we perceive reflects the state of mind within us. The range of perceptual possibilities is vast and extends from what can be called paranoia through pronoia and transnoia. With paranoia, we are consumed with anger, project it outward, and see a hostile, terrifying world filled with people conspiring to attack us. With pronoia we see the love and kindness within us mirrored by the people around us, who seem eager to help in whatever ways they can. With transnoia the world and all people are perceived as expressions of the transcendent and as part of a vast plan to awaken and enlighten us. Spiritual practices heal paranoia, and by opening the eye of the soul, they allow us to live and love in pronoia and transnoia.

CHAPTER 25

EXERCISES IN SACRED SEEING

You live in illusions
and the appearance of things.
There is a Reality,
you are that Reality.
When you recognize this
you will realize that you are no thing
and being no thing, you are everything.

—*Kalu Rinpoche,*
twentieth-century Tibetan Buddhist

To recognize the sacred is not so much to see new things as it is to see things in a new way. The sacred is not separate or different from all things, but rather hidden within all things. To see the spiritual in ourselves and the world is to recognize what is always already present. This new way of seeing is an innate gift that needs to be cultivated.

EXERCISE 8: OPEN TO THE SACRED IN NATURE

A certain Philosopher asked St. Anthony [the first and most famous of the Desert Fathers]: Father, how can you be so happy when you are deprived of the consolation of books? Anthony replied: My book, O philosopher, is the nature of created things, and any time I want to read the words of God, the book is before me.

Certain sites in nature have long been recognized as spiritually potent. Places of great beauty—stark deserts, majestic mountains, great forests, the meeting places of land and sea—can all be sources of spiritual inspiration and renewal, though with our overly busy lives we rarely give ourselves time to draw on them.

This exercise is simple and enjoyable. Find a place in nature that feels particularly appealing to you, and give yourself sufficient time to enjoy it. You might find it helpful to begin and end with a prayer or ritual, and you might wish to spend part of your time in meditation. There is no need to do much. Simply open yourself to the surroundings and appreciate the magnificence of the scenery, the varieties of plant and animal life, and their impact on your heart and mind. For many people, such experiences feel naturally healing and lead to a recognition of the sacredness of nature.

EXERCISE 9: RECOGNIZE THE INNER LIGHT

Seat yourself comfortably, close your eyes, and take a moment to relax. Take some slow, deep breaths to release any tension. You may wish to do the breath or insight meditation for a few minutes to further calm yourself.

Now visualize someone you love standing in front of you. Take a moment to experience the warm feelings you have for this person. Imagine that from some part of the person's body, perhaps the heart or the forehead, light radiates. Allow this light to grow in intensity. Eventually the whole body radiates and bathes in this light until it becomes so brilliant the body almost disappears.

Now imagine that standing next to your radiant friend is someone you do not like. See the light from your friend illuminating and filling this person until he or she begins to radiate light just as your friend does. Recognize the same radiance in them both.

Now begin to feel their radiance illuminating and filling you until your body begins to fade into the background as you also become a radiant source. In this vision there is no difference between you, your friend, and the disliked person. You have united with them in what Taoism calls "the radiance of the Tao within," which yoga knows as "the inner radiance which is free from sorrow."

This radiance may begin to dislodge feelings of anger towards the disliked person. Likewise, the feelings of affection for your friend may extend to include both your enemy and yourself. If this happens, you can glimpse the possibility of loving all people equally.

Enjoy this experience as long as you can. Then open your eyes. Stand up gently so that you maintain your feelings, and bring them with you into your activities.

EXERCISE 10: SURROUNDED BY SAINTS

If people are truly sacred—for example, Buddhas, children of God, or expressions of the Tao—what would happen if we treated them as such? Certainly the great religions encourage us to do so. A Buddhist proverb says, "If we are to be free we must make each person we meet our ultimate object of reverence."

For this exercise decide on a certain time period, perhaps an hour or a day, and try to see and treat everyone you meet as a holy person. You might wish to see them, as did Mother Teresa, as Christ in disguise or as Buddhists do, as Buddhas who do not know they are Buddhas. How would you relate to such people? Obviously with reverence, kindness, and delight.

This is not a one-way street. As we see and treat others, so do we see and treat ourselves. Seeing the sacred in others helps us recognize the sacred in ourselves.

EXERCISE 11: SEE TEACHERS EVERYWHERE

If we choose to, we can see everyone as our teacher. Those people who have admirable qualities can inspire us; those with de-

structive qualities can remind us of our shortcomings and motivate us to change. Confucius was very clear about this:

> When walking in the company of two other men I am bound to be
> able to learn from them. The good points of the one I copy; the
> bad points of the other I correct in myself.

When we meet kind people, we can develop feelings of gratitude and use those people as role models to inspire our own
kindness and generosity. We can also learn from unkind people.
Seeing how sensitive we are to criticism and hostility, we can remember how sensitive others are and resolve to treat them gently. We can also practice forgiveness and find how much better
this feels than smoldering with resentment for days.

To begin this exercise, select an initial time period such as a
morning or a day. During that time, try to see each person you
meet as a teacher bringing you an important lesson. Your challenge is to recognize what that lesson is, then to learn as much as
you can from this person. At the end of the day, look back and
review your interaction with each person, the lessons each one
brought, and what you learned.

As exercises like these are repeated, the eye of the soul gradually opens and we become increasingly aware of the sacred
within us and around us. Every person becomes a teacher and a
reminder of our spiritual nature, while every experience becomes
a learning opportunity. Then transnoia blossoms and we see the
world as a sacred schoolhouse designed to heal and awaken us,
and to teach us how to heal and awaken others. What greater
gift could the world offer?

CHAPTER 26

THE HIGHER REACHES
OF VISION

Master Tung Kwo asked Chuang:
"Show me where the Tao is to be found."
Chuang Tzu replied;
"There is nowhere it is not to be found."
—*The Way of Chuang Tzu*

Dedicated practice brings both a remarkable continuity and an extraordinary depth of awareness. What were once rare glimpses of the sacred blossom into recurrent recognitions and ultimately a continuous presence. The secret of success is to use more and more activities as opportunities for awakening so that spiritual practice grows from an occasional activity to being part of every activity.

The Buddha gave a beautiful example of this when approached by an elderly grandmother. She explained she would very much like to live a spiritual life but that she was too old and infirm to withstand the rigors of a monastery and too consumed with household duties to set aside long periods for meditation. What could she do? "Respected grandmother," replied the Buddha:

Every time you draw water from the well for you and your family, remain aware of every single act, movement, and motion of your hands. As you are carrying home the water jug atop your head, be aware of every step of your feet; as you do your chores, maintain continuous mindfulness and awareness every single instant, moment after moment, and you too will become a master of meditation.

ECSTATIC VISION AND THE DARK NIGHT OF THE SOUL

As spiritual practice matures, as the moments of clear awareness increase, the eye of the soul opens and begins to recognize the sacred in all things. One of the most famous accounts is that of William Wordsworth, who described both the ecstasy of this gift and the pain of its passing.

> There was a time when meadow, grove, and stream
> The earth and every common sight,
>   To me did seem
>   Apparelled in celestial light,
> The glory and the freshness of a dream.

Wordsworth, who did not have a systematic contemplative practice, was unable to sustain this ecstatic vision and finally lamented, "The things which I have seen I now can see no more."

The loss of these experiences can be devastating. After glimpsing a vision of the world that has brought unprecedented meaning and joy to life, after tasting the indescribable bliss of one's true nature, life bereft of these gifts can seem shallow and insipid. This is the dark night of the soul described by St. John of the Cross. And there is only one cure: to continue practicing, refining your awareness and purifying your heart, trusting that, as Maimonides promised, "One who satisfies these conditions—such a person will undoubtedly perceive only things very extraordinary and divine."

TRANSFORMING FLASHES OF ILLUMINATION INTO ABIDING LIGHT

For those who persist, initial glimpses gradually become a recurrent vision, peak experiences extend into plateau experiences, altered states of consciousness become altered traits of consciousness, and flashes of illumination transform into abiding light. The desired state, such as mindfulness or awareness of God, becomes an increasingly natural habit. While before the mind automatically fell into unconscious distraction, now it starts to fall into clear awareness. Where before constant effort was required, now a mere intention may suffice.

This is a crucial stage of advanced practice. In Buddhism it is known as *effortless effort*, in Taoism as *wu wei* (nondoing), and in Sufism as *continuance* (the ability to remain in divine communion in the midst of worldly activities). Sufism describes this development beautifully as a process by which remembrance (the effort to be always mindful of God) and remembrance of the tongue (*japa*, or recitation of the name of God) become remembrance of the heart (transient mystical experience) and finally remembrance of the soul (where recitation and mindfulness become constant). Eventually this remembrance continues even throughout the night.

DREAM YOGAS

The world's religions have long regarded dreams as spiritually significant. For thousands of years, shamans, yogis, and prophets have been guided by them, and the Jewish Torah proclaims:

> Hear my words; when there are prophets among you, I the Lord make myself known to them in visions, I speak to them in dreams.

Usually spiritual dreams occur infrequently. However, a person doing intensive practice day after day develops a formidable mental momentum, and the effects of practice—whether prayer, mindfulness, mantra, or koan—begin to penetrate into dreams. Finally there arrives a time when the practice continues unbroken throughout day and night. In the words of St. Isaac the Syrian:

> Then prayer never stops in a man's soul,
> whether he is asleep or awake.
> In eating or drinking, sleeping or doing something,
> even in deep sleep his heart sends forth without effort
> the incense and sighs of prayer.
> Then prayer never leaves him,
> but at every hour, even if externally silent,
> it continues secretly to act within.

At first the prayer or other exercise emerges into dreams. Subsequently practitioners start to have lucid dreams: their awareness is now so powerful they recognize they are dreaming while still dreaming.

Lucid dreams have remarkable potential, the greatest of which is to continue one's spiritual practice throughout the night. Eight hundred years ago Tibetan Buddhists developed a highly refined dream yoga. Ibn Arabi, widely regarded as Islam's greatest mystic–philosopher, declared:

> A person must control his thoughts in a dream. The training of this alertness...will produce great benefits for the individual. Everyone should apply himself to the attainment of this ability of such great value.

But even dream yogas and meditation, astonishing as they are, are not the summit of sleeping practices. Even more remarkable experiences are possible. You can witness your dreams—and you can remain aware during nondream sleep.

To "witness" your dreams is to observe them calmly and with equanimity without being caught up in them. In this way the practitioner cultivates imperturbable awareness both day and night. The result is, as Patañjali explained:

> the mind begins to experience the Self as separate from activity, and is naturally drawn towards Enlightenment.

In addition, advanced practitioners are able to maintain awareness, not only during dreams, but also during nondream sleep. According to Aurobindo:

> It is even possible to become wholly conscious in sleep and follow throughout from beginning to end or over large stretches the stages of our dream-experience; it is found that then we are aware of ourselves passing from state after state of consciousness to a brief state of luminous and peaceful dreamless rest, which is the true restorer of the energies of the waking nature, and then returning by the same way to the waking consciousness.... A coherent knowledge of sleep-life, though difficult to achieve or keep established, is possible.

When this capacity matures, awareness remains unbroken throughout the day and night. Practitioners are able to watch themselves fall asleep, dream, rest in dreamless pure awareness, and eventually awaken the next morning, all without losing consciousness. Plotinus named this ability "ever-present wakefulness"; TM meditators describe it as "cosmic consciousness," and psychologists call it "subject permanence." Hinduism goes so far as to call this state of consciousness *Turiya,* meaning "the fourth," implying that it is a fourth state beyond the usual three states of waking, dreaming, and dreamless sleep.

When this state is stabilized, spiritual vision is awakened, and remains awake throughout day and night, throughout every experience and activity. The body may sleep or sicken, experiences may come and go, but consciousness is no longer limited or affected by them, and shines continuously in unbroken, lucid, luminous awareness, aware of all things and limited by none. Ken Wilber, the author of many remarkable books on spirituality, psychology, and science, describes his own experience of this condition:

This constant consciousness through all states—waking, dreaming, and sleeping—tends to occur after many years of meditating; in my case about 25 years. The signs are very simple: you are conscious during the waking state, and then, as you fall asleep and start to dream, you still remain conscious of the dreaming. This is similar to lucid dreaming, with a slight difference: usually, in lucid dreaming, you start to manipulate the dream—you choose to dream of sex orgies, great food or flying over mountains or what not. But with constant witnessing consciousness, there is no desire to change anything that arises. You simply and innocently Witness it. It's a choiceless awareness, a mirror-like awareness, which equally and impartially reflects whatever arises. So you remain conscious during the dream state, witnessing it, not changing it (although you can if you want; usually you don't want). Then, as you pass into deep, dreamless sleep, you still remain conscious, now you are aware of nothing but vast pure emptiness, with no content whatsoever. But "aware of" is not quite right, since there is no duality here. It's more like, there is simply pure consciousness

210 ESSENTIAL SPIRITUALITY

itself, without qualities or content, or subjects or objects, a vast pure emptiness that is not "nothing" but is still unqualifiable....

Since the ego exists mostly in the gross state, with a few remnants in the subtle, then once you identify with constant consciousness—or that which exists in all three states—then you break the hold of the ego, since it barely exists in the subtle and does not exist at all in "causal emptiness" or in the deep sleep state which is one type of emptiness. You cease identifying with ego, and you identify with pure formless consciousness as such, which is colorless, spaceless, timeless, formless—pure clear emptiness. You identify with nothing in particular, and therefore you can embrace absolutely everything that arises. Gone with the ego, you are one with the All.

You still have complete access to the waking state ego, but you are no longer *only* that. Rather, the very deepest part of you is one with the entire Kosmos in all its radiant glory. You simply *are* everything that is arising moment to moment. You do not see the sky, you are the sky. You do not touch the earth, you are the earth. You do not hear the rain, you are the rain. You and the universe are what the mystics call One Taste.

Lucidity Meets the Laboratory

These are astounding claims, and they beg an obvious question. Are they true? Can practitioners really remain aware throughout the night? In 1997, a remarkable sleep study provided the answer. Researchers observed a group of very advanced TM meditators, all of whom claimed to be continuously aware 24 hours a day. When observed while they slept through the night, their brain waves showed a pattern never seen before: a combination of fast waking rhythms superimposed on the very slow rhythms of deep sleep, suggesting, just as they claimed, that these meditators remained alert and aware throughout the night. Contemporary science has validated ancient wisdom; continuous lucidity has been observed in the laboratory.

The central message of the great religions can be summarized very simply as, "Wake up!" Signs of this awakening have now been glimpsed by science.

Cultivate Spiritual Intelligence

DEVELOP WISDOM AND UNDERSTAND LIFE

Happy are those who find wisdom....
She is more precious than jewels,
and nothing you desire can compare with her....
Her ways are ways of pleasantness,
and all her paths are peace....
Get wisdom, get insight: do not forget.

—Jewish Torah

CHAPTER 27

WHAT IS WISDOM?

Knowledge studies others,
Wisdom is self-known.

—*Lao Tsu*

Our world is awash with information, and we are drowning in data. Each day sees new discoveries, and a single newspaper tells more about the world than someone a few centuries ago learned in a lifetime.

Yet something is missing. We have knowledge aplenty, but wisdom? That is another story. A mere glance at the extent of suffering and insanity in the world makes it painfully clear that wisdom is in desperately short supply.

This lack is doubly sad because wisdom is essential not only for sane lives and societies, but also for awakening. No wonder it is so highly valued by all the great religions. Both Jews and Christians claim "the greatest good is wisdom," while the Koran declares that "those to whom wisdom is given; they truly have received abundant good." In Hinduism the cultivation of wisdom constitutes one of the major spiritual paths or yogas, while in Buddhism wisdom is sometimes regarded as the preeminent spiritual capacity. What is wisdom and how do we foster it?

WHAT WISDOM IS NOT

Let us begin by clearing the ground and saying what wisdom is not. Wisdom is not simply intelligence or knowledge, nor is it equivalent to dramatic experiences or personal power. All these can be valuable but are also quite distinct from wisdom.

Intelligence

Intelligence is the ability to learn, understand, and think clearly and logically. These are crucial capacities and can be employed to cultivate and express wisdom. However, wisdom is much more than simple intelligence, because wisdom results from applying intelligence to understanding the central issues of life.

Knowledge

Likewise, wisdom is more than knowledge. Taoism is very clear that "He who is learned is not wise." Whereas knowledge simply acquires information, wisdom requires understanding it. Knowledge looks at things objectively; wisdom examines them subjectively to recognize their implications for life and how to live life well. Knowledge informs us, wisdom transforms us. Knowledge is something we have, wisdom something we must become. Knowledge is expressed in words, wisdom in our lives. Knowledge empowers; wisdom empowers and enlightens. Buddhism claims:

> One momentary glimpse of Divine Wisdom
> born of meditation is more precious
> than any amount of knowledge.

Dramatic Experiences

Dramatic experiences, even powerful spiritual ones, are also not proof of wisdom. Anyone who does long-term, intensive spiritual practice will sooner or later be visited by remarkable experiences, including ecstatic visions, powerful emotions, and penetrating insights. Yet visions and insights can be wrong, and all experiences eventually disappear. Powerful experiences are not necessarily proof of wisdom, nor do they all necessarily lead to wisdom. What is crucial is how we relate to and learn from our experiences. This is one of the vital secrets of spiritual practice.

Spectacular experiences can either seduce us or inspire us. If they seduce us, we become attached and try to prolong and repeat them rather than letting go and growing beyond them. We then forget that, in the words of St. Gregory of Nyssa: "The graces that we receive at every point are indeed great, but the path that lies beyond our immediate grasp is infinite."

Even more destructive is to use powerful experiences not for self-transcendence, but for self-aggrandizement to make ourselves seem special, important, or enlightened. This can happen very swiftly. Many times I have had some deep insight, and then in the very next moment caught my mind swelling with pride and planning how to announce my discovery to the world. This is *spiritual materialism*, the tendency to become attached to spiritual experiences and pervert them to egocentric purposes. The following Zen story is a useful antidote.

> A young monk suddenly jumped up from his meditation cushion and ran to his teacher's room. Without even pausing to take off his shoes, he barged in on his teacher, who was sitting reading, and breathlessly announced that he had just seen a vision of a golden Buddha radiating light.
>
> "Don't worry," replied the teacher without even looking up from the book. "If you keep meditating it will go away."

Of course, deep experiences can lead to wisdom. But they must be carefully examined, tested, discussed with a teacher, and used for learning and nonattachment. Wisdom can grow from experience but is considerably more than just experience.

Personal Power

Wisdom is also more than personal power. A powerful teacher can be very seductive to students who believe that power and charisma must be signs of spiritual maturity.

This is far from true. Teachers come in all shapes and sizes. Some have commanding personalities; others are quiet and retiring. It is crucial not to mistake personality and power for profundity.

Power can be all the more seductive if it involves apparent psychic abilities. The existence of psychic abilities has been one of the most fiercely debated topics in science, with enormous amounts of hot air and insults hurled back and forth for over a century. Anyone who believes scientists always operate calmly and rationally can be cured of this belief by reading the literature on parapsychology. Growing evidence seems to support the existence of psychic capacities, though the effects are usually very small.

The great religions agree that psychic powers are possible. They also agree, however, that these powers are not signs of wisdom or spiritual maturity and are infinitely less important than the goal of liberation. The great religions tend to view psychic abilities as mere sideshows, not to be deliberately sought. If the powers do emerge, they should be used sparingly and only for the good of others. An ancient myth makes this point well.

> The Buddha and his disciples once came to a river where they patiently waited for a boatman to offer them a ride. While they waited, the Buddha taught a group of lay people who gathered around him. Suddenly a yogi who had devoted years to developing psychic powers appeared. Wanting to impress the crowd, he walked across the river and back again, and then challenged the Buddha to match his feat.
>
> "Tell me," asked the Buddha. "How much is the boat fare across the river?"
>
> "Not much, just a few coins," answered the surprised yogi.
>
> "And that's how much your psychic powers are worth," responded the Buddha.

Defining Wisdom

Wisdom is deep understanding and practical skill in the central issues of life, especially existential and spiritual issues.

Existential issues are those crucial and universal concerns all of us face simply because we are human. They include finding meaning and purpose in our lives; managing relationships and aloneness; acknowledging our limits and smallness in a universe vast beyond comprehension; living in inevitable uncertainty and mystery; and dealing with sickness, suffering, and death. A person who has developed deep insights into these issues—and skills for dealing with them—is wise indeed.

THE TWO ASPECTS OF WISDOM

Ever since the ancient Greeks pondered it, wisdom has been considered to have two distinct but interlocking elements: a visionary or understanding aspect and a practical or applied aspect.

Vision and Understanding

The visionary aspect of wisdom comes from seeing deeply and clearly, penetrating below surface appearances to recognize the deeper nature of things and life. To do this requires highly refined awareness characterized by clarity, subtlety, and penetrating power. This penetrating power comes in large part from concentration, and in classical Buddhism concentration is described as the preceding or immediate cause of wisdom.

Vision provides the intuitions from which understanding is born. Clear, concentrated vision sees things as they are, and understanding is born from actively investigating and analyzing the way things are. Investigation is so illuminating that Buddhists list it as one of the seven factors of enlightenment, those qualities and capacities of mind essential for deep awakening. A neo-Confucian sage promised: "If one plumbs, investigates into, sharpens, and refines himself, a morning will come when he will gain self-enlightenment."

Likewise the great neo-Confucian Wang Yang-Ming reported his own enlightenment came when he realized the significance of the phrase "investigate things so that knowledge may be extended to the utmost."

By investigating things, wisdom is able to identify crucial principles and implications for living well. At a simple level, it recognizes cause-and-effect relationships such as, "This kind of behavior leads to suffering ; that way of thinking promotes happiness." At a more sophisticated level, wisdom is able to create whole psychologies and philosophies that precisely formulate and explain the visionary insights of wisdom and their practical applications.

The visionary aspect of wisdom sees and explores three things: life, mind, and the nature of reality.

LIFE

Wisdom explores and reflects on the nature of life, especially on the causes of happiness and the causes and cures of suffering. It sees that there is an enormous amount of unnecessary suffering in the world, most of it caused by people blinded by destructive forces such as greed or hatred. Wisdom sees that some actions—for example, unethical or greedy ones—lead to short-term pleasure and much greater long-term pain, whereas others—for example, being ethical and generous—lead to enduring well-being. So often people fail to recognize this, so they live in ways that thwart the possibility of happiness.

Visionary wisdom sees that conventional ways of living are rife with suffering. Practical wisdom begins when a person recognizes there must be a better way to live and commits to finding it. The quest to awaken begins.

MIND

Wisdom recognizes the awesome power of the mind to both create and cloud our experience, to produce ecstasy and suffering, and to learn or stagnate. Once you appreciate the all-consuming power of the mind, learning how your mind works and how to train it become vital goals.

Wisdom sees that the untrained mind is wild and uncontrolled. But it also recognizes that the mind can be trained, tamed, transformed, and transcended, and that this is the essential means for fostering happiness, love, altruism, and liberation. Training your mind becomes a pressing priority; this training in turn further fosters the growth of wisdom.

THE NATURE OF REALITY

By probing deeply into their own experience, wise people see deeply into the fundamental nature of reality. In doing so, they begin to rediscover aspects of the perennial philosophy. For them this is no mere theoretical knowledge, but is rather a direct personal recognition born of their penetrating explorations of life, the world, and the mind.

Wise people learn a great deal that remains hidden to the ordinary person, yet paradoxically they also learn there are limits to learning. Knowledge is always partial, the intellect limited, our understanding finite in an infinite universe of unfathomable mystery. Recognition and acceptance of these limits are aspects of wisdom and also, as we will see, essential means for developing it.

Practical or Applied Wisdom

Practical wisdom is skill in living, especially in responding to the central, existential issues of life. It is a way of living that expresses the visionary and understanding aspects of wisdom. At its deepest it is living *sub specie aeternitatas*, under the aspect of eternity, or as Taoists would say, "in alignment with the Tao."

Vast vision and profound understanding lead to an appreciation of "natural law," and also of "natural ethics" and the "natural lifestyle." These are, respectively, legal systems, ethics, and lifestyles rooted in, harmonious with, and awakening us to the fundamental nature of reality.

The Confucian ideal of the noble person or holy person (*sheng-jen*) embodies these ideas. The noble person, it is said, "complies perfectly with all the principles, lives in harmony with nature and society, and is the peerless teacher of an age."

People at all stages of development may strive to be ethical and kind, but perhaps only mystical experience and its resultant wisdom provide an unequivocal answer to the fundamental question, "Why be moral?" Without a direct recognition of our unity with all people and all life, we can only try to think our way into justifying a moral life, by considering ideas of justice and different people's viewpoints. Such reasoning is obviously very valuable but may also be limited, and the pioneering researcher of moral development, Lawrence Kohlberg, concluded:

> Not even the highest possible stage of justice reasoning can adequately answer the question "Why be moral?"...the only ethical-ontological orientation that appears capable of generating a fully adequate resolution to ultimate moral questions "Why be moral?" "Why be just in a world that is seemingly unjust?" is a cosmic perspective.... This orientation appears also to rely upon some type

of transcendental or mystical experience—experience of a level at which self and the universe seem unified.

Mystical experience provides the foundation for mature wisdom, which in turn fosters mature transpersonal ethics, motivation, emotions, and service. Wisdom therefore leads us to live harmoniously and compassionately with others. These centuries-old claims have recently found support from researchers who concluded that the wise people they studied "transcended personal agendas and turned to collective or universal issues." Buddhism calls this the union of wisdom and compassion, because wisdom naturally finds expression in service to others.

CHAPTER 28

AWAKENING WISDOM

Wisdom is radiant and unfolding
and she is easily discerned by those who love her,
and is found by those who seek her.
She hastens to make herself known
to those who desire her....
To fix one's thoughts on her is perfect understanding....
The beginning of wisdom is the most sincere desire for
    instruction....
The multitude of the wise is the salvation of the world.

—*Wisdom of Solomon*

Where do we go to become wise? Not to universities, where knowledge alone reigns supreme. Nor to our leaders, who so often worship politics and power and imperil our planet. Rather, we turn to the spiritual heart of the great religious traditions, which holds the accumulated wisdom of thousands of years and thousands of sages. The keys to wisdom lie there.

PREPARING FOR WISDOM

If you have read this far and done the previous practices, you have already done a great deal to develop wisdom. Refining motivation and relinquishing attachments allow wiser choices. Ethical living and transforming emotions reduce the clouding effects of anger, guilt, and fear. This is crucial. As the Torah points out, "Wisdom will not enter a deceitful soul." Concentration and clear perception sharpen awareness and recognize skillful choices and actions. The net result is a mind less burdened by the past, less clouded by craving, more focused and clear, and able to penetrate deeply and understand profoundly. The mind becomes an agile instrument for developing wisdom. This development starts with a crucial recognition.

The Wisdom of Ignorance

> The fool who thinks he is wise is a fool indeed.
> —*The Buddha*

Wisdom is born of paradox. If we would be wise, we must first recognize that we are not. We are motivated to learn only when we know we do not know. The importance of this wisdom is beautifully portrayed in a classic Zen story about the meeting of a knowledgeable professor and a wise Zen master.

The professor introduced himself to the Zen master and announced that he would like to learn something of Zen.

"Ah, very good!" said the Zen master. "Please come in." After they were seated, the Zen master began by speaking about the vital importance of ethical living in Zen.

"Ah, yes," interrupted the professor. "Ethics is a fascinating topic, isn't it. I've studied several branches of it. In fact, I actually wrote a book on it," and he gathered speed and launched into a lecture on the various theories of ethics.

"Ah, I see," said the Zen master gently, when at last the professor stopped to draw a breath. "In Zen the correct motivation for saying or doing anything is very important and so we try to say only what is truly helpful."

"Well, there are several theories which hold that view," exclaimed the professor. "However, I must say that I find each of them flawed," and he promptly delivered a long lecture on different theories of motivation.

"Hmm, I see," said the Zen master, when finally the professor paused for a minute. "Would you like some tea?"

"Why, yes, thank you," replied the professor. The Zen master smiled and poured until the professor's cup was full, poured until the tea filled the saucer, and continued pouring while the tea ran over the table. The professor, a man rarely lost for words, was stunned into silence. But when the tea started pouring into his lap, he leaped up yelling.

"Stop! Can't you see the cup is full? It can't take any more!"

"Why, yes, I can see that," smiled the Zen master. "And can't you see that your mind is completely full of old ideas and so can't take in new ones? Therefore, you can't possibly learn about Zen."

The recognition that we don't know is more than an insight into ourselves; it is an invaluable insight into reality. The universe is so incomprehensibly vast, life so inconceivably profound, and our minds so relatively limited that our lives and the universe are a great and wondrous mystery. Huston Smith summarized our situation: "We are born in mystery, we live in mystery, and we die in mystery."

Recognizing our ignorance in the face of this immense mystery is an accurate reflection of our human condition. It's actually an enormous relief. That was certainly my own experience. For years I regretted my feelings of ignorance and mystery, assuming they were signs that something was amiss with me or my spiritual practice, and that if I practiced properly they would disappear. It was a real relief when I finally realized these feelings were reflections of reality rather than necessarily signs of inadequacy.

Recognizing our ignorance can be a great gift. It empties our hearts of pride and prejudice, and opens our minds to new possibilities, leaving them clean and empty vessels into which wisdom can flow. The fear of not knowing is then replaced with awe and delight in the never-ending wonder of life. We see that, as Lao Tsu exclaimed, "From wonder into wonder/Existence opens." One Christian text recommends the following reflection as a means for releasing old concepts and opening to the sacred. It is best read slowly and quietly, allowing the words to work their healing effects.

Let us be still an instant, and forget
all things we ever learned, all thoughts we had,
and every preconception that we hold
of what things mean and what their purpose is.

Let us remember not our own ideas
of what the world is for.
We do not know....
Simply do this:
be still, and lay aside all thoughts
of what you are and what God is;
all concepts you have learned about the world;
all images you hold about yourself....
Do not bring with you one thought the past has taught,
nor one belief you ever learned before from anything.
Forget this world, forget this course,
and come with wholly empty hands unto your God.

SOURCES OF WISDOM

Those who would, may reach the utmost height—but they
must be eager to learn.

—The Buddha

Where do we find wisdom? Eventually, everywhere: in every
person, situation, and experience to which we bring an open in-
quiring mind. Yet although it is possible to learn from all people
and all things, religious traditions especially recommend five
sources. The traditions advise us to seek wisdom:

1) in nature
2) in silence and solitude
3) from the wise
4) in ourselves
5) from reflecting on the nature of life and death

We will consider the first four sources here, and the reflections
on life and death in the next chapter.

Nature: Birthplace of the Sacred

It is all too easy to forget what is truly important in our lives.
Wordsworth summarized our plight:

The world is too much with us; late and soon,
Getting and spending, we lay waste our powers;
Little we see in Nature that is ours;
We have given our hearts away...

Spiritual seekers the world over recognize the trap of losing our hearts in the hustle and bustle of daily life and recommend nature as a healing antidote. The Christian Desert Fathers, shamans, yogis, Taoists, and American Indians all agree that nature sensitizes us to the sacred and is a superb setting for self-discovery and the birth of wisdom. American Indians value vision quests (periods of prayer and fasting in the wilderness). They hold that "the only true wisdom lives far from mankind." Their conclusion echoes that of the Christian St. Bernard, who claimed:

> What I know of the divine sciences and of Holy Scriptures I learnt in woods and fields. I have had no other masters than the beeches and the oaks. Listen to a man of experience: thou wilt learn more in the woods than in books.

Whether it is a mountain peak, a forest valley, or an ocean shore, somehow nature sifts the trivia from our minds and reminds us of the timeless and important.

Silence and Solitude

> It is in the silence of the heart that God speaks.
> —*Mother Teresa*

The spiritual power of nature or of any situation can be further enriched by silence and solitude. Many people fear being alone and do everything possible to avoid it. But solitude is very different from loneliness. Loneliness is a painful feeling of lacking something. Solitude is a deliberate choice to take time alone in order to foster and enjoy serenity, sensitivity, and the other benefits that ensue.

These benefits have been recognized for thousands of years. Consider the examples of the religious founders: Buddha's long years of meditation in the forest, Mohammed's prayer in a cave, or Jesus's forty days in the wilderness. All would have agreed with the Native Americans that: "The power of solitude is great and beyond understanding."

In solitude—even more so in silent solitude—we escape the superficial demands of society that, according to the Koran, are "but diversion and distraction" from spiritual life. Silence allows the mind to rest. Then the inner chatter of thoughts and fantasies ceases and inner silence mirrors the outer silence.

When silence reigns both within and without, we can hear what can never be spoken, the wisdom that waits beyond words. "For is not silence the very voice of the Great Spirit?" asked Black Elk, a Native American wise man. Certainly wise people the world over have thought so. According to Father Thomas Keating, "Silence is the language God speaks and everything else is a bad translation." Taoism holds out the promise:

In stillness [the mind] becomes clear.
In clarity, it becomes bright—and this brightness
is the radiance of the Tao within.

An early Zen master warned that when we seek the sacred:

The more you talk and think about it,
The further astray you wander from the truth.
Stop talking and thinking,
and there is nothing you will not be able to know.

Religions sing the praise of silence and solitude, and modern psychologists have joined the chorus. Their research confirms ancient claims that periods of solitude foster reflection and refreshment, and they have found further benefits, including enhanced creativity and physical health.

Periods of silence and solitude can be interspersed with periods of companionship and discussion. Each can enrich the other, and each of us must find the balance that best nurtures and awakens us. The great religions agree that the most enriching of all friendships are with the wise.

The Wise

Who better to teach wisdom than the wise? But who are the wise? Obviously, the great religious founders such as the Buddha, Lao Tsu, Confucius, Jesus, and Mohammad; also the great men and women of old who preserved and invigorated these traditions, such as the prophets of Israel, the sages of China, and the yogis of India.

But we need not remain fixated on the past or assume that wise people became extinct thousands of years ago. If valued and cultivated, wisdom can flower in people of all times and places. The Wisdom of Solomon, one of the apocryphal books of the Bible, declares that wisdom "hastens to make herself known to those who desire her." The twentieth century produced many wise and compassionate people. The vast majority of them are unknown, while some—such as Gandhi, Mother Teresa, and the Dalai Lama—are household names. To study the lives of such people is to learn from their example; to meet them is to be inspired by their presence; to hear or read their words is to drink from their mouths. In the recently discovered Gospel of Thomas, Jesus is quoted as saying:

> He who will drink from my mouth will become like me.
> I myself shall become he, and the things that are hidden will be revealed to him.

Ramakrishna concluded:

> The most effective discipline, however, is friendship and constant companionship with god-conscious men and women.

Jewish wisdom recommends:

> Let your house be a meeting place for the wise...
> and drink in their words with thirst.

As usual, the Buddha summarized it beautifully:

> If you are awake in the presence of a master
> One moment will show you the way.... follow the awakened
> And set yourself free.

Saints and sages are in short supply, but fortunately modern technology offers a novel solution. We no longer have to walk hundreds of miles to glimpse a saint. Now we can invite wise people from around the world into our homes and drink in their words through books, tapes, and videos. Of course, only a few of the people who put out books and tapes are deeply wise. As always, careful discernment and discriminating shopping in the spiritual marketplace are essential.

Not only saints and sages can inspire us. There are many degrees of wisdom, and those only a few steps ahead can help, as can friends traveling the path with us. "To make friends with the straight, the trustworthy in word and the well-informed is to benefit," declared Confucius. Such friendships, born of a shared love of the sacred, can be unique in their depth, honesty, and love. "What brings happiness?" and "What should we prize most dearly?" asked Shankara. "Compassion and Friendship with the holy," he replied. The Buddha urged, "Find friends who love the truth."

KNOW YOUR SELF

Self-knowledge is the shortest road to the knowledge of God.

—*Islamic sage*

The fourth arena that wisdom explores is self-knowledge. As practice deepens, we gradually awaken to a startling realization: We do not really know ourselves. Of course, we know our habits and the personality we put on each day and pretend is our self. But we come to realize that we don't really know our own inner depths, how our mind works, and our deepest Self.

So many wise people have urged, pleaded, even begged us to "know yourself." "I must first know myself," exclaimed Plato, and when a disciple asked Mohammad, "What am I to do that I may not waste my time?" he replied, "Learn to know yourself."

The rewards of self-knowledge are profound because our Self—our true spiritual Self—is the doorway to the sacred. St.

Augustine prayed, "Let me know myself, Lord and I shall know you," while Mohammad promised, "Those who know themselves know their Lord."

What does it mean to "know yourself?" We can think of three levels of self-knowledge: outer, inner, and deep.

1) To know our outer self is to know the self and mask we show to the world: our surface emotions, habits, and personality. This is the self visible to everyone.

2) Our inner self is visible only to ourselves. However, to know it well requires that we consciously look inward. Our secret hopes and fears and fantasies live here, hidden from others and partly hidden from ourselves.

Our self-image, the picture of who and what we think we are, also lives here. This is not who we really are but merely a superficial belief or image. One of our costliest spiritual errors is that we mistake this puny self-image for our deep self.

3) Our deep self is our true Self: the Atman, Buddha nature or *imago dei* that is the goal of spiritual practice.

Finding the Secret of Life

One of the most frequent worries that nags beginners on the spiritual path is that there is some secret of life that eludes them; some secret knowledge that could answer their deepest questions; some understanding that would unlock the deepest mysteries. There is such a secret, but it is so close, so obvious, that few recognize it. As Lao Tsu said:

> My way is so simple to feel, so easy to apply,
> That only a few will feel or apply it.

We overlook the secret of life because we look for it in the wrong place. When we finally turn attention inward, we discover that we are not who we thought we were. To know ourselves is to recognize that we are far, far more than we believed. It is to exchange our shabby self-image for our true Self and to discover that our true Self is a sacred Self and a doorway to the Divine. What is the secret of life? You are!

Learning to Know Your Self

How do we learn to know our Self? In one sense all spiritual practice is geared towards this discovery. However, three techniques are especially important: meditation, studying oneself, and self-acceptance. We have already discussed meditation as a vital tool for clear awareness; it is also a powerful aid to self-knowledge. In the words of Sri Nisargadatta Maharaj:

> We are slaves to what we do not know;
> of what we know we are masters.
> Whatever vice or weakness in ourselves we discover
> and understand its causes and its workings,
> we overcome it by the very knowing.
> The primary purpose of meditation is to become conscious
> and familiar with our inner life.
> The ultimate purpose is to reach the source of life.

The power of inner exploration and meditation is increased by also studying our outer self. This means giving careful attention to everything we say and do. It means trying to learn from every experience. We observe what we say and do, our habits and relationships, strengths and weaknesses, successes and failures. In this way every experience, every person, every interaction becomes a lesson, and the world becomes a schoolhouse for the soul.

According to Jewish sages, "The wise man learns from every phrase he hears, from every event he observes, and from every experience he shares." Through doing this, "You will be able to use every experience as a means of drawing closer to God."

This effort to learn from all experiences is a superb exercise. It takes little extra time or effort, and yet it transforms each experience—and eventually one's entire life—into a continuous opportunity for learning.

Self-Acceptance

The third key element for deep self-knowledge is self-acceptance. We hear much about the importance of accepting others, and appropriately so. We hear very little, however, about self-acceptance, probably because it is confused with pride and smugness. Self-acceptance does not mean puffing ourselves up or feeling superior to other people. Rather, it means relinquishing self-attack and condemnation.

According to both modern psychology and some areas of ancient wisdom, self-acceptance is vital to psychological and spiritual health. One of Western psychotherapy's most important discoveries is the enormous amount of neurotic pain caused by self-condemnation and the equally enormous healing that self-acceptance can bring.

We tend to think that attacking ourselves for our failings will remove them. Actually, these attacks make us cling defensively all the harder to old familiar ways. "Condemnation does not liberate, it oppresses," observed Carl Jung, "and so acceptance of one's self...is the acid test of one's whole outlook on life." Research shows that self-acceptance is one of the very best predictors of life satisfaction.

Some religious groups argue for a very different perspective. According to them, we are all miserable sinners who deserve self-condemnation and contempt.

Certainly we have all made foolish mistakes. However, mistakes are far better used as an opportunity for learning than for self-loathing, which can be a terrible barrier to well-being and growth. We need a middle way between inflated pride on the one hand and self-loathing on the other. The middle way is simply to see ourselves as we are, without exaggerating either our virtues or our failings. This is simple self-acceptance. Self-acceptance does *not* mean denying our shortcomings or giving up our efforts to heal them. It does mean recognizing and working on our shortcomings without attacking and belittling ourselves for having them.

CHAPTER 29

EXERCISES
IN WISDOM

Nothing indeed in this world purifies like wisdom.
—*the Bhagavad Gita*

"The world is the activity of one's teacher," say Tibetan Buddhists. This is transnoia: the view that the world and all life experiences are calls to learn and awaken. The challenge is to open to and learn from these experiences.

EXERCISE 1: COMMIT TIME TO SILENCE AND SOLITUDE

For most of us the real challenge is finding uninterrupted time for silence and solitude. Any time we have to ourselves is usually filled with work, errands, or distractions. This is unfortunate, since the Jewish Torah points out:

> Wisdom...depends on the opportunity of leisure.
> Only the one who has little business can be wise.

Therefore, it is valuable to commit to quiet time alone, even if only a few minutes each day or an hour a week. This can be in any pleasant environment, although nature may prove especially valuable.

You might begin by consciously dedicating the time to your healing or awakening. If there is a particular question or concern you want to focus on, by all means do so. You may wish to read a little to inspire you, but the time is best spent mostly in quiet reflection, perhaps mixed with some meditation or prayer.

EXERCISE 2: REFLECT ON "THE FOUR MIND-CHANGERS"

Imagine you are about to begin one of the longest and most intense spiritual exercises any human being ever undertakes: you are about to begin a Tibetan Buddhist three-year retreat. For three years and three months, you and a small group of fellow practitioners will stay in a secluded house and devote yourselves day and night to continuous spiritual practice. How do you begin? What exercises develop the wisdom and motivation to inspire you for three long years?

What you do is spend the first month reflecting on four profound ideas. These ideas are known as "the four mind-changers" because they help us understand the nature of life and change our minds and lives accordingly. They are reflections on these facts:

- Life is inconceivably precious.
- Life is short and death is certain.
- Life contains inevitable difficulties.
- Our ethical choices mold our lives.

These ideas are also found in the other great religions, but Tibetan Buddhists regard them as fundamental.

Begin by taking time to relax and quiet the mind. Then read through one idea and its accompanying discussion slowly and thoughtfully. Allow related ideas and associations to come to mind. If emotions emerge—such as gratitude for life or fear of death—explore them. Consider what implications the idea has for your life and whether you wish to make any changes. Give yourself time to savor the idea and its implications. When you are ready, move on to the next idea.

Life Is Inconceivably Precious   The gift of life is priceless, and those of us blessed with what Tibetans call "free and well-favored lives" are extraordinarily fortunate. Free of the terrible difficulties—

such as dire poverty or disabling disease—that plague so many people, we are free to follow our deepest desires and find happiness for ourselves and others. This freedom is a remarkable gift. It is even more remarkable also to have "well-favored" lives, favored with the time and resources, teachers and friends that support spiritual practice. Our challenge is to make optimum use of this priceless opportunity, not to be seduced by petty obsessions and trivial goals, but rather to seek the greatest of all goals: our awakening and the awakening and welfare of others.

Life Is Short and Death Is Certain   When we look unflinchingly at life, we see that we and all things eventually die. No one gets out of here alive. Ashes to ashes, dust to dust; such is the fate of all living things. As one wry joke puts it,"Life is a sexually transmitted disease with a fatal prognosis."

Death comes to everyone, and at the end life seems so unbelievably short. My eighty-three-year-old aunt echoed the bewilderment of millions of elderly people when she lamented, "It's such a surprise to wake up and find that you're old."

It's not that we haven't been warned. Sage after sage has pleaded with us to realize how brief and unpredictable life is. Our lives last "but a moment," say the Taoists; they are "soon gone...they come to an end like a sigh...like a dream," cry the Jewish psalms. "What is your life?" asks the Bible, and replies, "you are a mist that appears a little while and then vanishes." Shankara made the same point by asking, "What roll quickly away, like drops of water from a lotus leaf?" to which he responded, "Youth, wealth and the years of a person's life."

The sages' goal in emphasizing the brevity and uncertainty of life is not to depress us, but rather to inspire us. Without recognizing our mortality, we tend to squander our lives in petty pursuits, tranquilize ourselves with trivia, and forget what really matters in life. When we recall, as Christian monks remind us, "Death is certain, the hour uncertain," then we remember we don't know how long we have, and we are inspired to live more fully, more boldly, and more impeccably.

This is why a brush with death can be so life-transforming; it strips away our denial of mortality and shocks us into reassessing our lives. The great astronomer Carl Sagan had just this experience and afterward wrote:

> I recommend almost dying to everyone; it's character-building. You get a much clearer perception of what's important and what isn't, the preciousness and beauty of life.

Those confronted with AIDS say it stands for Accelerated Individual Discovery of Self and produces "enlightenment at gunpoint."

Life Contains Inevitable Difficulties   Life is not only short, but difficult. There are times of great joy, love, triumph, and delight, moments when we are beside ourselves with happiness. But there are also times of inevitable sorrow: of sickness and loss, of grief and despair. There are also incomprehensible amounts of unnecessary sorrow: of senseless oppression and torment, slaughter and suffering. None of us escapes life unscathed. It is crucial to recognize this and not gloss over the inevitable difficulties of life, because "If a way to the Better there be, it exacts a full look at the Worst." This is why religious scholar Jacob Needleman concluded, from his survey of world religions:

> The perception of the suffering inherent in the human condition, the perception of man's inhumanity to man: this moment of awareness has been spoken of in all traditions as a tremendous moment. It is a tremendous moment because it is the recognition of suffering—both ours and the world's—which gives birth to both compassion and the urge to awaken. These motives propel us to spiritual practice and thereby eventually allow us to escape suffering and to relieve the suffering of others.

Our Ethical Choices Mold Our Lives   All that we say, do, or think affects our lives and creates consequences that haunt or help us. Burn with rage, and anger sears itself into our brains; speak with love, and love conditions our minds. This is the principle of karma. Ethical living is absolutely essential to our well-being. We have already examined these principles in a previous chapter and need not discuss them further here, except to add the words

of the Buddha: "Wherever we go, wherever we remain, the results of our actions follow us."

The four mind-changing thoughts contain some of the most
important of life's secrets. Tibetan Buddhists recommend reflecting on them repeatedly, even daily, knowing that their seeds of
wisdom gradually transform not only our minds but also our lives.

EXERCISE 3: SPIRITUAL READING

This exercise extends the previous one by reading and reflecting
on spiritual writing. We usually read to acquire information, but
reading can also cultivate wisdom. By reading and reflecting on
the words of the wise, their ideas and perspectives gradually become our own. Each of the great religions has a treasury of the
sayings of the sages and urges us to read and reflect on their
words.

The way in which wisdom literature is best read is very different from our usual approach, so different that Christians call
it *Lectio Divina*, divine reading. Father Thomas Keating, the
originator of Centering Prayer, explained:

> We tend to read the Scriptures as if they were just another book to
> be consumed. Lectio is just the opposite. It is the savoring of the
> text, a leisurely lingering in divine revelation.
>
> With sacred reading we are seeking insight rather than facts,
> transformation rather than information. Consequently, the read-
> ing is slow and reflective, a few sentences or even words at a time.

To begin, choose some writing that resonates with you. It
might be an ancient sacred text, the words of a modern sage, or
perhaps some of the quotations in this book. Read from your se-
lection slowly and reflectively, allowing the words to sink into your
depths. If related thoughts arise, feel free to ponder them; if insights arise, explore them; if feelings surface, accept them; if hopes
or prayers emerge, pray them. Of course, if you become lost in irrelevant thoughts or fantasies, simply return to reading. Done in
this way, sacred reading merges into meditation and prayer.

EXERCISE 4: RECOGNIZE YOUR TEACHERS AND THEIR GIFTS

Who are the people who have been your greatest teachers? They may have been family members, friends, coaches, or even children. They may even have seemed at the time to be adversaries or people you disliked.

As you remember them, write their names down. Then list the special qualities that made these people so helpful and the lessons you learned from them. Next, reflect on the qualities in you that made you receptive to their wisdom.

Finally, allow feelings of gratitude and appreciation for these teachers to emerge. At some time, you may wish to express these feelings to them. This will obviously be a gift to them, but it will also be a gift to you, because to express gratitude is to strengthen it.

EXERCISE 5: ENJOY THE COMPANY OF THE WISE

This exercise is very simple. Make a list of those people you know personally who seem wise or who want to learn and become wise. Then consider how you could spend more time with them. Could you visit them or invite them to visit you? Could you assist them in some way or work on a project together? Could you start a group to study this book together and encourage each other to do the exercises? Choose an approach you would enjoy, and begin.

EXERCISE 6: DISCOVER YOUR PHILOSOPHY OF LIFE

Like many great saints, Gandhi was both simple and profound and could convey important ideas in a few words. Once he was seated on a train; as it began to move a reporter rushed up to him and begged, "Do you have a message for the people?" Gandhi was observing one of his days of silence, days when he would communicate only a few words, and then only by writing. Leaning out the window as the train gathered speed and the breathless reporter ran along beside it, Gandhi scribbled, "My life is my message."

Gandhi's life of simplicity and service was his message, and each of our lives is also a message, a reflection of the philosophy that underlies it. Whether we know it or not, each of us has developed and lives by a philosophy of life. This philosophy includes beliefs about the nature of life and ourself, what is beautiful and true, and what is worth devoting our life to. Much of this philosophy lies deep within us, unconscious and unrecognized, but some of it can be brought to awareness rather easily.

Gandhi demonstrated this possibility. Asked what his philosophy of life was, he needed only three words: "Renounce and rejoice." Renounce or let go of attachments, and rejoice in the freedom and delight that a life free from craving offers.

To discover your own guiding philosophy, first relax, then close your eyes. When you feel calm, gently ask, "In approximately three words, what is my philosophy of life?" Then allow a response to emerge from the depths of your mind. There is no need to struggle or try to figure out an answer. That would be using the intellect, which is not the deepest part of your mind. Rather, simply remain quiet yet alert and patiently trust your inner wisdom to provide a valuable response. When it does, you will discover some of the deepest principles guiding your life.

EXERCISE 7: REVIEW YOUR LIFE

Periodically reviewing your life and behavior is widely regarded as extraordinarily beneficial—and essential for a deep spiritual life. Without it we blunder along without learning from our experiences or our mistakes. "Those who ponder upon their conduct bring much good to themselves," holds an ancient Jewish saying. This pondering is best done in the spirit of gentle inquiry aimed at understanding and accepting, rather than judging and condemning oneself. Self-inquiry should not be confused with self-condemnation; self-examination aims at learning, not punishment.

Rabbi Nachman urged:

> Make sure to set aside a specific time each day to calmly review your life. Consider what you are doing and ponder whether it is worthy that you devote your life to it.

It is helpful to have a systematic method. The end of the day is a particularly valuable time for self-examination, since then we can review the full day's activities and their lessons. One approach is to sequentially review the day from the time you got up. It is not necessary to recall all your activities; the major events and experiences will suffice. As each activity comes to mind, simply reflect on it and see what you can learn from the way you felt and acted. Jewish tradition calls those who faithfully do this evening review "masters of nightly recollection."

It is crucial to remember the goal of the review, and of all self-examination: The goal is to learn, not to blame; to grow in wisdom, not to fall into guilt; to appreciate our strengths as much as to recognize our weaknesses. We can learn as much, and sometimes even more, from our mistakes as from our good choices, as the following story makes clear.

> After a long, hard climb up the mountain, the spiritual seekers finally found themselves in front of the great teacher. Bowing deeply, they asked the question that had been burning inside them for so long: "How do we become wise?"
>
> There was a long pause until the teacher emerged from meditation. Finally the reply came: "Good choices."
>
> "But teacher, how do we make good choices?"
>
> "From experience," responded the wise one.
>
> "And how do we get experience?"
>
> "Bad choices," smiled the teacher.

Regular self-reflection fosters good choices. Wisdom and well-being flourish, while painful feelings, such as worry and guilt, gradually wilt. As Confucius pointed out, "If, on examining himself, a man finds nothing to reproach himself for, what worries and fears can he have?"

EXERCISE 8: CORRECTIVE VISUALIZATION

When self-examination reveals foolish things we said or did, how are we to heal them? It is useful to correct as many aspects of the problem as possible. For example, if we hurt someone, the first priority may be to apologize. As we discussed in the chapter on ethics, this will help heal the relationship. If we damaged or destroyed something, it may be helpful to repair or replace it. This will heal the loss.

It is also important to heal any destructive emotions or habits that caused the foolishness in the first place. One useful method for this is corrective visualization, a technique suggested more than a hundred years ago by a Jewish teacher, and now widely used by psychotherapists. Here we visualize ourselves handling the situation more skillfully.

Take a few minutes to relax. Recall a time when you spoke or acted in a way you now regret. As vividly as you can, imagine yourself back in that same situation. Visualize the place you were in and the people who were there. Recall what you were doing and how you felt. Then allow yourself to watch the scene unfold and watch yourself make the error and observe the consequences.

Now restart the visualization from the beginning and again allow the scene to unfold. However, this time see yourself making a wiser choice and notice how you feel as you do so. For example, perhaps a friend made a hurtful comment and you flew into a rage and lashed back, thereby damaging the friendship. In replaying the scene you might see yourself taking three deep breaths and then making a joke about the comment. If you wish, you can replay the scene several times and try different types of skillful responses. Just a few minutes doing this exercise can bring a sense of healing, offer new insights, and begin to establish healthy new habits.

EXERCISE 9: CONTACT YOUR INNER TEACHER

We think of wisdom as something we must learn, and that is partly true. Yet the great religions also assure us that wisdom already resides within us. Our minds are extraordinary miracles—"the greatest of all cosmic wonders," according to Carl Jung—and contain untapped sources of wisdom and understanding. We know more than we know we know. The inner source of wisdom has been called by many names: for example, the Hindu's "inner guru," the Tibetan Buddhist's "personal deity," the Christian Quaker's "still small voice within," or the psychologist's "higher self." Whatever the name, the implications are the same. We have within us remarkable wisdom that will guide and help us if we learn how to recognize and draw on it. The following exercise is one way to do so.

Close your eyes and relax. Imagine yourself in a beautiful place, perhaps your favorite beach, mountain, or garden. See yourself there and enjoy the feelings this special place evokes.

In just a moment you are going to invite into that place an extraordinarily wise person. It may be a great spiritual teacher, or it may be an unknown wise man or woman. Whoever it is, this person will embody qualities such as great wisdom, love, and complete acceptance of you just as you are.

Invite this wise person into your place of beauty and introduce yourself. Take time to savor the experience of being in the presence of a person of deep wisdom and boundless love. What does it feel like to be with someone who understands and loves you completely? What fears and defenses melt into nothingness in the presence of someone who accepts you just the way you are?

Here is an opportunity to learn and get advice about anything that concerns you. Take a moment to think of the questions you would most like to ask. Then ask your first question and wait quietly for the answer. There is no need to try to make anything happen. Simply relax and allow the wisdom within you to respond. When you are ready, ask your next question, wait for a response, and continue with any further questions.

Next, ask the wise person if he or she has anything to tell you. Again, just relax and wait for an answer. Then ask if there are any questions the wise person has for you.

Finally, ask the wise person if he or she will be available to you in the future at any time you request help or do this exercise. Then express your thanks for the gifts of this meeting.

Now imagine yourself beginning to merge with the wise person so that your bodies, hearts, and minds melt into one. Actually you already are one, because the sage and the qualities such as love and wisdom are creations and part of your own mind. Feel that you have absorbed the qualities of the wise person and explore the experience. What is it like to be wise? What does it feel like to be fearless and to have no need to defend yourself in any way? What is it like to feel boundless love and care for all people, including yourself? And what does it feel like to accept and love yourself completely, just as you are?

After you have savored this experience, gently open your eyes. Try to make the transition slowly and gently so you can bring back the qualities you experienced.

Take a moment to reflect on the fact that these feelings— wisdom, fearlessness, love, and acceptance—are not new or foreign to you. They are actually aspects of yourself that you projected onto the wise person. True, these qualities are not fully developed or always accessible to you yet, but they are available and await your attention to grow and flourish.

This exercise can be repeated whenever you wish to experience and nourish positive qualities. It can also be done when you need guidance with a difficult question or choice, and it is especially valuable during times of confusion.

CHAPTER 30

THE HIGHER REACHES OF WISDOM

Those who know others are wise,
Those who know themselves are enlightened.

—*Lao Tsu*

In addition to the visionary and practical wisdom recognized by philosophers, there is a still more profound transcendental wisdom that gradually illuminates spiritual practitioners. This transcendental wisdom flowers as practitioners assimilate the novel insights each stage of development unveils. The challenge is to incorporate these insights into an ever wider, deeper, and more comprehensive understanding of mind, self, and reality. We can briefly trace the major insights and challenges that face practitioners as they penetrate through three major stages: subtle, pure consciousness, and nondual.

SUBTLE WISDOM

As awareness becomes more lucid, it penetrates into the subtle depths of the psyche, far below the usual conscious mind, and far below even the realms of the unconscious usually explored in psychotherapy. Here the practitioner uncovers transpersonal forces that are initially faint and subtle, but have enormous transformative power: archetypal images, sacred visions, and emotions such as boundless love and compassion.

These experiences foster and require a new level of wisdom. Practitioners must learn how to open to and work with these powerful transformative energies. At the same time, they must avoid the traps of becoming entranced by them or becoming grandiose and inflated at having them. Practitioners must learn how to assimilate these novel experiences into their understanding of reality and find ways to express this understanding in their lives. The central insight of subtle wisdom is that the psyche is multilayered, and that within its depths are powerful transpersonal forces that must be appropriately experienced, integrated, and expressed.

THE WISDOM OF PURE CONSCIOUSNESS

As awareness becomes still more penetrating, it breaks through into the realm of pure consciousness, Mind, or Spirit. Here there are no objects, thoughts, or things, no time or change, no minds to suffer or bodies to decay and die. There is only the bliss of unbounded awareness, transcendent to space and time, eternally free.

At this stage exclusive identification with the body and mind is gone. Practitioners never again wholly believe the dream that they are merely separate egos, bound to and by the body, and inevitably doomed to die with it. Shankara described this recognition as one in which "The knower of the Atman does not identify himself with his body. He rests within it, as if within a carriage." The practitioner discovers that though all *things* change and all *bodies* die, there is a realm beyond things and bodies, and therefore beyond all change, suffering, and death.

This understanding naturally weakens attachments to the world and its transient pleasures, which pale in comparison to the bliss of the Divine. In Shankara 's words: "a man is free from worldliness if he has realized Brahman, the infinite bliss." For such a person, the advice of Jesus now makes perfect sense:

Do not store up for yourselves treasures on earth where moth and rust consume and where thieves break in and steal; but store up for yourselves treasures in heaven where neither moth nor rust consume and where thieves do not break in and steal. For where your treasure is, there your heart will be also.

The key insight of this level of wisdom is that a sacred realm of pure awareness is our true nature and our home, and that by awakening to it, suffering can be transcended and divine bliss directly known. The challenge of this level is to stabilize this insight and to reorient your behavior so you experience and express this realization in more and more of your life.

NONDUAL WISDOM

At the level of pure consciousness, the practitioner can experience either the world or the transcendent realm of awareness, but not both simultaneously. At the nondual stage, transcendent consciousness remains, but at the same time awareness of both inner and outer objects returns. However, these objects reappear in a radically new way. Now, as experiences arise, they are immediately, spontaneously, and effortlessly recognized as creations or manifestations of consciousness. Instead of appearing as separate, independent entities, all things are seen as expressions or projections of consciousness, the divine play or *lila* of God. Infinite consciousness, Mind, Brahman, or God is recognized as all beings, all things, and all worlds, or as Meister Eckhart put it, "All things become nothing but God." The moment he attained enlightenment, the sixth Zen patriarch exclaimed, "Who would have thought that all things are the manifestation of the Essence of Mind."

The seeker becomes a sage. She now looks out at the world and in at the mind, but wherever she looks sees only God. The Christian mystic Angela Foligno exclaimed:

The eyes of my soul were opened, and I beheld the plenitude of God, wherein I did comprehend the whole world, both here and beyond the sea, and the abyss and ocean and all things. In all these things I beheld naught save the divine power, in a manner assuredly indescribable; so that through excess of marveling the soul cried with a loud voice, saying, "This whole world is full of God!"

This recognition is the basis of the ecstatic cries of sages throughout the ages, cries such as "God is in all and all is in God" (Judaism) and "I have never seen anything without seeing God in it" (Mohammad). Likewise, the Sufi Baba Kuhi exclaimed:

> In the market, in the cloister—only God I saw.
> In the valley and on the mountain—only God I saw.
> Like a candle I was melting in his fire;
> Amidst the flames out flashing—only God I saw.
> Myself with mine own eyes I saw most clearly,
> But when I looked with God's eyes—only God I saw.
> I passed away into nothingness, I vanished,
> and lo, I was the All-living—only God I saw.

This is the recognition of nonduality, of the utter inseparability of spirit and matter, of mind and manifestation, of inner and outer, personal and transpersonal, sacred and profane, Self and God. According to Ramakrishna, this ecstatic vision is available to us all as soon as we prepare ourselves for it:

> This divinity of all beings, structures and dimensions can be clearly perceived by the organ of supreme vision that develops naturally as soon as the mind becomes pure enough.

WHO CHANTS THE NAME OF BUDDHA?

If all things are now experienced as inseparable aspects of the Divine, so too is the sense of self. The sense of one's self as an ego—a self limited to the body, forever separate from all things—dissolves in the blazing light of divine consciousness, to be replaced with a recognition of oneself, and everyone and everything, as aspects of the divine. According to the neo-Confucian sage Wang Yang-ming, this recognition "restore[s] the condition of forming one body with heaven, earth and the myriad things. The Sufi saint Nizami exclaimed:

> You imagine that you see me,
> But I no longer exist:
> What remains is the Beloved.

There is no longer a separate ego looking out at a material world, but only God looking at God, consciousness observing its manifestations, the Buddha aware of Buddha nature, Brahman enjoying his *lila*. The greatest of Islamic philosophers, Ibn Arabi, proclaimed this ultimate paradox:

> By Himself He sees Himself, and by Himself He knows Himself. None sees Him other than He, and none perceives Him other than He.... There is no other and there is no existence other than He.

Meister Eckhart exclaimed, "Here, in my own soul, the greatest of all miracles has taken place—God has returned to God!" Shankara cried out in absolute humility:

> I am neither this object, nor that. I am that which makes all objects manifest. I am supreme, eternally pure. I am neither inward nor outward. I am the infinite Brahman, one without a second.
>
> I am Reality without beginning, without equal. I have no part in the illusion of "I" and "You," "this" and "that." I am Brahman, one without a second, bliss without end, the eternal, unchanging Truth.

As usual, Chuang Tzu put it very simply:

> The ten thousand things and I are one.
> We are already one—
> what else is there to say?

The answer to the Zen koan "Who chants the name of Buddha?" is "Buddha."

This has been a point of enormous confusion, and many a sage has been burned, poisoned, or crucified because of it. "The Father and I are one," proclaimed Jesus, and was crucified shortly thereafter. "I am the truth" (one of the names of God), confessed the Sufi al-Hallaj, and he was also crucified.

This is not the ego inflation of megalomaniacs, like the Roman emperors who proclaimed themselves gods. Nor is it the ego disintegration of the severe psychotic, who cannot even find the boundaries of his own body. Nor is it blasphemy against God.

Rather, it is an awareness that there is only God: the recognition that all people, all creatures, all life—and certainly not the ego alone—live in and are lived by the Divine. Both the emperor and the psychotic think that they alone are divine, whereas the sage perceives all people as divine. The psychotic and the megalomaniac expect to be worshipped by everyone; the sage happily worships everyone. The psychotic suffers from ego disintegration; the megalomaniac suffers from ego inflation; the sage delights in ego transcendence. To confuse them is to commit the "pre/trans fallacy:" the trap of confusing prepersonal regression with transpersonal progression. What a world of difference between them!

THE LIBERATING POWER OF WISDOM

Transcendental wisdom has many levels and many names, names such as *hokhmah* (Judaism), *prajna* (Buddhism), *jnana* (Hinduism), *mar'ifah* (Islam), and *gnosis* (Christianity). Whatever its name, wisdom is a spiritual capacity of enormous liberating power. Seeing the way we and reality really are corrects the false beliefs and delusions that lock us into our self-defeating sense of self and ways of being. These myriad delusions—such as that there is no reality other than the physical, that we are merely skin-encapsulated egos, and that craving and attack can bring enduring happiness—create our suffering. By dissolving these delusions, wisdom dissolves our mental prison, reduces our suffering, and speeds our awakening.

By loosening the bonds of egoism, wisdom also fosters concern and compassion for others.

EXPRESS SPIRIT IN ACTION

EMBRACE GENEROSITY AND THE JOY OF SERVICE

Where there is hate, let me bring Love—
Where there is offense, let me bring Pardon—
Where there is discord, let me bring Union—
Where there is error, let me bring Truth—
Where there is doubt, let me bring Faith—
Where there is darkness, let me bring Light—
Where there is sadness, let me bring Joy—
because it is in giving oneself that one receives;
it is in forgetting oneself that one is found....

—*St. Francis of Assisi*

CHAPTER 31

THE SPIRIT OF SERVICE

If I am not for myself, who will be?
But if I am only for myself, what am I?
And if not now, then when?
—*the Jewish sage Hillel*

We have all heard that, as both Jesus and Mohammad emphasized, "It is more blessed to give than to receive." But somehow it doesn't always feel that way. Giving, whether of our time, money, or possessions, can feel more like a hardship than an opportunity.

If the great religions are right and giving can be a source of great satisfaction, why does it so often feel like a sacrifice? A crucial part of the answer is that just like living ethically and lovingly, openhearted giving is a skill to be cultivated and can be difficult at first. However, generosity matures as we mature and eventually flows spontaneously and enjoyably as spiritual life deepens.

IN PRAISE OF SERVICE

The great religions all sing the praises of generosity and service. "Make it your guiding principle to do your best for others," urged Confucius. When Mohammad was asked, "What actions are most excellent?" he replied, "To gladden the heart of a human being, to feed the hungry, to help the afflicted, to lighten the sorrow of the sorrowful, and to remove the wrongs of the injured." Both Mohammad and Jesus were uncompromising. Mohammad never said no when asked for anything, and Jesus urged,

"Give to everyone who begs from you and do not refuse anyone who wants to borrow from you."

Helping those in need may be even more important than preserving sacred objects and rituals, as Rabbi Israel Salanter demonstrated. Rabbi Salanter was a brilliant nineteenth-century Jewish reformer who invented several techniques for transforming difficult emotions such as anger. He once shocked his colleagues when he found a seriously ill student whose illness was being poorly treated.

> Rabbi Salanter asked the people who prayed in the young man's synagogue, "Why aren't you taking better care of him?"
>
> "Our community doesn't have any money," they replied. Rabbi Salanter then screamed at them, "You should have sold the fancy cover on the ark in which the torah scrolls are kept and used the money to help this person!"
>
> Rabbi Salanter seemed to be quite angry, but someone heard him whisper to himself, "External anger only. External anger only."

We All Want to Help

The great religions regard helping one another as more than mere obligation; they see it as a central human desire. In the monotheistic traditions of Judaism, Christianity, and Islam, love and service of others are often given equal status with love and service of God. In Buddhism, compassion is seen as an inherent aspect of our nature.

Psychologists are beginning to agree. For a long time psychologists held a particularly dim view of altruism and argued that people helped others merely to feel good about themselves or to look good to others. Recent experiments paint a far more pleasant picture: Human beings seem to be genuinely altruistic. We all have a desire to help.

Barriers to True Generosity

However, the great religions recognize that this desire may initially be quite weak and delicate. It is all too easily suffocated by conflicting forces such as greed or emotions of fear and anger.

These powerful forces scream for gratification and all too easily obliterate concern for others. The sad result is either miserliness or a mask of false generosity. When greed rules our minds, we compulsively acquire all we can, and the thought of parting with our precious possessions fills us with dread.

Under the sway of attachment and fear, even giving to others can spring from unhealthy motives. We can become attached to people just as easily as to possessions. Then we may shower these people with gifts in a desperate attempt to gain their affection. This may look like generosity, but it is actually a form of manipulation driven not by a joyful desire to share, but by a desperate need to be liked. Giving becomes a manipulative ploy in the service of our own neediness.

The Growth of Generosity

How can we transform generosity and service from a painful burden to an enjoyable spiritual opportunity? Through the seven practices.

They strengthen the qualities of mind, such as love and gratitude, that foster generosity, while weakening barriers, such as greed and anger, that inhibit it. Both ancient wisdom and modern psychology agree that the desire to help and the pleasure it brings grow as we grow. Jack Kornfield concludes:

> Whether it is generosity with our time, our possessions, our money, or our love, the principles are the same. True generosity grows as our heart opens, grows along with the integrity and health of our inner life.... Great generosity springs naturally out of a sense of health and wholeness of our being.

The great religions suggest that this growth of generosity develops through stages. Buddhism describes three stages:

1) *Tentative Giving:* Here we offer our gifts hesitantly and ambivalently, fearful that we might miss them later, and more concerned with our own fears than another's needs.

2) *Brotherly or Sisterly Giving:* Here we give willingly, happy to share our blessings with others, motivated by their well-being as well as our own.

3) *Royal Giving:* Generosity is now so highly developed, so effortless and spontaneous, that we naturally want to give the best of what is ours to maximize the happiness of others. Others' well-being is now as important as our own, and their happiness can only increase ours. At this stage it is clear that serving others can be a spiritual practice, a privilege, and a joy.

THE JOY OF SERVICE

Mother Teresa's nuns offer dramatic examples of royal giving and the joy it produces. Theirs is an austere lifestyle. They leave the comforts of home and live like the poorest of the poor people they serve. At their central house in Calcutta they are packed three or four to a room, and their only personal possessions are two dresses and a bucket for washing. They eat the same food as the poor, and despite the suffocating Indian heat they have no air conditioning. They rise before dawn and spend their days working in the slums. It is an existence that most of us would regard as difficult, if not downright depressing. Yet when a television interviewer visited Mother Teresa, he exclaimed:

> "The thing I notice about you and the hundreds of sisters who now form your team is that you all look so happy. Is it a put-on?"
>
> "Oh no," she replied, "not at all. Nothing makes you happier than when you really reach out in mercy to someone who is badly hurt."
>
> "I swear," wrote the interviewer afterward, that "I have never experienced so sharp a sense of joy."

The Nobel Prize–winning Indian poet Rabindranath Tagore summarized the practice in two lines.

> I awoke and saw that life was service.
> I acted and behold, service was joy.

Another Nobel Prize winner, Albert Schweitzer, who devoted his life to treating the poor and sick of Africa, agreed and warned: "The only ones among you who will be truly happy are those who have sought and found how to serve."

Of course, we don't have to be nuns or Nobel Prize winners to serve and reap the rewards of service. Even small gifts or simple acts of kindness can produce an enduring glow. When people are asked to recall acts of generosity they feel good about, they are often surprised by how simple or apparently small some of the most memorable ones were.

As I write this, it is the beginning of a new year. As I look back over last year I am surprised to realize that one of the things I feel best about is a gift I gave. My mother loves to travel by ship but was unable to afford it. For her eightieth birthday I gave her the gift of a cruise to Alaska, a place she had long wanted to visit. It was a bit of a financial stretch, but now I am delighted to have done it.

Helper's High

Psychologists have found striking evidence that supports religious claims for the benefits of generosity. Generous people tend to be happier and psychologically healthier than selfish individuals and to experience a "helper's high." As people age, they increasingly find it is their legacy—their contributions to the world and future generations—that gives meaning and satisfaction to their lives. Taking time to make others happy makes us feel better than devoting all our efforts to our own pleasures. Psychologists call this "the paradox of pleasure," and there are several reasons for it.

Our service to others serves us in several ways: It weakens negative forces and strengthens positive ones within our minds. When we share our possessions, time, or energy, we loosen the heavy chains of greed, jealousy, and fear of loss that bind us to our egos. Likewise, when emotions such as love and happiness are expressed as kindness, they grow stronger in the process.

We also experience ourselves what we intend for others. If we boil with hatred and revenge, it is our minds that are convulsed and torn by the anger long before we vent it on someone else. On the other hand, when we desire happiness for others, thoughts of happiness first fill our own minds, then overflow into caring action. This is one reason why generosity can alleviate painful feelings and help lift depression. One of the editors who reviewed this book wrote to me:

> This chapter makes an extremely crucial spiritual point and I've found myself nodding along with your statements—that behaving gener-

ously breeds contentment in oneself, that it fosters a desire to give more. This type of feedback loop matches very closely my own experiences over the past year. I've spent six months dragging myself out of a depression, and for the past few months have been flourishing. The turning point came when I spent a day with two Buddhist teachers I was interviewing for a book. Both of them were so generous to me and so obviously happy that I was inspired to be more generous myself. Perhaps I didn't completely play the Buckminster Fuller game [described later] of "how much good can one person do?" but I certainly played it in part. What astounded me was how easy it has been and how quickly the internal reward system kicked into place.

The Buddha claimed that if we understood the benefits of generosity as deeply as he did, we would not want to eat a single meal without offering to share it.

SERVICE AS THE SUPREME PRACTICE

So esteemed are generosity and service that some traditions regard them as the essence of spiritual life, the practice upon which all other practices converge. From this perspective, a crucial goal of spiritual life is to equip oneself to serve effectively. Even the supreme goal of enlightenment is sought, not for oneself alone, but to better serve and enlighten others.

With this goal in mind, some practitioners temporarily withdraw from involvement in the world in order to pursue their spiritual practice as intensely as possible. They do this in the hope of awakening quickly and thereby being able to awaken others. If they succeed, these seekers become sages and the sages dedicate themselves to the welfare of all people and all life.

With their own questions answered, the confusion of the world begs to be cleared. With their own pain healed, the suffering of others tugs at their hearts. With their own egocentric motives cleansed, the desire to serve assumes prominence. The sages are now ready and motivated to return to society and contribute.

This two-step process of secluded practice followed by service is what historian Arnold Toynbee called "the cycle of withdrawal and return." In his study of world history, Toynbee observed that the cycle marked the lives of the people who had contributed most to civilization. He asked:

> Who are... the greatest benefactors of the living generation of mankind? I should say: Confucius and Lao Tsu, the Buddha, the prophets of Israel and Judah, Zoroaster, Jesus, Mohammed and Socrates.

In short, those people who had a profound spiritual realization then devoted their lives to service.

There are many metaphors for the cycle of withdrawal and return. One of the best known is the ascent and descent of a mountain. The seeker climbs a mountain and from that lofty site gains a new transcendent perspective on life and the world, which can be brought back and shared with others. In the West, the great exemplar is Moses, who supposedly climbed Mount Sinai, spoke with God, and brought back the Ten Commandments to the Israelites.

The great mythologist Joseph Campbell called this final phase of return and service "the hero's return." In Zen it is described as "entering the marketplace with help bestowing hands." In Christianity it is the culmination of "the spiritual marriage" with God and is known as "fruitfulness of the soul." Having united with God in ecstatic love, this spiritual marriage now bears fruit as the mystic reenters the world to heal and help. Evelyn Underhill, one of the great scholars of Christian mysticism, wrote that the sage:

> accepts the pains and duties in the place of the raptures of love; and becomes a source, a "parent" of fresh spiritual life.... This forms that rare and final stage in the evolution of the great mystics, in which they return to the world which they forsook; and there live, as it were, as centers of transcendental energy.... To go up alone into the mountain and come back as an ambassador to the world, has ever been the method of humanity's best friends.

Humanity's greatest and most effective friends do two things: they awaken, and they share their awakening with the world.

Service as Means

Service is not only an expression *of* awakening, but also a means *to* awakening. Few of us are likely to withdraw from the world for a prolonged period and to go through one great cycle of withdrawal and return. Most of us will go through many cycles, withdrawing for perhaps an hour each day, a day each week, and for some weeks each year. Such rhythms are built into many traditions—for example, the Sabbath in Judaism and Christianity—and provide multiple opportunities to withdraw and return.

There is certainly no need to wait for enlightenment before serving, although I initially made the mistake of thinking I should wait, at least before beginning to teach. Inspired by heroic tales of great sages who gave their all and were finally enlightened after long periods of intensive solitary practice, I postponed doing any spiritual teaching for many years.

Finally my wife brought me down to earth as only a spouse can do. Drawing attention to my many retreats and years of practice, she pointed out that at my current rate of progress I was likely to die long before I ever taught a word. Eventually I learned, as Abraham Maslow concluded from his study of psychologically healthy people:

> the best way to become a better helper is to become a better person. But one necessary aspect of becoming a better person is *via* helping other people. So one must and can do both simultaneously.

Difficulties Are Potential Contributions

Wonderful talents and profound spiritual insights are priceless gifts, but we don't need them to serve effectively. Even those things we regard as our failings and deficiencies can contribute if we are willing to acknowledge them openly and use them to help others. One of my favorite examples comes from Rachel Remen, who was asked to treat one of the angriest people she had ever met. The patient was a star college athlete whose life had been a dream: a winning record, enormous recognition, fast cars, and many women. Then he developed a pain in his right leg. He was diagnosed with cancer and just two weeks later his leg was amputated.

The surgery saved his life but ended his life as he knew it. He became depressed, very angry, and self-destructive. He dropped out of school, began abusing drugs and alcohol, alienated former friends, and barely managed to survive one car crash after another. His former coach referred him to Rachel.

Hoping to encourage him to show his feelings about himself, I gave him a drawing pad and asked him to draw a picture of his body. He drew a crude sketch of a vase, just an outline. Running through the center of it he drew a deep crack. He went over and over the crack with a black crayon, gritting his teeth and ripping the paper. He had tears in his eyes. They were tears of rage. It seemed to me that the drawing was a powerful statement of his pain and the finality of his loss. It was clear that this broken vase could never hold water, could never function as a vase again. It hurt to watch. After he left, I folded the picture up and saved it. It seemed too important to throw away.

As he worked with Rachel Remen, the young man began to heal. At first he had no interest in helping other patients and was filled with rage towards doctors and medical staff. However, over time he began to feel the first stirrings of concern for others suffering like himself. He began to visit young people on the surgical wards with problems like his own and was delighted to find that he could reach them in ways that others who had not suffered as he had could not. In time he began helping patients' families, and the surgeons began referring people to him. He was developing a kind of ministry, and as he did his anger faded.

In our final meeting, we were reviewing the way he had come, the sticking points and the turning points. I opened his chart and found the picture of the broken vase that he had drawn two years before. Unfolding it, I asked him if he remembered the drawing he had made of his body. He took it in his hands and looked at it for some time. "You know," he said, "it's really not finished." Surprised, I extended my basket of crayons toward him. Taking a yellow crayon, he began to draw lines radiating from the crack in the vase to the very edges of the paper. Thick yellow lines. I watched, puzzled. He was smiling. Finally he put his finger on the crack, looked at me, and said softly, "This is where the light comes through."

The light comes through whatever part of ourselves we use to help others. As Rumi said:

Your defects are the ways that glory gets manifested....
That's where the light enters you.

CHAPTER 32

DEVELOP A GENEROUS HEART

All that one gives to others one gives to oneself.
If this truth is understood, who will not give to others?
—*Ramana Maharshi*

THE PRINCIPLES FOR CULTIVATING GENEROSITY

The first six practices lay the groundwork for generosity. Here are the central principles for cultivating generosity directly.

Seek Inspiration from Others

A recurring theme throughout this book has been the powerful influence others have on us and how inspiring fellow practitioners can be. The Buddha went so far as to say:

> With regard to external factors, I do not envision any other single factor like friendship with admirable people in being so helpful.

The great Jewish sage Maimonides explained why admirable people are so helpful:

> Man is created in such a way that his character traits are influenced by his neighbors and friends, and he follows the customs of the people in his country. Therefore, a man needs to associate with the just and be with the wise continually, in order to learn [from] their actions.

Moods and motives are catchy. To encounter someone who exudes love and joyful generosity is an inspiration and a delight. The few hours I spent with Mother Teresa and the Dalai Lama continue to inspire me years later, while films of them have inspired people around the world. Such is the power of those who devote their lives to awakening and service.

We do not have to cross the earth in search of saints; if we look around us we find that the world is full of unsung heroes. You probably know some of them yourself: the people who quietly work extra hours at schools or hospitals, visit the sick, serve meals to the homeless, or staff volunteer organizations. Befriending and working with such people is an excellent way of gaining inspiration and making their qualities our own.

Find How You Would Like to Help

Here is a little-known secret about service: It's okay to have a good time. In fact, it's more than okay—it's a gift to everyone. It is a gift to yourself because service then is a pleasure rather than a chore. It is a gift to others because you not only share your time but also your happiness. After all, who wants to be assisted by someone who is grumpy and resentful about giving?

The first step is to get in touch with your feelings and find out how you would *like* to help. For this it is crucial to set aside any tyrannical thoughts about what you *should* do and any limiting beliefs about what you *cannot* do, and to simply recognize what you would *like* to do. Often what you would really like to do is also what makes best use of your unique talents. It may take time and perhaps experimenting with different types of service to find out what most appeals to you.

I discovered this for myself when I first awoke to the horrors of the global crises we are creating. Visiting Asia and working with Mother Teresa startled me into recognizing the terrifying extent of overpopulation, poverty, and starvation. Shortly afterward I saw the film, *The Last Epidemic*, about the catastrophic effects of nuclear war, and I was blasted out of my unconscious complacency. How could I, who fondly believed I was socially concerned, have been so asleep about the extent of the global problems we face?

How could I have been so asleep for so long about the urgency of our situation? Now that I knew, what could I do?

For months I learned as much as I could. I read, went to lectures, and talked with people. I also learned what people were doing to help, joined some of the many concerned organizations, and admired the many dedicated volunteers working in ways large and small to contribute solutions. Yet while I greatly respected all these contributions, I kept feeling there must be something unique and strategic I could add.

I puzzled over this for many months until finally it hit me. I could write about the psychological roots of our global problems: the psychological forces within us and between us that create our crises and that must be understood and healed if these crises are to be truly healed. I am a psychiatrist, and I find writing stimulating and satisfying. This would be a strategic contribution that would make use of my skills and which I would enjoy. The result was the book, *Staying Alive: The Psychology of Human Survival.*

All of us have a unique sacred service to do, and with time and persistence it becomes apparent. By finding our sacred service—the work that helps others but also nourishes ourselves—we follow the advice of a Jewish sage who emphasized how important it is "to begin with oneself but not to end with oneself."

The Right Motivation for Giving

The motivation with which we do anything is crucial. We may help one person and walk away feeling wonderful. We may help someone else and later seethe with resentment. If so, it's a safe bet that our actions were contaminated by inappropriate motives.

When we give with the hope of getting something back, because we are motivated by guilt, or because we are afraid to say no, we set ourselves up to suffer. Externally, it may look like generosity. But such giving feels very different and afterward can inflame regret and resentment. The underlying motives with which we give determine their emotional and spiritual effects.

It is so important to explore our motives for giving. If we find feelings of openheartedness and genuine caring, giving is a wonderful way to express and strengthen them. But if we find a contracted heart, tension, or annoyance, perhaps it might be better to first take time to explore and resolve these feelings. Often it is essential to say "yes" to a request and to give as generously as we can. At other times it may be completely appropriate to say "no, this does not feel right." Jack Kornfield points out:

> There is no formula for the practice of compassion. Like all of the great spiritual arts, it requires that we listen and attend, understand our motivation, and then ask ourselves what action can really be helpful.... Instead of holding the ideal that we should be able to give endlessly with compassion for all beings "except me," we find compassion for all beings including ourselves.

Start Small

Another key principle for developing a generous heart is to be willing to start in small ways. This strengthens generosity and helps us to give more wholeheartedly later on. The Buddha was very aware of this, and so when a rich but stingy man came to him he recommended a gentle program of gradually increasing giving. First the Buddha encouraged him to give small gifts to his family, next to friends, and finally to beggars and strangers. Then the Buddha urged him to gradually increase the size of his gifts. To the rich man's surprise, he found himself enjoying the gratitude he received and eventually even the act of giving itself.

It is fine to start small. We would all like to end world hunger and wars. It might make sense, however, to start by bringing a meal to a sick neighbor, working with a charitable group, or supporting an abandoned orphan in a war-torn country. Mother Teresa repeatedly urged:

> Don't look for spectacular actions.
> What is important is the gift of yourselves.
> It is the degree of love you insert in your deeds.

Compared to the magnitude of suffering in the world, our contributions may seem insignificant, but to the people who receive them, they may be life-saving.

THE YOGA OF AWAKENING SERVICE

When combined with the right motivation, service is transformed into awakening service, or what Hindus call *karma yoga*. Karma yoga has two aspects, both aimed at changing and purifying motivation.

Acting for a Higher Purpose

The first aspect is to do our service and work in the world, not for ourselves alone, but for a higher purpose. This purpose might be the good of one's family or the welfare of the world, but the traditional goal is to express and fulfill the divine will. The *Bhagavad Gita* declares:

> work is holy
> When the heart of the worker
> Is fixed on the Highest....
> Action rightly performed brings freedom.

Of course, this idea is not unique to Hinduism. St. Paul, for example, urged, "do everything for the glory of God."

Releasing Attachment

The second element of karma yoga is to release attachments to the results of our contributions. Usually, when we contribute something, we have definite ideas about the outcome we want and the recognition and rewards we deserve. This is a recipe for disaster. If things work out differently from what we expect, or if we are not lavished with praise, our attachments go unfulfilled and we suffer accordingly. This is one reason why Confucius recommended so strongly that we "put service before the reward you get for it."

How much we suffer depends on whether we are run by, or learn from, our attachments. On the one hand, if we mindlessly cling to our attachments we may boil with anger or slide into depression. On the other hand, we can recognize these emotions as a wakeup call. They are the screams of our frustrated ego, reminding us that we can stay attached and continue to suffer, or let go and come to peace.

One way to reduce attachment to recognition is to do good works quietly, without the fanfare and trumpet-blowing that would draw attention, swell our egos, and puff up pride. "So whenever you give alms," urged Jesus, "do not sound a trumpet before you, as the hypocrites do." In fact, both Jesus and Mohammad used almost identical words when they recommended, "When you give alms, do not let your left hand know what your right hand is doing, so that your alms may be done in secret."

Awakening service is a delicate balancing act. We work and contribute wholeheartedly, yet at the same time we try to relinquish attachment to our fixed ideas of how things should turn out and to our attachment to recognition. The *Bhagavad Gita* summarizes the challenge as follows:

> Do your duty, always; but without attachment.
> That is how [one] reaches the ultimate Truth;
> by working without anxiety about results.
> In fact... many others reached enlightenment
> simply because they did their duty in this spirit.

Learn from All That You Do

Adding a third component to awakening service makes it still more potent. By learning as much as we can from serving, we simultaneously grow in wisdom and effectiveness.

To do this means bringing a desire to learn and grow to all that we do. Each act of service and every result of that service becomes a source of learning. With this attitude each success or failure and each emotional reaction becomes a kind of feedback. If the project we are working on turns out well, we try to learn why. If we make a mistake, which of course we will, many times, we explore this also. Our mistakes can prove just as valuable as our triumphs, sometimes even more so. With this perspective there is no need for guilt or self-blame; these are merely sorry substitutes for learning. Sufis call one who has learned to accept and learn from any outcome a "contented self." A person at this advanced stage is a living example of Confucius's claim "The person of benevolence never worries."

These three elements—dedicating efforts to a higher goal, relinquishing attachments to specific outcomes, and learning from experience—are the keys to effective awakening service. By combining them, we create a spiritual technique of enormous power. Through awakening service we simultaneously purify motivation, weaken cravings, serve as best we can, and learn how to serve and awaken more effectively in the future.

One enormous advantage of awakening service is that it transforms daily activities into spiritual practices. With its help we need not change *what* we are doing so much as *how* and *why* we are doing it. Awakening service is a superb practice for those busily engaged with work and families. With this approach, work and family, far from being distractions from spiritual life, become central to spiritual life, and each project or family activity can be transformed into a sacred act.

A beautiful example comes from Sri Anandamaya Ma, a twentieth-century Indian saint who mastered multiple spiritual paths. Although she had only two years of schooling and referred to herself as "a little unlettered child," she spoke beautifully and profoundly and her students included renowned scholars, philosophers, and statesmen. She described her relationship with her family:

> This body has lived with father, mother, husband and all. This body has served the husband, so you may call it a wife. It has prepared dishes for all, so you may call it a cook. It has done all sorts of scrubbing and menial work, so you may call it a servant. But if you look at the thing from another standpoint you will realize that this body has served none but God. For when I served my father, mother, husband and others, I simply considered them as different manifestations of the Almighty and served them as such. When I sat down to prepare food I did so as if it were a ritual, for the food cooked was after all meant for God. Whatever I did, I did in a spirit of divine service. Hence I was not quite worldly though always engaged in household affairs. I had but one ideal. To serve all as God, to do everything for the sake of God.

As with all practices, awakening service initially requires effort. But over time the effort becomes spontaneous and service becomes joy. Gradually, awakening service extends to encompass our lives and each activity within its healing, awakening embrace. As it does so, we begin to recognize who we really are, and the words of an ancient Hindu saying ring increasingly true:

When I forget who I am I serve you.
Through serving I remember who I am
And know I am you.

CHAPTER 33

EXERCISES IN GENEROSITY AND SERVICE

Be kind to all.... The best people among you
are the ones who are benefactors to others.

—Mohammad

EXERCISE 1: TURN WORK INTO SERVICE

Remember the story of the people carving stones? One of them
was killing time, another building a cathedral and doing awakening service. It is an important tale because it makes clear that the
same action, the same job, can be done for utterly different reasons. Both these people were going through exactly the same
motions. The first probably went home grumpy, kicked the cat,
and dreaded getting out of bed the next morning to face another
day of drudgery. The other likely left work feeling happy, fed the
cat, and awoke the next morning looking forward to another day
of contribution.

Do you want to kill time or build a cathedral, to see what you
are doing as drudgery or contribution? The crucial point is that we
have a choice. The same actions can be seen in quite different ways
because it is we who decide on the meaning and significance of
what we do. Much of what we do each day is already service.
Whether it is cleaning, cooking, or accounting, a lot of it is for the
benefit of other people, whether they are clients, friends, or family.
Whether we do it as service or drudgery, however, is up to us.

Take a few minutes to think of your daily activities. Is there one you would like to do for a day in a spirit of service? It could be a complex technical task at work or something as simple as shopping.

Choose an activity. Then think of ways in which it helps people. Perhaps your work will allow others to get their work done more easily; perhaps the shopping will feed your family and friends. Concentrate on these benefits, then choose to see and do your task as a service to these people.

With practice, the rewards of helping become increasingly obvious. As they do, you may wish to see more and more activities from the perspective of service until it becomes a natural way of life.

EXERCISE 2: USE THE POWER OF DEDICATION

By changing our motives, we transform our actions and ourselves. We have already discussed a Tibetan Buddhist method for transforming motivation. Here you pause for a moment before each major activity, whether it be reading or cleaning. Then, instead of simply proceeding automatically with only your own well-being in mind, you dedicate the activity to your own awakening so that you can better help and awaken others.

At the end of the activity, you pause again. This time you offer whatever benefits you have gained from doing the activity to the benefit of all people and even to all life. It is as though you try to give away the benefits—whatever you learned, whatever qualities such as love or patience you acquired—to everyone else.

This may seem like a sacrifice—after all, why try to give away what you worked so hard to gain? When you recall the way the mind works, however, you realize that this is a skillful strategy that, paradoxically, benefits everyone, including yourself. Remember that what you want for others you experience and strengthen in your own mind. Give away qualities such as love or patience that you gained from helping or meditating, and they, together with generosity, flower more fully.

When you feel ready, experiment with beginning and ending some of your activities with dedications. One place to start is with your quiet time of reflection, meditation, or prayer. Here, in the sensitivity that sacred silence offers, you are most likely to remember to do the dedications and to be able to feel the benefits they bring.

As these benefits become apparent, you may wish to dedicate more activities—for example, work, play, cooking, and eating—in this way. This transforms these activities and also makes it clear that even the most humble of daily activities can serve the process of awakening.

EXERCISE 3: CHANGE PAIN INTO COMPASSION

The smog in Calcutta—home to Mother Teresa's center for the dying—is horrendous, and as I was leaving I noticed an unpleasant tickle in my throat. Sure enough, by the time I reached Benares, one of India's holiest cities and the place where many Hindus come to die, I had developed bronchitis. I lay in my hotel room for most of the day, thousands of miles from anyone I knew, feeling lonely, sick, and sorry for myself.

Late that night I came to a startling realization. I might be mildly ill, but at least I had medicine, food, and a comfortable bed. However, below my window, on the streets and in the gutters, lay literally thousands of homeless, penniless, sick, and dying people. Suddenly my own problems seemed very minor, and my heart went out to the suffering paupers below me. Compassion replaced self-pity.

Research shows that this kind of "downward comparison," comparing oneself with someone who is worse off, is an effective strategy for combating feelings of pain and depression. It can also be an effective means for cultivating compassion.

To do this exercise, think of some difficulty you are having; it could be physical, psychological, or spiritual. Next, think of people who are suffering even more from the same kind of difficulty or related ones. If you know specific individuals suffering in this way, bring them to mind. Think of all the suffering your difficulty has brought you. Then think of all the suffering these people must be experiencing. Allow yourself to feel their pain. Recognize that just as you want to be free of pain, so do they. Let compassion for them arise as you hope or pray that they become free of pain.

EXERCISE 4: PRACTICE ALL-EMBRACING KINDNESS

The essence of this exercise is very straightforward: Simply try to be as kind as you can to as many people as you can during a specific time. This period of time could be an hour, a morning, or a day. If you wish, you can extend your help to include creatures as well as people. Mother Teresa devoted practically every waking moment of her life to this exercise and summarized it by saying, "Let no one ever come to you without leaving better and happier."

Of course, the specific forms your kindness takes will depend on the situation. Many of your actions will probably be very simple, such as visiting a friend in need of comfort, smiling at a stranger, or helping a child who has fallen. In places such as a crowded room, you may only be able to smile at people. Actually, this is not a small gift. A group of poor people who had neither money nor food to spare asked Mohammad's son-in-law how they could help others. He advised them simply to smile and make others feel cared for.

The goal is to be as helpful as you can, no matter how small or insignificant your help may seem. Gandhi probably did as much good as anyone who lived in the twentieth century. Yet he observed from his direct experience, "Almost anything you do will seem insignificant, but it is very important that you do it."

EXERCISE 5: AWAKENING SERVICE

Awakening service, or karma yoga, involves three steps, each of them a potent force for awakening in its own right. We have already discussed these and need only summarize them briefly.

The first step is to begin by dedicating an activity to a purpose larger than your own satisfaction. For some, this larger purpose might be the welfare of their family; for others, helping the poor; for still others, it might be, as St. Paul recommended, "for the glory of God." The second step is to relinquish attachments to your ideas of how things ought to turn out. The third is to learn from the process.

For example, imagine you feel worn and tired from the day's work and long for a quiet evening with your family. By remembering to dedicate this time not just to your own well-being and awakening, but also to the welfare of your family, you can transform the evening into a time of awakening service. To make everything enjoyable for people, you buy some food, clean the house, and wait eagerly for everyone to come home.

They come home, all right. One immediately announces he is going to a movie, two others grab most of the food as they leave for a party, and another says she needs to visit a sick friend. There you are with a clean house, a few scraps of leftover food, and only the dog for company.

Now comes the big question: Do you simmer with anger about everyone's selfishness and mope around the house feeling sorry for yourself? Or do you recognize your attachments to how you think the evening should be, take a moment to laugh and release them, learn as much as you can from the situation and your reactions, and then settle down for a relaxing evening in a pleasantly quiet house? Do you suffer or enjoy, lament or learn? Awakening service offers a choice.

A simple way to begin this exercise is by choosing a contribution you are already making. It is helpful if this contribution is one you make regularly, so that you have multiple opportunities to learn from it. For example, perhaps you visit a sick neighbor daily or help at school each week. By dedicating this to a larger purpose, looking for and releasing attachments to a particular outcome, and learning from the whole process, you transform your contribution into awakening service.

EXERCISE 6: HELPER'S HIGH: GIVE ANONYMOUSLY

The great religious traditions speak of the deep satisfaction of giving, while psychologists speak of "helper's high." If we can ex-

perience this high for ourselves, we begin to learn how rewarding helping others can be.

Often the good feelings that flow from the act of giving itself
become mixed with feelings related to rewards such as being
praised or receiving a gift in return. It can be a valuable learning
experience to give an anonymous gift we know will not result in
praise or return gifts. Anonymous giving has long been praised
by the great religions. The Jewish Talmud describes how, in ancient times, generous people would come at night to leave food
at the doors of the needy.

A friend of mine had a delightful experience of "helper's high"
and a potent lesson in the power of anonymous giving when he
was on a spiritual retreat. The food at the retreat was rather
sparse and plain, so when he received a cake in the mail he was
ecstatic. However, after eating a piece he began to think of the
other people at the retreat, all of whom would enjoy a treat just as
much as he would. After a moment's hesitation, he went into the
kitchen and placed a piece of cake in each person's bowl. Then he
hid and watched the expressions of astonishment and delight as
each person filed into the kitchen and found not an empty bowl,
but an unexpected delicacy. This happened twenty years ago and
he says that he can't recall the taste of the cake he ate himself, but
he still remembers with delight the look on people's faces that
day. He has had twenty years of enjoyment from one cake.

Of course, parents practice anonymous giving regularly.
They fill Christmas stockings with presents from Santa Claus
and then enjoy their children's delight. Most of us do it sometimes—such as when we send money to charity—but it can be
useful to do it as an exercise.

Is there a gift you could give anonymously? If so, make it and
observe the feelings that arise. Then, if possible, observe the people enjoying your gift and the further feelings this evokes in you.

EXERCISE 7: TAKE TIME FOR AWAKENING SERVICE

The power of any practice can be amplified by committing a specific period to it. For this exercise, devote whatever time you se-

lect—perhaps an hour, a morning, or a day—to awakening service. This time and practice will be enriched by each of the following four steps:

1) Begin by dedicating the time and all that you do during it.
2) Then, wherever you are, whoever you are with, and whatever you are doing, look for ways to help.
3) Whatever you do, try to do it in a spirit of service.
4) Whenever you serve, try to do it as awakening service in which you learn from each activity while releasing attachments to the way things turn out.

Committing to a period of awakening service does not necessarily mean making drastic changes in your life. You don't have to quit your job and forget your family in order to work in the slums. Perhaps you will take a day off to serve. Or perhaps you'll go through your usual routine, using each meeting, phone call, and situation as an opportunity for helping.

On the surface, your day may seem routine. You may smile at more people or give more compliments. You might give up your place in line to a person in a hurry, give a donation to a beggar, or offer to help someone with a project, but externally not much may seem unusual.

But inside is a different story. Now you have a larger purpose for your day and all you do. Now each activity becomes a source of satisfaction, each meeting a spiritual encounter, each twinge of fear or anger a clue about a lurking attachment, and each experience a welcome opportunity for learning.

Of course, there will be times when you forget your purpose and slide back into the semiconscious habits that consume most of our days. That is to be expected. If we could do this practice of service—or any of the other practices—perfectly, we would be saints and sages. But since we are ordinary human beings, we simply try to practice what the saints and sages do, knowing we will often fail, but also knowing they once struggled and failed as we do now, and that each effort, each exercise, each dedication carries us one step closer to recognizing that our true nature is the same as theirs.

CHAPTER 34

THE HIGHER REACHES
OF GENEROSITY

I worship and serve God in the form of the poor, the sick, the
ignorant and the oppressed.
—*Vivekananda, nineteenth-century Hindu sage*

Years ago, a young man fell to the lowest point of his life. Tor-
mented by doubts and depression, he stood on a bridge and ago-
nized about whether to throw himself to his death. If he killed
himself, his pain would end. But if he lived, then what? What
would make life worth living? What could give his life sufficient
meaning and value to be worth facing his difficulties and despair?

In a flash, the answer came to him. He would devote his life
to the challenge of finding out just how much good one person
can do.

Some sixty years later, Buckminster Fuller, known to the
world as Bucky, died of natural causes. During those six decades
he had patented over two thousand inventions, written twenty-
five books, and achieved an international reputation as one of the
century's greatest inventors, designers and thinkers. The answer
to his question "How much good can one person do?" is, A lot.

Of course, Bucky was far from the first person to discover the
game of trying to contribute as much as possible. Wise people have
enjoyed it for thousands of years and recommend contributing and
awakening as the two greatest games any human being can play.
Nothing, they claim, offers such meaning and value to life.

Modern contemplatives agree and urge us to "Seek, above
all, for a game worth playing.... Having found the game, play it

with intensity—play as if your life and sanity depended on it. (They *do* depend on it.)" Awakening, contributing, and finding out how much good we can do are definitely games worth playing. The Bucky Fuller game is one all of us can play. We don't have to be geniuses like Bucky, and we certainly don't have to be saints. The Bucky Fuller game is really just a logical extension of previous exercises. Instead of dedicating an hour or a day to optimal service, however, we simply allow this goal to infuse more and more of our lives.

This doesn't necessarily mean helping harder, but it may mean helping smarter. An enjoyable challenge of the Bucky Fuller game is to look for ways in which our contributions can be most effective, our service most strategic and beneficial. As the old saying goes, "Give people a fish and you feed them for a day; teach them how to fish and you feed them for life."

Gandhi was a master of this game, and his simple but strategic actions changed the world. One beautiful example was his response to the British salt tax. The British had passed a law requiring all Indians to buy salt rather than taking the free and plentiful salt lying on every beach. When Indian leaders came to him for advice on how to respond, Gandhi replied that he did not yet know what should be done. He therefore went into solitude to ponder the matter.

After several days of silent reflection and prayer, an answer flashed into his mind. He announced that he would break the law by taking some ocean salt. Then he simply started walking across India to the ocean. Day after day he walked, while news of his journey spread like wildfire around the country and then around the world. Finally he reached the shore. There he bathed in the water, prayed, and then picked up a single handful of salt. Millions of people rushed to follow his example and the British salt laws collapsed.

Gandhi's strategy suggests the importance of taking time for quiet reflection before acting. When the mind comes to rest and awareness clears, we open ourselves to inspiration and can act more clearly and effectively. By combining contemplation and karma yoga, we go into ourselves to go more effectively out into the world, and we go out into the world in order to go more deeply into ourselves. Work in the world and work on ourselves then become alternating waves of one great flow of awakening and service that guide and fulfill our lives.

SERVICE AND SPIRITUAL VISION

As awakening and service continue, spiritual vision begins to awaken. As it does, we begin to recognize who we really are and who we are serving. We begin to recognize behind the masks of fearful faces, hungry bodies, and broken bones that we are actually serving Buddha, Christ, Elijah, and the children of God. Then we can understand and say with Mother Teresa:

> Actually we are touching Christ's body in the poor. In the poor it is the hungry Christ we are feeding, it is the naked Christ that we are clothing, it is the homeless Christ that we are giving shelter.

Those whose eyes of the soul are wide open no longer see a distinction between themselves and others. Now one Buddha cares for another Buddha, Christ shelters Christ, and one child of God feeds another. Generosity and service are now spontaneous and effortless responses, as natural as one hand helping another, for who would not want to help their Self? According to Ramakrishna, people at this stage:

> are constantly engaged, inwardly or outwardly, in the humble service of all creatures, whom they experience as transparent and beautiful vessels of the one Presence. In their holy company, the longing to know and merge with Truth arises and intensifies naturally.

To reach this realization may seem like a superhuman feat. Yet those who have reached it assure us that we are all capable of it and that the sacrifices involved are actually far less than the sacrifices involved in continuing to live unconsciously and selfishly. Gandhi said:

> I claim to be no more than an average person with less than average ability. I have not the shadow of a doubt that any man or woman can achieve what I have if they would make the same ef-

fort, cultivate the same hope and faith, and simply dedicate themselves to the truth.

A World in Need

As we open to the enormous amount of tragic yet unnecessary
suffering in the world, concern and compassion grow. We find
our circle of concern spontaneously extending—beyond our
family and friends, beyond our nation and particular religious
tradition—to eventually encompass all people and even all creatures. Einstein expressed this process as only a genius could:

> A human being is a part of the whole called by us universe, a part
> limited in time and space. He experiences himself, his thoughts
> and feelings as something separated from the rest, a kind of optical
> delusion of his consciousness. This delusion is a kind of prison for
> us, restricting us to our personal desires and to affection for a few
> persons nearest to us. Our task must be to free ourselves from this
> prison by widening our circle of compassion to embrace all living
> creatures and the whole of nature in its beauty.

So we look for ways, however small, to serve all living creatures and all of nature in its beauty. This can seem a daunting
process until we remember the words of the wise. Jewish wisdom
reminds us, "It is not for you to complete the work but it is up to
you to begin it."

We are not necessarily called to do world-shaking deeds, but
we are called to do what we can with as much wisdom, awareness, and love as we can. For it is increasingly clear that so much
of the pain of the world—whether it be from poverty, oppression, or pollution, from cruelty, addiction, or war—stems from a
lack of the very qualities that we are working to cultivate.

In Indian traditions, human consciousness is sometimes described as a vast ocean—an ocean muddied and darkened by the
fear, anger, greed, and ignorance that cloud our lives. Whatever
is dropped into this ocean creates waves that ripple out forever,
diminishing in size but never completely disappearing. Our task
is to drop into this ocean the most helpful gifts of wisdom,

awareness, and love that we can. Our little gifts will ripple out through the great ocean of human consciousness forever; they are boundless in their effects.

The Jewish tradition holds that each of us carries a spark of the Divine within us; Jesus called those who follow his example "the light of the world," while Basque shamans describe human beings as walking stars. As we do the seven practices, the sparks within us blaze and we become ever brighter stars. It becomes our priceless privilege to help shine away the darkness of pain and ignorance and to light each other's way, until the sea of human sorrow becomes a shoreless ocean of light.

CHAPTER 35

ENJOY YOUR SELF

AWAKENED HEART, AWAKENED MIND

Christ has no body now on earth but yours,
no hands but yours, no feet but yours,
Yours are the eyes through which is to look out
Christ's compassion to the world;
Yours are the feet with which he is to go about doing good;
Yours are the hands with which he is to bless men now.

—*St. Teresa of Avila*

The journey of awakening is the most remarkable adventure any human being can undertake. No other activity is ultimately so rewarding for ourselves or so helpful to others. Like any adventure, the more wholeheartedly we play, the more fulfilling it is. How, then, can we play the game of awakening fully and effectively?

In one sense, the answer is simple. It is, "Do the seven practices as fully as possible," for they constitute the very heart of spiritual practice and propel awakening. At this stage you already understand the seven practices and have begun to use them. The challenge now is to make them a regular and increasingly central part of your life.

Of course, the particular practice may vary from one month to another or even from one day to another. There is a rhythm to spiritual life, and each of us needs to use the gifts of growing sensitivity and clarity to realize the practice that is most appropriate at any given stage. At one time you may want to focus on emotions and relinquish anger, at another you may feel the need to study for greater understanding, later you may feel pulled to contribution and service. Ram Dass put it this way:

> There are stages at which you feel pulled into inner work and all you seek is a quiet place to meditate and get on with it, and then there are times when you turn outward and seek to be involved in the marketplace. Both of these parts of the cycle are a part of one's practice, for what happens to you in the marketplace helps in your meditation, and what happens in your meditation helps you to participate in the marketplace without attachment.... At first you will think of practice as a limited part of your life. In time you will realize that everything you do is part of your practice.

Even when everything becomes part of practice, it is still essential to set aside regular time free from the distractions and busyness of modern life. The important thing is to make practice a regular part of each day. Nothing takes the place of daily practice. Even deep insights and ecstatic states can fade into dim memories unless refreshed by the repeated inspiration regular practice brings.

Don't Delay: Start Today

Two thousand years ago a Jewish elder urged, "Do not say, 'When I have leisure, I will study!' Perhaps you will have no leisure." In our own time, an unknown poet with a sharp wit and keen insight into our ability to delay penned the following lines:

> Procrastination is a sin,
> it causes endless sorrow.
> I really must give it up,
> in fact I'll start tomorrow.

The solution? Start today, even if in a small way, and make practice a part of every day.

MAKE PRACTICE THE
FIRST PRIORITY OF THE DAY

Long ago I learned this the hard way: If I do not make practice the first priority of the day, it doesn't happen. Either I begin my practice first thing in the morning and block out some specific time later in the day, or else the day slips into history before I begin.

Now I have a regular routine. When I wake up, I shower, and then begin my practice immediately. At some time later in the day I tell people I will be unavailable for the next half-hour, hide in my room or office, lock the door, and turn off the phone. In this way I can create an oasis of quiet time in the middle of a busy day.

Of course, you may prefer a different routine, and it is important to find the schedule that works best for you. Many parents report that the secret of success for them is to get up before their children do and to use this time for quiet reflection, meditation, or spiritual reading. You need to have a routine of some kind with sacred time carefully set aside. Otherwise the world's distractions and demands will consume every open moment and leave you astounded to find that yet another day, month, year, or even decade has disappeared into oblivion with only a few scattered moments devoted to spiritual practice.

FIND SPIRITUAL FRIENDS
AND COMMUNITIES

One of the great tragedies is that so few people know it is possible to awaken, still fewer understand how to do it, and even fewer seriously attempt it. In most communities there is little support for the values and practices we are cultivating.

That is why it is so valuable to find friends who are on similar paths and who share the same values. Such friends are an enormous gift. They can offer inspiration and encouragement, share insights and discoveries, and during difficult times offer comfort and support. When people come together with a shared commitment to use their relationships to foster each other's learning, spiritual growth accelerates dramatically. The Buddha recommended:

> If the traveler can find
> A virtuous and wise companion
> Let him go with him joyfully
> And overcome the dangers of the way.
> But if you cannot find
> Friend or master to go with you....
> Travel on alone
> Rather than with a fool for company.

FIND A GUIDE

Spiritual friends are extremely valuable. But a friend who has practiced longer, traveled the path further, and understands it more deeply can be invaluable. Such a person, rich in wisdom and kindness, may become a guide or teacher. The Buddha said:

> Wise people tell you
> Where you have fallen
> And where you may yet fall.
> Invaluable secrets!
> Follow them, follow the way.

Of course, anyone can call him- or herself a teacher. It is wise to learn as much as possible about specific teachers before entrusting your practice, let alone your life, to them. Good teachers have done considerable practice themselves, and may have been certified to teach by their own instructors. They walk their talk, living and relating in ways consistent with their message. They treat everyone, including students, with kindness and respect. Their major concern is with awakening, rather than with ego traps such as fame or power. Good teachers openly acknowledge their mistakes and do not pretend to be perfect. This may be offputting to immature seekers looking for the perfect teacher. But there are no perfect teachers—there are only human beings who teach.

DON'T BE DISCOURAGED BY APPARENT SETBACKS

Here we are, trying to foster beautiful qualities such as love and compassion, when—*wham!* Suddenly everything seems to go wrong. Instead of love, the mind erupts with anger; instead of joy, painful memories swarm out of the unconscious like bats from a cave. It feels as though the practices are making things worse rather than better, that we are regressing instead of progressing.

Not to worry. This is a natural, normal, and valuable healing process. The practices work not only by cultivating positive qualities, but also by uncovering and bringing to healing awareness old, painful memories and emotions. This frees us from the prison of past pain and opens us to present possibilities.

There is rarely any need to fear these eruptions. There is certainly no need to judge them, or to punish yourself for having them. If they feel particularly strong or even overwhelming, by all means discuss them with a teacher, or with a psychotherapist who understands spiritual practice. If necessary, do less practice or a different kind of practice for a while. These difficulties will pass and in retrospect will probably seem challenging but valuable processes of healing and purification.

START AGAIN

Sooner or later it happens to everyone: We become overly busy, get caught up in a family emergency, or simply have an attack of laziness. The result: We stop practicing. The trap at this stage is to feel guilty and inadequate, to lament that we have failed and are forever doomed to fail again, so why even bother restarting?

From a spiritual perspective, "failure" is just another learning opportunity, and sometimes one of the most valuable. By exploring the factors—such as a harried schedule or beliefs like "I can't do this"—that caused us to stop, we can learn much about ourselves and our lives. Investigating a harried schedule may show that we feel guilty about saying no to requests; feelings such as inadequacy may reveal how we attack and underestimate ourselves. Once we recognize these traps we can gently laugh at and learn from them, and then, wiser and stronger, start the practice again.

PRACTICE FOR THE BENEFIT OF EVERYONE

The power of practice depends in part on why it is done. This is why practicing for the well-being and awakening of everyone, including ourselves, is more potent than practicing for ourselves alone. To focus solely on our own well-being is to separate ourselves from others and to starve beneficial qualities such as love and generosity.

To practice for the benefit of all people—even all creatures—is to expand our circle of care and to cultivate emotions such as love and kindness. Over time it becomes increasingly obvious that the happiness of others is our own and that to practice for the benefit of all is not a sacrifice but rather a delight. Our spiritual work not only helps us but is, according to Ramana Maharshi, "the best help you can possibly render to others." Our task is simply to do our practice as fully as we can. In this way we gradually learn to awaken ourselves, to love and serve life in all its infinite forms, to see the sacred in all things, and to care for our troubled world.

❈

Our world is in desperate need of healing. But it also rests in good hands, because it rests in yours. And in you rests the Source of all healing, and all that is needed to awaken you and the world.

SOURCE NOTES

Quotations marked with an asterisk* have been modified to remove sexist or archaic terms.

Chapter 1: Unveiling the Sacred
When you seek God...Yûnus Emre: In Vaughan-Lee, 1995, p. 20.
Our years come to an end...: Psalms 89, 90 in the *Bible, New Revised Standard Version* (NRSV).
  All quotes are from this version unless indicated otherwise.
All at once I found myself...: Richard Bucke, 1901/1969.
The kingdom of God is within you: Jesus, Luke 17:21(King James Version).
Those who know themselves know their Lord: Mohammad, in Perry, 1981, p. 855.*
He is in all, and all is in Him: Idel, 1988, p. 245.
Those who know completely their own nature...: Mencius, in Creel, 1953, p. 92.*
In the depths of the soul....: R. Wilhelm, in Baynes, 1967, p. 505.
Atman and Brahman are one: A frequent theme in the Hindu scriptures, the Upanishads.
Look within, you are the Buddha: Buddhist saying.
Not by reasoning...: Katha Upanishad 1.2.4.
the arguments of the wise...St. John of the Cross, in de Nicalis, 1989, pp. 135–137.

Chapter 2: Discovering the Seven Practices
By exhaustively examining one's own mind...: Mencius, in Creel, 1953, p. 210.
Even wise men...: Chuang Tzu, in Feng & English, 1974, p. 65.
A darkened glass,...: St. Paul, 1 Corinthians 13:12.
most excellent of all virtues...: Mohammad, in Syed, 1962, p. 51.

Chapter 3: Using This Book
The fragrance of blossoms soon passes...Loy Ching Yuen, in Harvey, 1996, p. 32.
the world was created...: Archbishop James Ussher, in Nerf & Navasky, 1984, p. 3.
man was created by the Trinity on...: Dr. John Lightfoot, in Nerf & Navasky, 1984, p. 3.
Start in a modest way...: Rabbi Yerachmiel, in Hoffman, 1985, p. 102.
However many holy words you read...: The Buddha, in Byrom, 1976, p. 7.

Chapter 4: Spiritual Practices: What Do They Do and How Do They Do It?
Little by little...: Rumi, in Barks, 1995, pp. 70–71.
metaphors of transformation: In R. Metzner, 1998.
a consensus trance: Tart, 1986.
a shared hypnosis: Harman, 1988.
a collective psychosis: Walsh, 1984.
A psychological study...: Milgram, 1974.
to die to one story...: Huston, 1982.
This is why it is so...: This summary of Aurobindo's ideas is by his biographer, Satprem, 1968,
  p. 35.

PRACTICE ONE: TRANSFORM YOUR MOTIVATION
All you want is to be happy....: Nisargadatta, 1973, vol 1.

Chapter 5: The Secret of Happiness
To a land where people cease from coveting...: Lao Tsu, in Bynner, 1944/1980, p. 48.
You use all your vital energy...: Chuang Tzu, in Feng & English, 1974, p. 108.
It is difficult for a person ....: Mohammad, in Syed, 1962, p. 58.*
For what is a man profited, if he shall gain...: Jesus, Matthew 16:26 (Bible, King James Version).
Strangely, however, there is...: Myers, 1992, p. 39.
Our becoming much better off...: Myers, 1992, p. 34.
The richest among you...: Mohammad, in Angha, 1995, pp. 21, 23.
You are deceived...: Longchenpa, 1975, p. 29.
As I took such small quantities...: The Buddha, in Narada, 1980, p. 25.
The rain could turn to gold...: The Buddha, in Byrom, 1976, pp. 70–71.
To be too fond of this world...: Joseph Kimichi of Narbonne, in Perry, 1981, p. 148.
No one can serve two masters....: Jesus, Matthew 6:24.
You shall not covet: Exodus 20:17.
The learning of the great person...: Wang Yang-ming, in Chan, 1963, p. 660.*
ever-rising desires...: Myers, 1992, p. 65.
What destroys craving?: Shankara, in Prabhavananda & Isherwood, 1945/1978, p. 134.
How is heaven attained?: Shankara, in Prabhavananda & Isherwood, 1945/1978, p. 134.
I have read many writings...: Meister Eckhart, in Colledge & McGinn, 1981, p. 285.
Renounce and rejoice!: Gandhi. This story was told by Ram Dass.
No one is happier...: Meister Eckhart, in M. Walshe, 1981, p. 128.

Chapter 6: Exercises to Reduce Craving
Free yourself from greed...: Mohammad, in Angha, 1995, p. 72.
Suffering is a call...: Nisargadatta, 1973, Vol. 1, p. 233.
Weak [attachments] can be removed by...: Nisargadatta, 1973, Vol. 1, p. 112.
We are what we think....: The Buddha, in Byrom, 1976, p. 3.

Chapter 7: Find Your Soul's Desire
Where your treasure is...: Jesus, Matthew 6:21.
When we are established...: Patanjali, 2:39, in Shearer, 1982, p. 82.
Our hearts are restless...: St. Augustine, in Feuerstein, 1989, p. 48.
The only real rest comes...: Rumi, in Barks, 1995, p. 75.
Theories of human nature...: Allport, 1964, p. 27–44.
As hunger and thirst arise...: Ramakrishna, in Hixon, 1992, pp. 223, 187, 78.
At fifteen, I set my heart upon learning: Confucius II:4, in Waley, 1938/1989, p. 88.
Strive first for the kingdom...: Jesus, Matthew 6:33.

Chapter 8: Exercises to Redirect Desires
Ecstasy assumes...: Aurobindo, 1922, p. 339.
Consider what you are doing...: Rabbi Nachman, in Hoffman, 1985, p. 99.
There are as many ways...: Mohammad, in Fadiman & Frager, 1997, p. 92.
Each and every human being...: Jewish wisdom.
fell at each other's feet...: Sultan Walad (Rumi's son), in Schimmel, 1987, p. 483.
Why should I seek...: Rumi, in Barks, 1995.
Everyone has been made for...: Rumi, in Perry, 1981, p. 336.

Chapter 9: The Higher Reaches of Desire
No drives, no compulsions...: Chuang Tzu in Merton, 1965, p. 101.*
There is pleasure...: The Buddha, in Byrom, 1976, p. 111.
All of humankind are children...: Rumi, Mathnawi, 1, 4329–30, in Helminski, 1998, p. 12.
effortless being: This is the title of a translation of Patanjali's Yoga Sutras by Shearer, 1989.
Not to act...: Clifford, 1988, p. 13.
Less and less do you need...: Lao Tsu, 38, 48, in Mitchell, 1992.

Most desires arise from...: Shearer, 1989, p. 23.
to experience Divine Bliss...: Ramakrishna, in Hixon, 1992, p. 65.

PRACTICE TWO: CULTIVATE EMOTIONAL WISDOM

Love all people...Confucius in Cleary, 1992, 1:7, p. 121.

Chapter 10: The Gift of Love
It is well known...: Maimonides, in Hoffman, 1985, p. 18.
the idea of love...: J. B. Long, 1987, p. 31.
love God with all your heart...: Deuteronomy 6:5.
love one another...: Jesus, John 15:12.
my kingdom is not of this world: Jesus, John 18:36 (King James Version).
Father, forgive them: Jesus, Luke 32:34.
and every living being is your neighbor: Gandhi, in Hirayana, 1973, p. 23.
As a mother watches over her child...: The Buddha, The Metta Sutra, in Kornfield and Frons-
    dal, 1993, p. 7.
If I speak in the tongues...: St. Paul, 1 Corinthians 13:1–8.
The sublime and ineffable state...: Ramakrishna, in Hixon, 1992, p. 152.
Everything from ruler...: Wang Yang-ming, in Chan, 1963, p. 661.

Chapter 11: The Challenge of Difficult Emotions
Never let the sun go down....: St. Paul, Ephiseans 4:26.
The goal is balance...: Goleman, 1995, p. 56.
In truth, the one thing...: Rabbi Nachman, in Buber, 1970, p. 37.
cognitive incapacitation...: Goleman, 1995, p. 62.

Chapter 12: Exercises to Reduce Fear and Anger
There are no chains like hate...: The Buddha, in Byrom, 1976, p. 97.
has emotions but no ensnarement: Wang Pi, in Yu-Lan, 1948, p. 238.
responds to things...: Wang Pi, in Yu-Lan, 1948, p. 238.
The superior person...: Ch'eng Yi, in Yu-Lan, 1948, p. 288.*
Hate never yet dispelled hate...: The Buddha, in Byrom, 1976, p. 4.
I found myself...: Greenspan, 1998, p. 39–40.
The greatest victor...: Lao Tsu, in Bynner, 1944/1980, pp. 68, 69, 70.
Who do you imagine to be...: Mohammad, in Syed, 1962, p. 62.*
Why do you see the speck...: Jesus, Matthew 7:3–5.
There was a certain elder who...: In Merton, 1960, p. 61.
For most people...: Kornfield, 1993, p. 205.
At the end of the way...: The Buddha, in Byrom, 1976, p. 70.
Only pursue an offender...: Lao Tsu, in Bynner (Trans.), Verse 62, 1944/1980, p. 34.
Malice will never drive out malice....: In Merton, 1960, p. 43.
Forgive those who wrong you....: Mohammad, in Syed, 1962, p. 91.*
What could you want....: Anonymous, 1992, Vol. 2, p. 213.

Chapter 13: Cultivate Love and Gratitude
Wherever you are...: Rumi, in Shah, 1971, p. 357.
When one reaches happiness...: Chuang Tzu, in Feng & English, 1974, p. 30.
Rejoice always: St. Paul, Thessalonians 5:16, 18.
As we recall the compassion....: Jewish Yom Kippur prayer on a Spirit Rock Meditation Center
    (Woodacre, California) card.
Fan Ch'ih asked about benevolence...: Confucius 12:22 in Lau, 1979, p. 116.
Do not look for bad company...: The Buddha, in Byrom, 1976, p. 30.
As you give so shall you receive: Anonymous.

Grant that I may not so much seek...: St. Francis of Assisi, in Perry, 1981, p. 608.
Put away all hindrances...: The Buddha, in Kornfield, 1993, p. 9.
Love your neighbor...: Leviticus 19:18, and A. Kaplan, 1985, p. 23.
Perfect love casts out fear: 1 John 4:18.

Chapter 14: The Higher Reaches of Love
The supreme purpose and goal....: Ramakrishna, in Hixon, 1992, p. 175.
God loves the world through us: Mother Teresa, in the film by J. Petrie, *Mother Teresa*, 1986.
A pencil in the hand...: Mother Teresa, in Grof, 1993, p. 225.
Dear Johnny. Thank you...: Mother Teresa. This story was told by Jan Petrie, producer of the superb film *Mother Teresa*.
You and I must come forward....: Mother Teresa, address to the United Nations, shown on a special broadcast edition of the film *Mother Teresa*, 1986.
the single most potent force...: J. B. Long, 1987, p. 31.
You shall love the Lord....: Deuteronomy 6:5
The tao that can be told....: Lao Tsu, in S. Mitchell, 1992, p. 1.
God is love: Ramana Maharishi, in Osborne, 1978, p. 165; Ramakrishni, in Hixon, 1992, p. 129; 1 John 4:16, NRSV.
the all-merciful, the all-compassionate: The Koran, 59: 22–23.
Both forms and proceeds...: Koller, 1985, p. 323.
There is no boundary....: Ramakrishna, in Hixon, 1992, p. 175.
Love is not different from the Self....: Ramana Maharishi, 1988, p. 165.
When the lover is annihilated...: Najm al-Din Kubra, in Vaughan-Lee, 1995, p. 201.
If we love one another...: 1 John 4:12.
become mad with love...: Ramakrishna, in Hixon, 1992, p. 296.
God is love...: 1 John 4:16.

PRACTICE THREE: LIVE ETHICALLY

Regard your neighbour's gain...: Tai Shang Kan Ying P'ien, in Penner, 1993, p. 43.

Chapter 15: The Value of Virtue
[A wise person] is good...: Lao Tsu, in Mitchell, 1992, p. 149.
Rare are those who understand virtue: Confucius, in Lau, XV:3, 1979, p. 132.
Do to others...: Luke 6:3.
That which is hurtful to you...: Steinberg, 1947, p. 12.*
A woman with heart disease...: Remen, 1996, pp. 75–76.
whatever you do, you do to yourself: The Buddha, in Byrom, 1976, p. 118.
It's hard to sit down...: Kornfield, 1995.
In the final analysis...: Smith, 1958, p. 185.
There are bound to be...: Confucius, in Lau, 1979, V:28, VII: 34.
Why did you not simply say...: Confucius, in Lau, 1979, VII: 19.
In the eating of coarse rice...: Confucius, in Lau, 1979, VII: 16.
How dare I claim to be a sage...: Confucius, in Lau, 1979, VII: 34.
At seventy, I could follow the dictates...: Confucius, 11:4, in Waley, 1938/1989.
It is morality that is supreme: Confucius, in Lau, XVII, 1979, pp. 147–8.
If...I had to take one phrase...: Confucius, II: 2, in Waley, 1938/1989.
Speak and act...: The Buddha, in Byrom, 1976, p. 3.

Chapter 16: What Is an Ethical Life?
We are visitors on this planet: The Dalai Lama, in Muller, 1996, p. 285.
In the beginning was the Word: John 1:1.
A group of Mark's classmates...: Sister H.P.M., The *San Francisco Chronicle*, 1997.

good words are worth much...: *San Francisco Chronicle*, 1997.
the gossips and double-tongued...: Ecclesiastes 28:13,18.
The truth will make you free: Jesus, John 8:32.
offend no one...: The Buddha, in Byrom, 1976, pp. 152, 158.*
When goodness is lost,...: Lao Tsu, in Mitchell, 1992, #38.*
Let anyone with ears to hear listen!: Jesus, Mark: 4:9.
I hate, I despise your festivals,...: Amos 5:21, 24.
What can a person do with the rites...: Confucius, 3:3 in Lau, 1979, p. 67.
all actions are judged by the motives...:Mohammad, in Syed, 1962, p. 57.
Harmlessness is a most...: Nisargadatta, 1973, Vol. 1, p. 198.
Not to mend one's ways...: Confucius, in Lau, 1979, XV:30, p. 136.
Alas for the man...: The Buddha, in Byrom, 1976, p. 152.
So when you are offering your gift...: Jesus, Matthew 5:23.
Trials are but lessons...: Anonymous, *Text*, Vol. 1, 1992, p. 620.

Chapter 17: Exercises in Ethical Living
Know that moral virtues...: Maimonides, in Hoffman, 1985, p. 71.
I can will what is right,...: St. Paul, Romans 7:18–19.
Do not belittle your virtues...: The Buddha, in Byrom, 1976, p. 46.*
Curb your tongue...: Lao Tsu, in Bynner, 1944/1980, p. 52.
Better than a thousand hollow words...: The Buddha, in Byrom, 1976, p. 41.
Be quick to do good....: The Buddha, in Byrom, 1976, p. 45.*

Chapter 18: The Higher Reaches of Ethical Living
Wish for others...: Mohammad, in Fadiman & Frager, 1997, p. 88.
Blessed are the pure in heart...: Matthew 5:8.
See yourself in others...: The Buddha, in Byrom, 1976, p. 49.
At first, precepts...: J. Kornfield, 1993, p. 298.

PRACTICE FOUR: CONCENTRATE AND CALM YOUR MIND

Control the mind....: Chuang Tzu, XXII:3, in Merton, 1965, p. 121.*

Chapter 19: Your Meandering Mind
May you develop mental concentration...: The Buddha, in Nyanatiloka, 1980, p. 37.
I was forced to recognize...: Walsh, 1977, p. 154.
man is not even master....: Freud, 1962, p. 252.
would be the education par excellence: William James, 1910/1950, p. 424.
Attention cannot be continuously sustained: William James, 1899/1962, p. 51.
Restless the mind is...: Prabhavananda & Isherwood, 1972, p. 85.
All scriptures without any exception...: Ramana Maharshi, 1955/1990.
Your wandering mind: Ramana Maharshi, 1988, p. 80.
More than those who hate you...: The Buddha, in Byrom, 1976, p. 75.
Religion is at best...: Dalai Lama, 1973.
We are all prisoners of our minds...: Ram Dass, 1979.
The bind is in the mind: Pier Villayet Khan, 1990, talk given at the International Transpersonal
    Association Conference.
Whatever is true, whatever is honorable,...: St. Paul, Phillippians 4:8.

Chapter 20: Develop a Peaceful Mind
Our essential nature...: Patanjali, in Shearer, 1989, p. 49. (1.4 and 1.3).
What is the most difficult task?: Shankara, in Prabhavananda & Isherwood, 1945/1978, p. 132.
Sometimes I want to die....: St. Teresa, in Bielecki, 1994, p. 34.
To know Tao meditate...: Loy Ching Yuen, in Harvey, 1996, p. 32.

Idleness is the enemy...: Rule of St. Benedict of Nursia, in Davis & Mesner, 1994, p. 259.
Meditation is the chief possession....: Muhasibi, in Vaughan-Lee, 1995, p. 83.
A person who does not meditate...: Rabbi Nachman, in Kaplan, 1982, p. 311.
The rush and pressure...: Thomas Merton, cited in a talk by Robert Lehman, 1998.
voluntary simplicity: This is a widely used term and is also the title of Duane Elgin's (1993) superb book on this topic.
Any natural act, if hallowed...: Buber, 1966, p. 20.
clumsy fellow who...: Lawrence, 1985, p. 61.
I renounced for [God's] love...: Lawrence, 1985, pp. 109–110.
The time of business does...: Lawrence, 1985, p. 8.
With regard to internal factors: The Buddha, in Thanissaro, 1996, p. 113.
To try and try again,...: Satprem, 1968, p. 34.
The breath that does not...: Kabir, in Vaughan-Lee, 1995, p. 63.
God's name cannot be heard...: Anonymous, 1992, Vol. 2, p. 334 (Lesson 183).
every revealed Name...: Ramakrishna, in Hixon, 1992, p. 41.
Repeat God's name...: Anonymous, 1992, Vol. 2, p. 334 (Lesson 183).
the presence of God: Keating, 1994.

Chapter 21: The Higher Reaches of Concentration and Calm
When, through the practice...: *Bhagavad Gita*, in Prabhavananda & Isherwood, 1972, p. 66.
the peace of God...: St. Paul, Philippians 4:7.
Let us bring our minds to rest...: LeMee, 1975, p. 4 (III.62.10)
Yoga is the stilling of the mind...: Shearer, 1:2, 1989, p. 49.
those who have gained tranquility...: *Bhagavad Gita*, in Prabhavananda & Isherwood, 1972, p. 45.
Be still and know...: Jewish Torah.
path leading to heaven...: Palmer et al., 1993, p. 109.
Be constant in prayer...: Cleary, 1993, p. 9.
pray without ceasing: St. Paul 1 Thessalonians 5:17.
What is necessary...: Ramakrishna, in Hixon, 1992, p. 116.
the whole act of living...: Aurobindo, 1922, p. 283.
suffused with the awareness...: Steinberg, 1947, p. 136.
I set out again,...: In Savin, 1991, pp. 35–36.
When water is still...: Chuang Tzu, in Giles, 1926/1969.

PRACTICE FIVE: AWAKEN YOUR SPIRITUAL VISION

Wherever you turn,...: Koran 2:115, in Cleary, 1993, p. 12.

Chapter 22: The Healing Power of Awareness
The true person sees...: Chuang Tsu, in Merton, 1965, p. 149.*
mindlessness occurs in...: Langer, 1982, pp. 60–71.
What can we gain...: Merton, 1960, p. 11.
A great deal of the distress...: James Bugental, 1978, pp. 124–125.
Close observation discloses...: Schumacher, 1977, pp. 29–30.
a veil lies over their minds: St. Paul, 2 Corinthians 3:15.
narrow chinks in his cavern: Blake, 1966.*
consensus trance: Tart, 1986, p. 85.
Be always mindful...: Abd'l-Khaliq Ghijdewani, in Vaughn-Lee, 1995, p. 104.
The best act of worship...: Abu Bakr Muhammad al-Wasiti, in Vaughan-Lee, 1995, p. 85.*
From this [meditation] are born...: Patanjali, 3:35–36, in Shearer, 1989, p. 103.
experience of the finer...: Patanjali, 1:35, in Shearer, 1989, p. 64.
O seeker, know that...: Sheikh Badrutdin, in Fadiman & Frager, 1997, p. 198.
We know the outer world...: Nisargadatta, 1973.*

This is the path to enlightenment: The Buddha, in Nanamoli, 1978, pp. 27, 29.
guarding the mind: Savin, 1991, p. 52.
Therapeutic progress depends…: Whitmont, 1969, p. 293.
Awareness—by and of itself—can be curative: Fritz Perls, 1969, p. 16.
Fully functioning people…: Carl Rogers, in Raskin & Rogers, 1995, p. 141.

Chapter 23: Exercises in Awareness
Mindfulness…is helpful everywhere: The Buddha, in Nyanaponika, 1962, p. 150.
Amongst people there are none…: Tsu-ssu, in Yu-Lan, 1948, p. 175. (Whether Tsu-ssu was actually the author is a matter of debate.)
Even the most mundane act…: Kaplan, 1985, pp. 143–44.
Get me a musician: 2 Kings 3:15.
a vehicle of experience…: Shankara, in Prabhavananda & Isherwood, 1972, p. 45.
method of internal observation: Wong, 1997, p. 199.
We are what we think…: The Buddha, in Byrom, 1976, pp. 3, 13.
It had been eight years…: Lloyd Burton.
to try and try again…: In Satprem, 1968, p. 34.
Let us run with perseverance…: Hebrews 12:1.

Chapter 24: Seeing the Sacred in All Things
Where there is no vision…: Proverbs 29:18.
The present fashion of applying…: Einstein, in Wilber, 1984, p. 5.
[The] mental and spiritual nature…: Eddington, in Wilber, 1984, p. 18.
a new manner of seeing…: Plotinus I, VI, 8.
and beheld with the eye of my soul…: St. Augustine, in Perry, 1981, p. 818.
It is with the interior eye…: St. Augustine, in Perry, 1981, p. 819.
Our whole business…: St. Augustine, in Perry, 1981, p. 819.
There is an eye of the soul…: Plato, *Republic* VII, 527E, in Perry, 1981, p. 816.
A sensible person…: Lao Tsu, in Bynner, 1955/1980, p. 31.
the Lord is in this place…: Genesis 2:16.
the kingdom of the Father…: Jesus, in the Gospel of Thomas, in Robinson, 1981, p. 130.
The sun was just coming up…: in Hoffman, 1992, pp. 31–33.
Those who are open-eyed…: Lao Tsu, 16, in Bynner, 1944/1980, p. 34.
Then it was if I suddenly saw…: Thomas Merton, in Kornfield, 1993, p. 311.

Chapter 25: Exercises in Sacred Seeing
You live in illusions…: Kalu Rinpoche, in a talk given by Joseph Goldstein at the Insight Meditation Society, Barre, MA, 1981.
A certain Philosopher asked St. Anthony…: In Merton, 1960, p. 62.
the radiance of the Tao within: Wong, 1997, p. 200.
If we are to be free…: Buddhist proverb.
When walking in the company…: Confucius, in Lau, VII: 22, 1979, p. 88.

Chapter 26: The Higher Reaches of Vision
Show me where the Tao is…: Merton, 1965, p. 123.
Every time you draw water…: The Buddha, in Surya Das, 1997, p. 302.
There was a time when…: Wordsworth, 1952, pp. 321–322.
The things which I have seen…: Wordsworth, 1952, p. 322.
One who satisfies these…: Maimonides, in Hoffman, 1985, p. 18.
Hear my words…: Numbers 12:6.
Then prayer never stops…: St. Isaac the Syrian, in Harvey, 1998, p. 63.
A person must control…: Ibn Arabi, in Shah, 1971, pp. 159–160.
witness: Mason et al., 1997, p. 103.

the mind begins to experience...: Patanjali, in Shearer, 1989, 4:26.
It is even possible...: Aurobindo, in Walsh & Vaughan, 1993, p. 84.
ever-present wakefulness: Plotinus, in Wilber, 1995.
cosmic consciousness: In Alexander & Langer, 1990.
This constant consciousness...: In Wilber, 1999, p. 55.

PRACTICE SIX: CULTIVATE SPIRITUAL INTELLIGENCE

Happy are those who find wisdom...: Proverbs 3:13, 17, 4:5.

Chapter 27: What Is Wisdom?
Knowledge studies others,...: Lao Tsu, in Bynner, 1944/1980, p. 46.
those to whom wisdom is given...: Koran II.269.*
He who is learned is not wise: In Perry, 1981, p. 739.
One momentary glimpse of Divine Wisdom...: Gampopa, 1958/1971, p. 65.
The graces that we receive...: Gregory of Nyssa, in Harvey, 1998, p. 46.
spiritual materialism: Trungpa, 1973.
Psychic abilities: For a review of scientific research see Broughton, 1991, and Radin, 1997.
If one plumbs, investigates into...: Lu Shiang-shan, in Creel, 1953, p. 213.
investigate things...: Wang Yang-ming, in Creel, 1953, p. 214.
complies perfectly with all the principles...: Rudolph, 1987, p. 401.
Not even the highest...: Kohlberg, in Alexander and Langer, 1990, p. 206.
transcended personal agendas and...: Staudinger & Baltes, 1994, p. 1147.

Chapter 28: Awakening Wisdom
Wisdom is radiant...: Wisdom of Solomon 6:12–13, 15, 17, 24.
Wisdom will not enter a...: Wisdom of Solomon 1:4.
The fool who thinks he is wise...: The Buddha, in Byrom, 1976, p. 25.
We are born in mystery...: Smith, 1991, p. 389.
From wonder into wonder...: Lao Tsu, in Bynner, 1944/1980, p. 25.
Let us be still an instant...: Anonymous, 1992, Vol. 1, 12:1–3; Vol. 2 (Lesson 189), 7:1–5.
The world is too much...: Wordsworth, 1952.
What I know of the divine sciences...: St. Bernard, in Brown, 1987, p. 31.
It is in the silence of the heart...: Mother Teresa, cited in Time, Sept. 15, 1997, p. 83.
The power of solitude...: Rasmussen, 1929, p. 114.
but diversion and distraction...: The Koran, in Cleary, 1993, p. 126.
For is not silence...: Black Elk, in Brown, 1987, p. 78.
Silence is the language God speaks: Fr. Thomas Keating, 1994, p. 44.
In stillness [the mind] becomes clear: Wong, 1997, p. 200.
The more you talk and think about it...: Sengstan, ND.
hastens to make herself known...: Wisdom of Solomon, 6:13.
He who will drink from my mouth...: Jesus, the Gospel of Thomas, in Robinson, 1981, p. 108.
The most effective discipline...: Ramakrishna, in Hixon, 1992, p. 170.
Let your house be...: Hoffman, 1985, p. 92.
If you are awake in the presence...: The Buddha, in Byrom, 1976, pp. 26, 29.
To make friends with the straight...: Confucius, 16:4, in Lau, 1979, p. 139.
What brings happiness?...: Shankara, in Prabhavananda & Isherwood, 1945/1978, p. 137.
Find friends who love the truth: The Buddha, in Byrom, 1976, p. 31.
Self-knowledge is the shortest road...: Aziz ibn Muhammad al Nasaji, in Perry, 1981, p. 859.
I must first know myself...: Plato, Phaedrus, 299E, in Perry, 1981, p. 859.
What am I to do...: Aziz ibn Muhammad al Nasafi, in Perry, 1981, p. 855.
Let me know myself...: St. Augustine, in Perry, 1981, p. 860.
Those who know themselves...: Mohammad, in Perry, 1981, p. 855.

My way is so simple...: Lao Tsu, 70, in Bynner, 1944/1980, p. 70.
We are slaves to what we do not know...: Nisargadatta, 1973, p. 15.
The wise man learns...: The Kobriner Rebbe, Rabbi Nachman, in Hoffman, 1985, p. 94.
You will be able to use every experience...: Rabbi Nachman, in Hoffman, 1985, p. 94.
Condemnation does not liberate...: Jung, 1958, p. 339.

Chapter 29: Exercises in Wisdom

Nothing indeed in this world... *The Bhagavad Gita*, in Prabhavananda & Isherwood, 1972.
Wisdom...depends on the opportunity of leisure...: Ecclesiasticus 38:24.
soon gone...they come to an end like a sigh...: Psalm 90.
What roll quickly away, like drops...: Shankara, in Prabhavananda & Isherwood, 1945/1978, p. 136.*
I recommend almost dying...: Carl Sagan, personal communication from Jack Kornfield.
If a way to the Better there be...: Thomas Hardy, 1926, p. 154.
The perception of the suffering...: Needleman, 1980, p. 217.
Wherever we go...: The Buddha, in Surya Das, 1997, p. 129.
We tend to read the Scriptures...: Keating, 1994, p. 47.
Make sure to set aside...: Rabbi Nachman, in Hoffman, 1985, p. 74.
If, on examining himself...: Confucius, 4:17, in Lau, 1979, p. 74.
the greatest of all cosmic wonders...: Jung, 1958, p. 357.

Chapter 30: The Higher Reaches of Wisdom

Those who know others are wise...: Lao Tsu, *Tao Te Ching* 33, in Perry, 1981, p. 159.*
The knower of the Atman...: Shankara, in Prabhavananda & Isherwood, 1945/1978, p. 122.
a man is free from worldliness...: Shankara, in Prabhavananda & Isherwood, 1945/1978.
Do not store up for yourselves...: Jesus, Matthew 6:19.
All things become nothing...: Meister Eckhart, in Wilber, 1995.
Who would have thought...: Hui Neng, sixth Zen patriarch, in Price & Mou-Lam, 1969, p. 19.
The eyes of my soul...: Angela of Foligno, in Harvey, 1998, p. 88.
I have never seen anything...: Mohammad, in Schuon, 1975, p. 89.
In the market, in the cloister...: Sufi Baba Kuhi, in Vaughan-Lee, 1995, p. 173.
This divinity of all...: Ramakrishna, in Hixon, 1992, p. 180.
You imagine that you see me...: Nizami, in Vaughan-Lee, 1995, p. 192.
By Himself He sees...: Ibn Arabi, in Vaughan-Lee, 1995, p. 179.
Here, in my own soul...: Meister Eckhart, in Harvey, 1998, p. 92.
I am neither this object...: Shankara, in Prabhavananda & Isherwood, 1978, p. 115.
The ten thousand things...: Chuang Tzu, in Feng & English, 1974, p. 35.
The Father and I are one: Jesus, John 10:30.
I am the truth: al-Hallaj, in Vaughan-Lee, 1995, p. 204.
pre/trans fallacy: Wilber, 1996, p. 198.

PRACTICE SEVEN: EXPRESS SPIRIT IN ACTION

Where there is hate...: The prayer of St. Francis, taken from a greeting card. A slightly different
    translation is in Perry, 1981.

Chapter 31: The Spirit of Service

If I am not for myself...: Hillel, in Hoffman, 1985, p. xiv.
Make it your guiding principle...: Confucius 1:8 in Lau, 1979, p. 60.
What actions are most excellent?...: Mohammad, in Syed, 1962, p. 51.
Give to everyone who begs...: Matthew 5:42.
Rabbi Salanter asked...: Hoffman, 1985, p. 34.
Whether it is generosity...: Kornfield, 1993, p. 217.

The thing I notice...: in Myers, 1992, p. 194.
Who are...the greatest benefactors...: Arnold Toynbee, 1948, p. 156.
accepts the pains and duties...: Evelyn Underhill, 1974.
the best way...: Maslow, 1970, p. xii.
Hoping to encourage him...: Remen, 1996, pp. 114–118.
Your defects are the ways...: Rumi, in Barks, 1995, pp. 141–142.

Chapter 32: Develop a Generous Heart
All that one gives...: Ramana Maharshi, 1988, p. 8.
With regard to external...: The Buddha, Itiruttaka Sutra, in Thannisaro Bikkhu, 1996, p. 113.
Man is created in such a way...: Maimonides, in Hoffman, 1985, p. 70.
There is no formula...: Kornfield, 1993, p. 224.
Don't look for spectacular actions...: Mother Teresa, cited in Serrou, 1980, p. 77.
work is holy...: *Bhagavad Gita*, in Prabhavananda & Isherwood, 1972, p. 47.
do everything for the glory of God: St. Paul, 1 Corinthians 10:31.
put service before the reward...: Confucius, 12:21, in Lau, 1979, p. 116.
So whenever you give alms...: Jesus, Matthew 16:3–4; Mohammad, in Syed, 1962, p. 56.
Do your duty always...: Prabhavananda & Isherwood, 1972, pp. 46–47.
The person of benevolence...: Confucius, in Lau, 1979, 9:29, p. 100.
This body has lived...: Sri Anandamaya Ma, in Atmananda, 1988.

Chapter 33: Exercises in Generosity and Service
Be kind to all...: Mohammad, in Angha, 1995.
Let no one ever come...: Mother Teresa, in Serrou, 1980, p. 76.
for the glory of God: St. Paul. 1 Corinthians 10:31.

Chapter 34: The Higher Reaches of Generosity
I worship and serve God...: Vivekananda, in Hixon, 1978, p. 189.
Seek above all...: DeRopp, 1968, p. 11.
Actually we are touching...: Mother Teresa, in Serrou, 1980, p. 77.
are constantly engaged...: Ramakrishna, in Hixon, 1992, p. 292.
I claim to be no more...: Gandhi, personal communication from J. Kornfield
A human being is part...: Einstein, in Goldstein, 1983, p. 126.

Chapter 35: Enjoy Your Self
Christ has no body now...: St. Teresa of Avila, in Harvey, 1998, p. 183.
There are stages...: Ram Dass, in Kornfield, 1993, p. 172–73.
Do not say, when I have leisure...: Hillel, in Hoffman, 1985, p. 101.
If a traveler can find...: The Buddha, in Byrom, 1976, p. 123.
Wise people tell you...: The Buddha, in Byrom, 1976, p. 31.
the best help you can...: Ramana Maharshi, p. 63.

FURTHER READING

The following books combine profundity with simplicity and accessibility. Additional texts can be found in the bibliography.

OVERVIEWS OF THE WORLD'S RELIGIOUS AND SPIRITUAL TRADITIONS

Smith, Huston. (1991). *The World's Religions.* New York: Harper & Row.
Hixon, Lex. (1978) *Coming Home: The Experience of Enlightenment in Sacred Traditions.* New York: Doubleday/Anchor.
Novak, Philip. (Ed.). (1996). *The World's Wisdom: Sacred Texts of the World's Religions.* San Francisco: HarperSanFrancisco.
Harvey, Andrew. (Ed.). (1996). *The Essential Mystics: Selections from the World's Great Wisdom Traditions.* San Francisco: HarperSanFrancisco.

BUDDHISM

Byrom, Thomas. (Trans.). (1976). *The Dhammapada: The Sayings of the Buddha.* New York: Vintage.

CHRISTIANITY

Harvey, Andrew. (Ed.). (1998). *Teachings of the Christian Mystics.* Boston: Shambhala.

CONFUCIANISM

Waley, Arthur. (Trans.). (1989). *The Analects of Confucius.* New York: Vintage.

HINDUISM

Prabhavananda & Isherwood, Christopher (Trans.). (1972). *The Song of God: Bhagavad Gita.* New York: New American Library.

ISLAM

Fadiman, James, & Frager, Robert. (Eds.). (1997). *Essential Sufism.* New York: HarperCollins.

JUDAISM

Besserman, Perle. (Ed.). (1984). *The Way of the Jewish Mystics.* Boston: Shambhala.

TAOISM

Lao Tsu. (1980). *The Way of Life.* (W. Bynner, Trans.). New York: Perigee.

BIBLIOGRAPHY

Alexander, Charles, & Langer, Ellen. (Eds.). (1990). *Higher Stages of Human Development*. New York: Oxford University Press.

Allport, G. (1964). The fruits of eclecticism: Bitter or sweet? *Acta Psychologica, 23,* 27–44.

Angha, N. (Ed.). (1995). *Deliverance: Words from the Prophet Mohammad*. San Rafael, CA: International Association of Sufism.

Anonymous. (1992). *A Course in Miracles, 2nd ed.* Tiburon, CA: Foundation for Inner Peace.

Atmananda. (1988). *Matri Darshan*. Westerkappeln, Germany: Mangalam-Verlag S. Schang.

Aurobindo, Sri. (1922). *Essays on the Gita*. Pondicherry, India: Sri Aurobindo Ashram Trust.

Aurobindo, Sri. (1970). *The Life Divine, 5th ed.* Pondicherry, India: Sri Aurobindo Ashram Trust.

Barks, Coleman. (Trans.) (1995). *The Essential Rumi*. New York: HarperCollins.

Baynes, Cary. (1967). *I Ching: The Chinese Book of Changes* (Richard Wilhelm, Trans.). Princeton, NJ: Princeton University Press.

Bible, New Revised Standard Version. (1991). New York: Oxford University Press.

Bielecki, Teresa. (1994). *Teresa of Avila*. New York: Crossroads.

Blake, William. (1966). The marriage of heaven and hell. In G. Keynes (Ed.), *Blake: Complete Writings*. London: Oxford University Press.

Broughton, Richard. (1991). *Parapsychology: The Controversial Science*. New York: Ballantine.

Brown, Joseph. (1987). *The Spiritual Legacy of the American Indian*. New York: Crossroad.

Buber, Martin. (1966). *The Way of Man*. Secaucus, NJ: Citadel Press.

Buber, Martin. (1970). *The Tales of Rabbi Nachman*. New York: Avon.

Bucke, Richard. (1969). *Cosmic Consciousness*. New York: Dutton. (Original work published 1901).

Bugental, James. (1978). *Psychotherapy and Process*. Reading, MA.: Addison-Wesley.

Bynner, Witter. (Trans.). (1980). *The Way of Life According to Lao Tzu*. New York: Putnam. (Original work published 1944).

Byron, Thomas. (Trans.). (1976). *The Dhammapada: The Sayings of the Buddha*. New York: Vintage.

Cerf, C., & Navasky, V. (1984). *The Experts Speak: The Definitive Compendium of Authoritative Misinformation*. New York: Pantheon Books.

Chan, Wing-Tsit (Trans.) (1963). *A Source Book in Chinese philosophy*. Princeton, NJ: Princeton University Press.

Cleary, Thomas. (Trans.). (1992). *The Essential Confucius*. New York: HarperCollins.

Cleary, Thomas. (Trans.). (1993). *The Essential Koran*. New York: HarperCollins.

Clements, Alan, & Kean, Leslie. (1994). *Burma's Revolution of the Spirit*. New York: Aperture.

Clifford, T. (Ed.). (1988). *The Lamps of Liberation: A Collection of Prayers, Advice and Aspiration*. New York: Yeshe Melong.

Colledge, Edmund, & McGinn, Bernard. (Trans.). (1981). *Meister Eckhart: The Essential Sermons, Commentaries, Treatises and Defense*. New York: Paulist Press.

Creel, Herrlee. (1953). *Chinese Thought from Confucius to Mao Tse-tung*. Chicago: University of Chicago Press.

Dalai Lama. (1973). *Universal Responsibility and the Good Heart*. Dharmsala, India. Library of Tibetan Works and Archives.

Dalai Lama. (1983). Talk given at the International Transpersonal Association, Davos, Switzerland.

Davis, Rebecca, & Mesner, Susan, (Eds.). (1994). *The Treasury of Religious and Spiritual Quotations*. Pleasantville, NY: Reader's Digest.

De Nicalis, A. (Ed.). (1989). *St. John of the Cross: Alchemist of the Soul*. New York: Paragon House.

DeRopp, Robert. (1968). *The Master Game*. New York: Delacorte.

Elgin, Duane. (1993). *Voluntary Simplicity* (2nd ed.). New York: Quill/William Morrow.

Evans-Wentz, W. (Trans.). (1958). *Tibetan Yoga and Secret Doctrines* (2nd ed.). Oxford: Oxford University Press.

Fadiman, James, & Frager, Robert. (Eds.). (1997). *Essential Sufism*. New York: HarperCollins.

Feng, Gia-Fu, & English, Jane. (Trans.). (1974). *Chuang Tzu: Inner Chapters*. New York: Vintage.

Feuerstein, Georg. (1989). *Yoga: The Technology of Ecstasy*. New York: Tarcher/Putnam.

Feuerstein, Georg. (1990). *Encyclopedic Dictionary of Yoga*. New York: Paragon.

Feuerstein, Georg. (1991). *Holy Madness*. New York: Paragon Press.

Freud, Sigmund. (1962). *Civilization and its Discontents*. New York: Norton.

Gampopa. (1971). *The Jewel Ornament of Liberation* (H. Guenther, Trans.). Boston: Shambhala. (Original work published 1958).

Giles, H. (Trans.). (1969). *Chuang-tzu, Mystic, Moralist, and Social Reformer* (2nd ed., rev.). Taipei: Ch'eng Wen. (Original work published 1926).

Goldstein, Joseph. (1983). *The Experience of Insight*. Boston: Shambhala.

Goleman, Daniel. (1995). *Emotional Intelligence*. New York: Bantam.

Greenspan, Miriam. (1998). Befriending the dark emotions. *Common Boundary* May/June, 34–43.

Grof, Christina. (1993). *The Thirst for Wholeness*. San Francisco: HarperSanFrancisco.

Hardy, Thomas. (1926). *Collected Poems of Thomas Hardy*. New York: Macmillan.

Harman, Willis. (1988). *Global Mind Change: The Promise of the Last Years of the Twentieth Century*. Indianapolis: Knowledge Systems.

Harman, Willis, & deQuincy, Christian. (Eds.). (1994). *The Scientific Exploration of Consciousness*. Sausalito, CA: Institute of Noetic Sciences.

Harvey, Andrew. (Ed.) (1996). *The Essential Mystics*. San Francisco: HarperSanFrancisco.

Harvey, Andrew. (Ed.) (1998). *Teachings of the Christian Mystics*. Boston: Shambhala.

Helminski, Kabir. (1998). I will make myself mad. *Parabola, 23* (2), 9–14.

Hirayana, M. (1973). *Outline of Indian Philosophy*. Bombay: George Allen & Unwin.

Hixon, L. (1978). *Coming Home: The Experience of Enlightenment in Sacred Traditions*. New York: Anchor/Doubleday.

Hixon, Lex. (1992). *Great Swan: Meetings with Ramakrishna*. Boston: Shambhala.

Hoffman, Edward. (1981). *The Way of Splendor*. Boston: Shambhala.

Hoffman, Edward. (1985). *The Heavenly Ladder: A Jewish Guide to Inner Growth*. San Francisco: Harper & Row.

Hoffman, Edward. (1992). *Visions of Innocence: Spiritual and Inspirational Experiences of Childhood*. Boston: Shambhala.

Huston, Jean. (1982). *The Search for the Beloved: Journeys in Sacred Psychology*. Los Angeles: Tarcher.

Idel, Moshe. (1988). *Kabbalah: New Perspectives*. New Haven, CT: Yale University Press.

James, William. (1950). *The Principles of Psychology*. New York: Dover. (Original work published 1910).

James, William. (1958). *The Varieties of Religious Experience*. New York: New American Library.

James, William. (1962). *Talks to Teachers on Psychology and to Students on Some of Life's Ideals*. New York: Dover. (Original work published 1899).

Jung, Carl. (1958). *Psychology and Religion: West and East* (R.F.C. Hull, Trans.) (Collected Works, Vol. II, Bollingen Series 30). New York: Pantheon Books.

Kaplan, Aryeh. (1982). *Meditation and Kabbalah*. York Beach, ME: Samuel Weiser.

Kaplan, Aryeh. (1985). *Jewish Meditation*. New York: Schocken Books.

Keating, Thomas. (1994). *Intimacy with God*. New York: Crossroad.

Koller, John. (1985). *Oriental Philosophies*. New York: Scribner.

Kornfield, Jack. (1993). *A Path with Heart*. New York: Bantam.

Kornfield, Jack. (1995). Talk given at Yucca Valley retreat, April, 1995.

Kornfield, J. & Fronsdal, G. (eds.). (1973). *Teachings of the Buddha.* Boston: Shambhala.

Landau, D. (1984, January). Citizen diplomacy. *New Age.*

Langer, Ellen. (1982). Automated lives. *Psychology Today, 16,* 16–71.

Langer, Ellen. (1989). *Mindfulness.* Reading, MA: Addison-Wesley.

Lau, D. (Trans.). (1979). *Confucius: The Analects.* New York: Penguin.

Lawrence, Brother. (1985). *The Practice of the Presence of God.* Old Tappan, NJ: Spire Books.

LeMee, Jean. (Trans.). (1975). *Hymns from the Rig-Veda.* New York: Knopf.

Long, J. Bruce. (1987). Love. In M. Eliade (Ed.), *The Encyclopedia of Religion, Vol. 9.* pp. 31–40. New York: Macmillan.

Longchenpa. (1975). *Kindly Bent to Ease Us, Part I: Mind* (H. Guenther, Trans.). Emeryville, CA: Dharma.

Maslow, Abraham. (1970). *Religions, Values and Peak Experiences.* New York: Viking.

Mason, Lynne, Alexander, Charles, Travis, F., et al. (1997). Electrophysiological correlates of higher states of consciousness during sleep in long-term practitioners of the transcendental meditation program. *Sleep, 20,* 102–110.

Merton, Thomas. (Ed.). (1960). *The Wisdom of the Desert.* New York: New Directions.

Merton, Thomas. (Ed.) (1965). *The Way of Chuang Tzu.* New York: New Directions.

Merton, Thomas. (1998). Cited in a talk by Robert Lehman to "The Spirit of Philanthropy" conference, Sedona, Arizona.

Metzner, Ralph. (1986). *Opening to Inner Light.* Los Angeles: Tarcher.

Metzner, Ralph. (1998). *The Unfolding Self: Varieties of Transformative Experience.* Novato, CA: Origin Press.

Milgram, Stanley. (1974). *Obedience to Authority: An Experimental View.* New York: Harper & Row.

Mitchell, Steven. (Trans.). (1992). *Tao Te Ching.* New York: HarperPerennial.

Mother Teresa. (1986). Address to the United Nations shown in a special broadcast edition of the film *Mother Teresa.*

Mother Teresa. (1997). *Time,* September 15, 83.

Muller, Wayne. (1996). *How, Then, Shall We Live?* New York: Bantam.

Murphy, Michael, & Donovan, Steven (1997). *The Physical and Psychological Effects of Meditation* (2nd ed.). Sausalito, CA: Institute of Noetic Sciences.

Myers, David. (1992). *The Pursuit of Happiness.* New York: Avon.

Nanamoli, Bhikkhu. (1978). *The Life of the Buddha.* Kandy, Sri Lanka: Buddhist Publication Society.

Narada. (1980). *The Buddha and His Teachings.* Kandy, Sri Lanka: Buddhist Publication Society.

Needleman, Jacob. (1980). *Lost Christianity.* Garden City, NY: Doubleday.

Needleman, Jacob. (1998). *Time and the Soul.* Garden City, NY: Doubleday.

Nisargadatta, Sri. (1973). *I Am That: Conversations with Sri Nisargadatta Maharaj,* 2 Vols. (M. Friedman, Trans.). Bombay: Chetana.

Nyanaponika Thera. (1962). *The Heart of Buddhist Meditation.* New York: Samuel Weiser.

Nyanaponika Thera. (1976). *Abhidhamma Studies.* Kandy, Sri Lanka: Buddhist Publication Society.

Nyanatiloka. (1980). *Buddhist Dictionary.* Kandy, Sri Lanka: Buddhist Publication Society.

Osborne, Arthur. (Ed.) (1978). *The Teachings of Ramana Maharishi.* New York: Samuel Weiser.

Ostermann, H. (1952). *The Alaskan eskimos, as described in the posthumous notes of Dr. Knud Rasmussen (Report of the Fifth Thule Expedition, 1921–24, Vol. X, No. 3).* Copenhagen: Nordisk Forlag.

Penner, Samuel. (1993). *The Four Dimensions of Paradise.* San Diego: Cyprus Press.

Perls, Fritz. (1969). *Gestalt Therapy Verbatim.* Lafayette, CA: Real People Press.

Perry, Whitall. (Ed.). (1981). *The Treasury of Traditional Wisdom.* Pates, Middlesex, UK: Perennial Books.

Prabhavananda & Isherwood, Christopher. (Trans.). (1953). *How to Know God: The Yoga Aphorisms of Patanjali.* Hollywood: Vedanta Press.

Prabhavananda & Isherwood, Christopher. (Trans.). (1972). *The Song of God: Bhagavad Gita* (3rd ed.). New York: New American Library.

Prabhavananda & Isherwood, Christopher. (Trans.). (1978). *Shankara's Crest-Jewel of Discrimination.* Hollywood: Vedanta Press. (Original work published 1945).

Price, A., & Mou-Lam, Wong. (Trans.). (1969). *The Diamond Sutra and the Sutra of Hui Neng*. Boston: Shambhala.

Radin, Dean. (1997). *The Conscious Universe: The Scientific Truth of Psychic Phenomena*. New York: HarperCollins.

Ram Dass. (1979). *Be Here Now*. San Cristobal, NM: Lama Foundation.

Ramana Maharshi. (1990). *Who Am I?* (T. Venkataraman, Ed.). Tiruvannamali, India: Sri Ramanasramam. (Original work published 1955).

Ramana Maharshi. (1988). *The Spiritual Teaching of Ramana Maharshi*. Boston: Shambhala.

Raskin, Neal, & Rogers, Carl. (1995). Person-centered therapy. In R. Corsini & D. Wedding (Eds.), *Current Psychotherapies* (5th ed.) (pp. 128–161). Itasca, IL: F. E. Peacock.

Rasmussen, K. (1929). *Intellectual Culture of the Iglulik Eskimos*. Copenhagen: Gyldendalske Boghandel, Nordisk Forlag.

Remen, Rachel. (1996). *Kitchen Table Wisdom*. New York: Riverhead Books.

Robinson, John. (Ed.). (1981). *The Nag Hammadi Library*. New York: Harper & Row.

Rudolph, Kurt. (1987). Wisdom. In M. Eliade (Ed.), *The Encyclopedia of Religion* (vol. 15, pp. 393–401). New York: Macmillan.

St. Nikodinos & St. Makarios. (Eds.). (1993). *Prayer of the Heart: Writings from the Philokalia* (G. Palmer, Philip Sherwood & Kallistos, Ware, Trans.). Boston: Shambhala.

Satprem. (1968). *Sri Aurobindo, or the Adventure of Consciousness*. New York: Harper & Row.

Savin, Olga. (Trans.). (1991). *The Way of a Pilgrim*. Boston: Shambhala.

Schimmel, Annemarie. (1987). Rumi, Jalal al-Din. In M. Eliade (Ed.), *The Encyclopedia of Religion* (vol. 12, pp. 482–485). New York: Macmillan.

Schumacher, E. (1977). *A Guide for the Perplexed*. New York: Harper & Row.

Schuon, Frithjof. (1975). *The Transcendental Unity of Religions*. New York: Harper Touchstone Books.

Schuon, Frithjof. (1976). *Understanding Islam*. London: Unwin.

Sengstan (Third Zen Patriarch). (n.d.) *Verses on the Faith Mind* (R. Clarke, Trans.). Sharon Springs, NY: Zen Center.

Serrou, Robert. (1980). *Teresa of Calcutta*. New York: McGraw-Hill.

Shah, Idres. (1971). *The Sufis*. Garden City, NY: Anchor/Doubleday.

Shearer, Peter. (Trans.). (1989). *Effortless Being: The Yoga Sutras of Patanjali*. London: Wildwood House.

Silesius, Angelus. (1976). *The Book of Angelus Silesius* (F.A. Frank, Trans.). New York: Vintage/Random House.

Smith, Huston. (1958). *The Religions of Man*. New York: Harper & Row.

Smith, Huston. (1991). *The World's Religions*. New York; Harper & Row.

Staudinger, Ursula, & Baltes, Paul. (1994). Psychology of wisdom. In R. Sternberg (Ed.), *Encyclopedia of Human Intelligence* (vol. 2, pp. 1143–1152). New York: Macmillan.

Steinberg, Milton. (1947). *Basic Judaism*. New York: Harcourt, Brace, Jovanovich.

Steinsaltz, Adin. (1980). *The Thirteen Petalled Rose* (Yehuda Hanegbi, Trans.). New York: Basic Books.

Surya Das. (1997). *Awakening the Buddha Within*. New York: Broadway Books.

Syed, M. Hafiz. (Ed.). (1962). *Thus Spake Prophet Muhammad*. Madras, India: Sri Ramakrishna Math.

Tart, C. (1986). *Waking Up*. Boston: Shambhala.

Thanissaro Bhikkhu. (1996). *The Wings to Awakening: An Anthology from the Pali Canon*. Barre, MA: Dhamma Dana.

Toynbee, Arnold. (1960). *A Study of History*. London: Oxford Press. (Original work published 1934).

Toynbee, Arnold. (1948). *Civilization on Trial*. New York: Oxford University Press.

Trungpa, Chogyam. (1973). *Cutting Through Spiritual Materialism*. Boston: Shambhala.

Underhill, Evelyn. (1974). *Mysticism*. New York: New American Library.

Vaughan-Lee, Lewellyn. (Ed.). (1995). *Traveling the Path of Love: Sayings of Sufi Masters*. Inverness, CA: Golden Sufi Center.

Waley, Arthur. (Trans.). (1989). *The Analects of Confucius*. New York: Vintage/Random House. (Original work published 1938).

Walsh, Roger. (1977). Initial meditative experiences: Part I. *Journal of Transpersonal Psychology, 9*, 151–192.

Walsh, Roger. (1984). *Staying Alive: The Psychology of Human Survival*. Boston: Shambhala.

Walsh, Roger, & Vaughan, Frances. (Eds.). (1993). *Paths Beyond Ego: The Transpersonal Vision*. New York; Tarcher/Putnam.

Walshe, M. (1981). *Meister Eckhart: German Sermons and Treatises* (3 vols.). London; Watkins.

Wang Yang-ming. (1963). In *A Source Book in Chinese Philosophy* (W. Chan, Trans.) (pp. 659–661). Princeton, NJ: Princeton University Press.

Whitmont, Edward. (1969). *The Symbolic Quest*. Princeton: Princeton University Press.

Wilber, Ken. (1981). *No Boundary*. Boston: Shambhala.

Wilber, Ken. (Ed.). (1984). *Quantum Questions*. Boston: Shambhala.

Wilber, Ken. (1995). *Sex, Ecology, Spirituality: The Spirit of Evolution*. Boston: Shambhala.

Wilber, K. (1996). *Eye to Eye: The Quest for the New Paradigm*. Boston: Shambhala.

Wilber, Ken. (1999). *One Taste*. Boston: Shambhala.

Wilber, Ken, Engler, Jack, & Brown, Daniel. (Eds.). (1986). *Transformations of Consciousness: Conventional and Contemplative Perspectives on Development*. Boston: New Science Library/Shambhala.

Wong, Eva. (1997). *The Shambhala Guide to Taoism*. Boston: Shambhala.

Wordsworth, William. (1952). Ode on Intimations of Immortality. In *Poems in Two Volumes of 1807* (H. Darbyshire, Ed.). Oxford: Clarendon Press.

Yu-Lan, Fung. (1948). *A Short History of Chinese Philosophy* (D. Bodde, Trans.). New York: Free Press/Macmillan.

INDEX

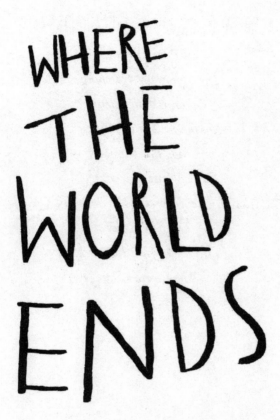